APR 2 9 2014

Charles Dickens's
Bleak House

DATE DUE

With its sus_____es Dickens's
*Bleak Hous*_____remarkable
novel.

Taking the _____novel offers:

- extensiv_____retations of
  the text,
- annotate_____itical works
  and the t
- cross-ref_____in order to
  suggest l
- suggestic

Part of the R_____tial reading
for all those b_____only a guide
to the novel, t_____aterial that
surrounds Dic

Janice M. All

Routledge Gu_____ost widely
studied autho_____ntexts and
criticism, high_____s that need
to be taken int

D0145671

Routledge Guides to Literature*

Routledge Guides to Literature offer clear introductions to the most widely studied authors and literary texts.

Each book engages with texts, contexts and criticism, highlighting the range of critical views and contextual factors that need to be taken into consideration in advanced studies of literary works. The series encourages informed but independent readings of texts by ranging as widely as possible across the contextual and critical issues relevant to the works examined, rather than presenting a single interpretation. Alongside general guides to texts and authors, the series includes 'sourcebooks', which allow access to reprinted contextual and critical materials as well as annotated extracts of primary text.

Also available in this series

For Andy and Sophie

Charles Dickens's
Bleak House
A Sourcebook

Edited by Janice M. Allan

Routledge
Taylor & Francis Group

LONDON AND NEW YORK

First published 2004
by Routledge
2 Park Square, Milton Park, Abingdon, Oxon OX14 4RN

Simultaneously published in the USA and Canada
by Routledge
711 Third Avenue, New York, NY 10017

Routledge is an imprint of the Taylor & Francis Group

Editorial material and selection © 2004 Janice M. Allan

Typeset in Sabon and Gill Sans by RefineCatch Ltd, Bungay, Suffolk

British Library Cataloguing in Publication Data
A catalogue record for this book is available from the British Library

Library of Congress Cataloging in Publication Data
Bleak House : A Sourcebook /
edited by Janice M. Allan.
        p. cm. – Routledge guides to literature
Includes bibliographical references and index.
    1. Dickens, Charles, 1812–1870. Bleak House – Handbooks, manuals, etc.
I. Allan, Janice M., 1966–   . II. Series.

    PR4556.R685 2003
    823'.8 – dc22

                                                      2003019868

ISBN 978-0-415-24772-6 (hbk)
ISBN 978-0-415-24773-3 (pbk)

Contents

2: Interpretations   43

Critical History   45

Early Critical Reception   56

Modern Criticism   62

3: Key Passages   99

Introduction   101

Key Passages   104

4: Further Reading   153

Illustrations

Annotation and Footnotes

Annotation is a key feature of this series. Both the original notes from the reprinted texts and new annotations by the editor appear at the bottom of the relevant page. The reprinted notes are prefaced by the author's name in square brackets, e.g. '[Robinson's note.]'.

Acknowledgements

I am grateful to Duncan Wu for the enthusiasm and genuine support he offered during the course of preparing this Sourcebook. I would also like to acknowledge the advice and help of many colleagues, including Sue Chaplin, Andrew Cooper, Robert Eaglestone, Hilary Haigh, Kate Holden, Brian Maidment, Hugh Robertson and David Taylor. In addition, I would like to thank everyone at Cambridge Road Nursery for giving me the peace of mind to work on this project. I owe an enormous debt of gratitude to my parents, especially my father and fellow academic, John Allan, for the insightful comments and suggestions he offered at every stage of this project. Like all who work on Dickens, I am indebted to the work undertaken by various scholars, especially J. Hillis Miller. I have also found Paul Schlicke's *Oxford Reader's Companion to Dickens* to be an invaluable source of information on Dickens's life and works.

It is difficult to imagine how this sourcebook would have been completed without the editorial assistance provided by Liz Thompson, Fiona Cairns, Diane Parker and Liz O'Donnell. Their patience, support and advice proved invaluable. I would also like to thank the various readers to whom Routledge sent this project; their comments have made this a better book.

The following publishers, institutions and individuals have kindly given permission to reprint material:

AMS PRESS INC. for Harvey P. Sucksmith, 'Sir Leicester Dedlock, Wat Tyler and the Chartists: The Role of Ironmaster in *Bleak House*' in *Dickens Studies Annual*, 1975, Vol. 4, pp. 123–6.

CAMBRIDGE UNIVERSITY PRESS and the author for Hilary M. Schor, *Dickens and the Daugher of the House*, 1999.

CAMBRIDGE UNIVERSITY PRESS and the author for Carolyn Dever, *Death and the Mother from Dickens to Freud*, 1998.

THE CHARLES DICKENS MUSEUM for the illustrations.

CONTINUUM for F.S. Schwarzbach, *Dickens and the City*, The Athlone Press, 1979.

CORNELL UNIVERSITY PRESS. Reprinted from Elizabeth Langland, *Nobody's Angels: Middle-Class Women and Domestic Ideology in Victorian Culture*. Copyright © 1995 by Cornell University. Used by permission of the publisher, Cornell University Press.

K.J. Fielding for *The Speeches of Charles Dickens*, Oxford, Clarendon Press, 1960.

PEARSON EDUCATION LIMITED for J. Hillis Miller, *Victorian Subjects*, Harvester Wheatsheaf/Duke University Press, 1991.

Jane M. Rabb for Jane R. Cohen, *Charles Dickens and His Original Illustrators*, Ohio State University Press, 1980.

UNIVERSITY OF CALIFORNIA PRESS for D.A. Miller, 'Discipline in Different Voices: Bureaucracy, Police, Family, and Bleak House' in D.A. Miller, *The Novel and the Police* © The Regents of the University of California, 1988.

Every effort has been made to trace and contact copyright holders. The publishers would be pleased to hear from any copyright holders not acknowledged here so that this section may be amended at the earliest opportunity.

Introduction

It is now universally recognised that *Bleak House* is one of the great novels of the nineteenth century. Combining a sustained attack on several of the most pressing issues of the day with a moving account of Esther Summerson's search for origins and selfhood, the narrative is remarkable in both scope and stylistic innovation. It is not surprising, therefore, that although Dickens did not sit down to write *Bleak House* until November 1851, 'the first shadows of a new story' were circulating within his mind as early as February of that year.[1] Such a long gestation period was not unusual for Dickens, nor were the feelings of heightened restlessness that he came to associate with the first stages of creative production. Plagued by feelings of 'Violent restlessness, and vague ideas of going I don't know where, I don't know why', Dickens, always energetic, threw himself into a frenzy of activity.[2] In addition to editing and contributing to his own weekly periodical, *Household Words* (see headnote to Cole, p. 34), he was busy rehearsing with his own theatre company for a royal performance of *Not So Bad as We Seem*, a play written by the popular novelist Edward Bulwer-Lytton. He was also managing and directing Urania Cottage, a home for fallen women established by the wealthy philanthropist Angela Burdett Coutts in 1847. In addition, Dickens was becoming more actively involved with issues of public health (see Contextual Overview, p. 15). In May 1851 he gave a speech to the Metropolitan Sanitary Association in which he stated his firm belief that 'Sanitary Reform must precede all other social remedies . . . and that even Education and Religion can do nothing where they are most needed, until the way is paved for their ministrations by Cleanliness and Decency' (see p. 37). Later in the same year, he was engaged in trying to locate an appropriate site upon which to erect model housing for the working classes. Dickens's active support for the Ragged School Movement – which aimed to provide a basic education to the poorest children – gave him ample opportunities to gain first-hand knowledge of the plight faced by abandoned and neglected children. As we

---

1   C. Dickens, letter to Mary Boyle, in G. Storey, K. Tillotson and N. Burgis (eds), *The Letters of Charles Dickens*, vol. 6, Oxford: Clarendon Press, 1988, p. 298.
2   C. Dickens, letter to Angela Burdett Coutts (see note 1), p. 463.

shall see, such social issues were to assume a prominent place within his new novel.

Picking up a copy of *Bleak House*, today's readers tend to be intimidated by its sheer volume. But we need to remember that the reading experience was quite different for Dickens's contemporaries. Like many of his novels, *Bleak House* was first issued in twenty parts (called numbers) over a period of nineteen months (the last being a double issue). The first number appeared in March 1852 and the last in September 1853. Each monthly number consisted of thirty-two pages of text, two illustrations contributed by Hablot Browne, better known as 'Phiz' (for a discussion of Browne's illustrations, see Cohen, **p. 77**), and more than a dozen pages of advertisements. On average, 34,000 copies of each monthly number were sold at the price of one shilling.[3] As reading aloud was a popular communal activity, the audience for this novel was actually much larger than such sales figures suggest.

Inevitably, serial publication had a pronounced effect on both the reading and the writing experience. As the average price of a three-volume novel was thirty-one shillings and sixpence (the equivalent of just under £100 today), they were well outside the reach of all but the most affluent readers. By both bringing down the overall price and allowing it to be spread over a considerable period, serialisation made the work accessible to a much larger and more diverse audience.[4] While his novels are unambiguously middle class in outlook (see Sucksmith, **p. 71** and Langland, **p. 84**), Dickens was read and admired by all classes, and this success was, in part, attributable to his mode of publication. Regardless of class, waiting impatiently for the appearance of the next monthly number must have been a frustrating experience. In addition, extending the reading process over nineteen months would not only tax the memory but also make it extremely difficult to trace the various themes, motifs and patterns that render *Bleak House* such a tightly constructed novel.

The reasons why Dickens preferred this form of publication were twofold:

> Partly it was to do with Dickens's need to be reassured by an ever-present sense of an audience. The monthly or weekly serialized form kept a writer in frequent and regular contact with the audience he was addressing. The other reason was money. Successful serialization was a very effective way of generating income for a writer and sustaining that income over a long period.[5]

There can be no doubt that by the time he came to write *Bleak House*, Dickens had become a master at 'successful serialization'. While the demands of serialisation might prove irksome, he was well accustomed to the rigid deadlines that meant finishing the number only days before publication. More importantly, he

---

3   S. Eliot, 'The business of Victorian publishing', in D. David (ed.), *The Cambridge Companion to the Victorian Novel*, Cambridge: Cambridge University Press, 2001, p. 44.
4   Eliot (see note 3), pp. 44–5.
5   Eliot (see note 3), p. 45.

had learned how to achieve the necessary balance whereby each number would function as a self-contained entity while, at the same time, being an integral element of a larger whole. This control over his material was, in part, achieved through the use of 'number-plans' in which he recorded chapter titles as well as a brief indication of the key events and characters that would play a role within them. As we shall see, contemporary reviewers of *Bleak House* criticised the novel for a lack of coherence (see, for example, Brimley, **p. 58** and *Illustrated London News*, **p. 59**). What the number-plans make abundantly clear, however, is that Dickens took great pains with the overall development and structure of this work.[6]

In the same month in which the final double number was issued, *Bleak House* was published as a single volume. Three further editions followed within Dickens's lifetime, in 1858 (Cheap Edition) 1868 (Library Edition) and 1869 (Charles Dickens Edition). Since then, countless editions have and will continue to appear – a testament to the novel's lasting popularity and importance.

As its title suggests, this sourcebook brings together a range of sources – historical and critical, contemporaneous and current – that will enable you to engage with Dickens's novel in a more informed manner. To help you to get the most from these sources, each one will be both introduced and annotated. You will see that the book is divided into four sections. The first offers a contextual overview of the key issues and events that preoccupied Dickens at mid-century. *Bleak House* is the most topical of novels and thus it is essential that the reader have a good grasp of the environment – social, economic and cultural – in which it was produced. The chronology will enable you to situate the novel within Dickens's personal and professional development, as well as in relation to the broader social and technological changes that occurred within his lifetime. The selection of contemporary documents that follows includes an extract from one of Dickens's many public speeches, as well as examples of his enormous journalistic output. You will also find extracts by the social critic and historian Thomas Carlyle, the sanitary reformer Hector Gavin and the lawyer Alfred Cole. In each case, I have chosen those sources that most directly address and inform the main concerns of the novel.

Section 2 explores the various readings and interpretations to which this novel has given rise. The opening chapter provides a general overview of the critical history of *Bleak House*, tracing the fluctuations in its critical and popular reception from the first reviews through to the present day. As this critical history suggests, *Bleak House* has provoked a variety of responses, both positive and negative. It has also been subject to many different types of readings generated by a variety of critical approaches. The range and diversity of possible approaches to the novel – a sign of its richness – is reflected in my selection of critical sources. At the same time, this selection has been guided by the needs and relative experience of undergraduate readers. The next chapter on contemporary reviews provides a good sense of how *Bleak House* was received by Dickens's first critics, while also

---

6 A complete set of number-plans for *Bleak House* is included in the Penguin editions of the novel.

No. X.   DECEMBER.   Price 1s.

BLEAK HOUSE

BY

CHARLES DICKENS.

WITH ILLUSTRATIONS BY H. K. BROWNE.

LONDON: BRADBURY & EVANS, BOUVERIE STREET.

AGENTS: J. MENZIES, EDINBURGH; MURRAY AND SON, GLASGOW; J. M'GLASHAN, DUBLIN.

The Author of this Work notifies that it is his intention to reserve the right of translating it.

Figure 1 Bleak House's blue wrapper.

reflecting the state of novel criticism at mid-century. The following chapter, devoted to modern criticism of the novel, offers a broad selection of interpretations, ranging from the historical and thematic through to the more recent theoretical readings of the text.

Section 3 opens with a brief outline of the novel's plot. Readers who are not yet familiar with the text will find it helpful to read this summary before engaging with the rest of the material contained within this sourcebook. The remainder of this section consists of a number of key passages from *Bleak House* itself. Each passage is prefaced by a commentary alerting you to any important textual or thematic features and indicating the passage's importance within the novel as a whole. In addition, these commentaries will relate the text back to the issues and concerns raised by the contemporary documents and the various critical sources.

To help you use your time most effectively, the final section offers suggestions on both preferred editions and further reading. There is a vast amount of material devoted to *Bleak House* and my suggestions represent nothing more than a starting point for your own research. Bearing the needs of an undergraduate reader in mind, the texts that I am recommending are both accessible and informative. The annotations should help you to identify those that will best suit your needs and interests.

1

Contexts

Contextual Overview

The world into which Dickens was born bears little resemblance to the one he left behind. A quick glance at the events outlined in the chronology below suggests the unprecedented material, technological and cultural advancements that occurred in the course of his lifetime. Mass industrialisation and urbanisation, the advent of the railway, the Reform movement, the growth of the British Empire and the publication of Charles Darwin's radical work on evolution, *On the Origin of Species* (1859), are just some of the more obvious factors that altered beyond recognition the ways in which the Victorians viewed themselves and their world. While certain of these developments undeniably constituted huge strides towards modernity and contributed to the contemporary belief in progress, they were also the source of much uncertainty and anxiety. Established beliefs and social structures – associated with the traditions and relative simplicity of village life – fell by the wayside and, for many, it was not clear what would, or could, take their place. To put it simply, the age of Dickens was, in the words of a contemporary observer, an 'age of transition'.[1]

From the myriad events and changes that made the nineteenth century such an extraordinary period, this chapter will concentrate on the contextual issues that most directly inform and influence Dickens's outlook at mid-century and, at the same time, provide the necessary background to the sources included in this section of the book. These documents deal with the need for sanitary and legal reform; Dickens's admiration for the Detective Branch; and contemporary constructions of a 'proper' femininity. What links these seemingly disparate documents is a set of underlying attitudes and assumptions most clearly associated with the burgeoning middle classes, of which Dickens was both a member and a spokesperson for its values.

---

1   H. Holland, 'The Progress and Spirit of Physical Science' [1858], cited in W.E. Houghton, *The Victorian Frame of Mind 1830–1870*, New Haven, Conn.: Yale University Press, 1974, p. 1.

A Neglected Child

Dickens's popularity amongst middle-class readers was, in large part, attributable to the fact that his novels were seen to celebrate the domestic virtues of hearth and home. Yet when one considers his actual treatment of the domestic realm, what is most obvious is the very absence of happy families. What we find in their stead is an alarming number of absent or irresponsible parents and a proliferation of literal or metaphorical orphans (for a discussion of the effect of maternal loss on Esther, see Dever, p. 88). Parental responsibility is a key theme within *Bleak House* (see, for example, Key Passages, p. 138) and the list of inadequate parents within this novel alone would include: Mrs Jellyby, Harold Skimpole, Miss Barbary, Mr Turveydrop, Lady Dedlock, the Lord Chancellor (in his position of *loco parentis* to Ada and Richard) and the brickmaker. The list of orphaned or neglected children is even longer, comprising Esther, Jo, the Jellyby children, Prince Turveydrop, Bart and Judy Smallweed, the Pardiggle clan and Charley and her siblings. These children – who like Judy Smallweed 'never owned a doll, never heard of Cinderella, never played at any game' (Chapter 21)[2] – are denied the innocent joys of childhood and forced prematurely into the adult world of care and responsibility. This preoccupation with the neglected child was far from unique to Dickens. Throughout the 1840s, the public was bombarded by representations of the horrific conditions faced by young children working in mines and factories and a large number of novelists were quick to capitalise on the sympathy and outrage generated by such reports. What is unique about Dickens's treatment of neglected children is that it was, at least in part, based on first-hand experience.

When Dickens's intimate friend and advisor John Forster (1812–76) published *The Life of Charles Dickens* (1872–4), it contained an autobiographical statement calculated to shock its readers. From this brief fragment, the world learned for the first time of the poverty and degradation Dickens suffered as a child (although a thinly veiled account of such experiences had already appeared in Dickens's most autobiographical novel, *David Copperfield* (1849–50)). Although his father, John, received a reasonable salary as a clerk in the Navy Pay Office, he was an imprudent man who struggled to live within his means. Matters came to a head in 1822 when John was transferred back to London from Chatham (near Rochester), a move that entailed a cut in salary at a time when he was already deeply in debt. Following a sale of their household goods, the family moved into rather cramped lodgings in the newly developed and semi-rural Camden Town. When the young Dickens joined them (he had remained in Chatham until the end of the school term), he found that his education was suspended. According to Dickens, 1823 was spent 'cleaning his [father's] boots of a morning, and my own; and making myself useful in the work of the little house; and looking after

---

2   C. Dickens, *Bleak House* [1852–3], ed. N. Bradbury, Harmondsworth: Penguin, 2003. All my references are to this edition. As readers will be using a variety of editions, all references (throughout this Sourcebook) will be given as chapter numbers.

my younger brothers and sisters (we were now six in all); and going on such poor errands as arose out of our poor way of living'.[3] His hopes of resuming an education were dealt a blow early in 1824 when James Lambert, a relative of his mother's, found him a situation at Warren's Blacking Factory (blacking was used for polishing boots). Just after his twelfth birthday, Dickens went to work for six shillings a week. Eleven days later, his father was arrested for debt and, like all insolvent debtors prior to 1849, imprisoned in the Marshalsea. As was usual at the time, his wife and the younger children joined him in prison shortly after and Dickens was sent to live in cheap lodgings on his own.

It has to be said that it was not unusual for boys of twelve to be sent out to earn a living, nor was the wage that Dickens received unusually low. Furthermore, the period during which Dickens was employed at the factory just exceeded one year. Yet the impression one receives from Dickens's admittedly vague pronouncement that 'I have no idea how long it lasted, whether for a year, or much more, or less', is one of prolonged if not infinite suffering.[4] It is impossible to say whether Dickens was consciously aware of the various exaggerations within his account (for example, he lowered his age from twelve to ten). What they do suggest is that these experiences were subjected to an imaginative reconstruction before they were presented to the reader, a reconstruction which foregrounds the irresponsibility of his parents, his own status as their helpless victim and his ongoing sense of betrayal more than twenty years later.

Elsewhere in this volume I will suggest the dangers and limitations of biographical criticism (reading the works through the life of the author) and I am certainly not suggesting that each and every neglected child within Dickens's novels constitutes a disguised version of the author himself. There is little doubt, however, that these experiences continued to exercise a profound yet ambivalent influence on his attitudes towards the treatment of children within the family and society at large, and his feelings about poverty and class. On the one hand, the neglected child looms large within Dickens's social critique and he consistently condemned society for casting aside those like the homeless Jo, *Bleak House*'s crossing-sweeper who earns a few pence by clearing a path through the mud and excrement that covered London's streets (for a discussion of the unsanitary conditions of London, see Gavin, **p. 32** and Schwarzbach, **p. 76**; for Dickens's representation of Jo, see Key Passages, **p. 127**). Still, I would argue that Dickens's early experiences also engendered a certain anxiety and defensiveness about his own class position. This uneasiness helps to explain certain inconsistencies and limitations within Dickens's social agenda, particularly the ways in which his ideas for reform were rigidly constrained by middle-class values and ideologies.

---

3   J. Forster, *The Life of Charles Dickens* [1872–4], 3 vols, London: Chapman & Hall, no publication date, p. 12.
4   Forster (see note 3), p. 26.

The Rise of the Middle Classes

No discussion of the Victorian period would be complete without a consideration of the burgeoning middle classes. These classes were themselves the product of the twin forces of industrialisation and urbanisation and, more specifically, the administrative, commercial, professional and service-sector needs to which these forces gave rise. For example, the mass production of goods created the need for shopkeepers to sell them throughout the nation and merchants to arrange for their sale abroad. Those who made their fortunes producing such goods required lawyers to manage their affairs, tutors to educate their sons, and so on. Encompassing such a diverse range of occupations, the middle classes were necessarily characterised by a number of internal divisions reflecting varying income levels, the relative status of various occupations, education and regional differences. Self-conscious about their recently achieved position, they were understandably preoccupied by the need to create a coherent class identity, an identity distinct from both the aristocracy and the working classes. Indeed, the middle classes' sense of themselves was, at least in part, based on this perception of being different from those above and below them; if it was difficult to identify what they were, it was at least possible to establish what they were not (for a discussion of class see Sucksmith, p. 71 and Langland, p. 84). The qualities that most clearly distinguished them from the other classes were a well-developed sense of morality, a pride in work and a competitive business spirit. Unsurprisingly, the first of these was associated with the middle-class woman, while the latter two belonged to her male counterpart.

Today's readers might find the middle classes' commitment to both the spiritual and the commercial somewhat problematic. However, among the middle classes the most common religion was Evangelicism. This was a popular branch of Anglicanism that emphasised conversion, good conduct, the literal interpretation of the Bible and the inherently sinful nature of humanity. According to Evangelical doctrine, the spiritual and the commercial were complementary. As the social historian Richard Altick suggests, 'Work, in a secular context, was the counterpart of faith in a religious one'.[5] Both were underpinned by an emphasis on duty, self-control, seriousness and self-sacrifice (these qualities are taken to an extreme by Esther, see Key Passages, p. 113). When secular and spiritual earnestness were combined, they defined a notion of respectability that, for many, remains a byword for the period as a whole. The middle classes had good reason to feel confident in their own superiority: they were the undisputed industrial and moral leaders of the nation. As such, they did their best to disseminate their values and practices throughout the working classes through social reform, religious conversion and, when necessary, social policing. Of course, one should not forget the role of literature in propagating middle-class ideologies. For example, Esther Summerson provides a model of 'proper' femininity for women of all classes to emulate. Some, like the brickmaker in *Bleak House*, resented such efforts as

---

5   R. Altick, *Victorian People and Ideas*, New York: W.W. Norton, 1973, p. 168.

unwanted intrusions into their private lives (see Key Passages, **p. 121**), while other aspiring members of the working classes were only too happy to embrace the behaviour and mores of their so-called betters.

Constructions of Gender and the Separate Spheres

During the eighteenth century, middle-class women held a variety of occupations outside the home. Yet by the 1830s, a growing national prosperity, coupled with a tendency to separate business premises from the home, led to the creation of two distinct and separate spheres: the public world of commerce and politics and the private world of the domestic environment. It should be noted, however, that the separation of these two realms was as much an ideological as an economic imperative. Indeed their separation was closely related to middle-class constructions of both gender and class.

Like the vast majority of his contemporaries, Dickens was confident in the belief that men and women were fundamentally different creatures. Scripture had always said as much but it was now confirmed by the supposedly irrefutable discourses of science and medicine. For example, when a doctor named Theodor Bischoff discovered, in 1843, that women were subject to spontaneous ovulation, his discovery 'was enlisted to provide a scientific explanation for what rapidly came to be considered woman's definitive characteristic – maternal instinct'.[6] In short, the Victorians believed that God and Nature had combined to endow men and women with fundamentally different – and inalterable – characteristics. Possessing a more fully developed intellect and rationality, as well as a basic need for action and competition, a man was, by his very nature, best suited for the public world of industry. Women, in contrast, were deemed to be blessed with a superior spirituality, an innate desire to nurture and a supreme selflessness that allowed them to gratify themselves only by gratifying others. The ethereal and virtuous nature of such a woman is captured in the title of Coventry Patmore's enormously popular poem *The Angel in the House* (1854–63). Such qualities, it was argued, made the private realm their natural and proper sphere of action, especially when they assumed the roles of wives and mothers. Although Esther only becomes a mother at the novel's conclusion, her ability and willingness to nurture others is consistently emphasised. For example, when Ada and Richard (the two wards of Chancery) and Esther arrive at the home of Mrs Jellyby (whose charitable activities lead her to neglect her own home and family), Esther immediately devotes herself to Mrs Jellyby's unhappy children. According to Ada, 'Esther was their friend directly. Esther nursed them, coaxed them to sleep, washed and dressed them, told them stories, kept them quiet, bought them keepsakes' (Chapter 6). Under the moral guardianship of a woman like Esther, the

---

6 M. Poovey, *Uneven Developments: The Ideological Work of Gender in Mid-Victorian England*, Chicago, Ill.: University of Chicago Press, 1988, p. 7.

home was able to function as a refuge and retreat from the physically and morally tainted world outside (this notion is challenged by Langland, p. 85). By mid-century, this construction of the home represented the dominant version of middle-class reality, while the corresponding image of femininity had been codified within a whole series of material practices that confirmed and upheld the sub-ordinate and dependent position of women. Perhaps the most obvious example of such practices was the Matrimonial Causes Act of 1857, which inscribed sexual inequality into the statute books. This Act allowed men to petition for a divorce on the grounds of adultery but granted a divorce to women only on the grounds of adultery *plus* incest, cruelty, bigamy, sodomy, bestiality, desertion or rape.

From a modern perspective, the role and sphere assigned to middle-class women in the nineteenth century appears both limited and limiting. We need to recognise, however, that for the Victorians, the public and private spheres were complementary: different but equal. Indeed, for a society that judged the health of the nation by the health of its families, the role of women was pivotal. As the social commentator Lynda Nead suggests, 'Regulation, control and peace in the home ensured national security and prosperity. The family home was defined as the nucleus of the state and breakdown in domestic order was understood in terms of total social disintegration.'[7]

In addition to playing a key role in the constitution of a national identity, this construction of femininity played an equally important role in the delineation of class (see Langland, pp. 86–7). A well-ordered and harmonious domestic environ-ment provided both the necessary balance and tangible reward for the productive labour that defined the middle-class male. Thus the financial failure of Mr Jellyby is explicitly linked to his wife's poor household management (Chapter 14). More importantly, as I suggest above, the notions of respectability and morality implied by both the feminine ideal and the domestic haven she maintained provided the foundation of a middle-class identity and system of values which distinguished them from both the aristocracy above them and the working classes below them. Indeed, the separation of the two spheres and the related constructions of mascu-linity and femininity had little relevance for either the aristocracy or the working classes. Not only did the aristocratic woman have an enviable degree of freedom – social, psychological and physical – compared to her middle-class counterpart, but the aristocracy in general were seen as the idle inheritors of an immorality that could be traced back to the excesses of the Regency. In the case of working-class women, who made an important, indeed indispensable, contribution to the family income, participation in the public realm was a necessity. This, and their prolific breeding – which was read as a sign of their unregulated sexuality and 'animalistic' natures – clearly distinguished them from the middle classes.

We must always remember, however, that gender roles never constituted a stable or unified body of beliefs and practices; they were both inherently contra-dictory and constantly contested. Leonore Davidoff and Catherine Hall, two his-torians of family life and class, highlight just some of the contradictions implicit in

7   L. Nead, *Myths of Sexuality: Representations of Women in Victorian Britain*, Oxford: Basil Blackwell, 1988, p. 33.

middle-class constructions of femininity. As they suggest, 'Their religion recognized their spiritual equality yet defended social and sexual subordination. Their class applauded self-assertion yet the feminine ideal was selflessness. Their supposed dependence and fragility was continually stressed yet they were expected to manage the "business" of motherhood and the efficient organization of the household.'[8] Yet because the feminine ideal established by the middle classes played such a pivotal role at so many levels, any deviation or transgression was perceived as a serious threat. Novelists, who had always been active in codifying and disseminating gender roles, responded to this threat by meting out appropriate poetic justice: 'deviant' women like *Bleak House*'s philanthropist, Mrs Jellyby, and her friend Miss Wisk (who campaigns for women's rights), were depicted as figures of ridicule and contempt (see 'Suckling Pigs', **p. 40** and Key Passages, **p. 114**).

Slums, Sanitation and Policing

Within the course of Dickens's life, Britain transformed itself from a predominantly agricultural nation into the acknowledged industrial leader of the modern world. While it is slightly misleading to refer to such developments as an Industrial Revolution – the process was more piecemeal than the term implies – there is no denying the sheer scale of the changes wrought on Britain's economy, political systems, landscape and inhabitants. Industrialisation, together with the technological advancements that made it possible, had the potential to better the lives of all. Even the working classes benefited from the advent of mass-produced goods, wider employment opportunities and the increase in leisure and cultural activities that flourished in the new urban environments. Yet such advantages hardly offset the horrific squalor in which a significant portion of the population lived, worked and died.

One of the most striking effects of industrialism was the process of mass and rapid urbanisation as rural workers, tempted by higher wages and the lure of new opportunities, left their native villages for towns and cities that were neither equipped nor prepared to accommodate them. This situation was compounded by the influx of Irish and European immigrants, who flocked into Britain's industrial centres throughout the 1840s. With no means of transportation, these workers were forced to live in close proximity to the workplace, while low or uncertain wages confined them to the cheapest housing available. As a result, domestic overcrowding within slum districts was a fact of life for a large percentage of the urban population. Within such districts, the norm was for one or more families to inhabit a single room within houses that were haphazardly packed together, tumbling down and poorly ventilated (see Gavin, **p. 32** and Key Passages, **p. 120**).

To make matters infinitely worse, even the most basic sanitary provisions were

---

8   L. Davidoff and C. Hall, *Family Fortunes: Men and women of the English middle class 1780–1850*, London: Routledge, 1997, p. 451.

almost non-existent; cesspools and shared privies routinely overflowed and saturated the surrounding area. Water, if available at all, had to be collected from a communal pump, which often operated for no more than an hour a day. Nor should one forget that the source of this water supply (generally a river) was more than likely to be the depository of raw sewage. Within such environments, it is hardly surprising that disease was rampant. Infected water supplies, the accumulation of human and animal excrement, poor ventilation, sanitation and hygiene, and the overcrowding which precluded the possibility of separating the sick from the healthy all contributed to the rapid spread of communicable diseases such as cholera, smallpox, typhoid and typhus. Almost 42,000 people died during the smallpox epidemic that spanned 1837–40,[9] while epidemics of cholera occurred in 1832, 1848–9 and again in 1853–4. In the 1848–9 outbreak some 16,000 people died in London alone.[10]

Largely ignorant of the manner in which such diseases spread, many Victorians still subscribed to the 'miasmic' theory, which associated bad smells with the presence of disease. This at least served to establish a putative connection between environment and disease, thereby placing housing reform at the centre of the Public Health Movement. As the fate of Esther Summerson makes clear (she catches a fever from Jo, the crossing-sweeper), the threat of contamination paid little heed to demographic or class boundaries (see Carlyle, **p. 31** and 'Speech to the Metropolitan Sanitary Association', **p. 36**). The middle-class response to sanitary reform was thus motivated as much by fear and self-interest as by Evangelical or paternalistic notions of duty. It is worth noting that while paternalism acknowledged a degree of middle-class responsibility, it also constructed the working classes as children who, if needing help, also required guidance and control.

The history of the Public Health Movement was fraught with political tensions, practical difficulties and obstructionism. Despite the obvious need for reform established by the myriad reports and investigations of both official and voluntary sanitary workers such as Hector Gavin (see **p. 32**), attempts to introduce interventionist legislation were opposed by those who upheld the doctrines of self-help and a *laissez-faire* economy, as well as by local ratepayers. The doctrine of self-help was founded on the assumption that every individual was able to improve their standing through hard work, discipline and good conduct. Thus, it relieved the state of any responsibility for its subjects. A *laissez-faire* economy, in turn, allows for no government interference, arguing that the market will always look after itself and determine its own level.

It must also be noted that both the scale and severity of the problems faced by public health workers were unprecedented: inexperience and a lack of specialised knowledge hindered their efforts. Nonetheless, in 1848 the first Public Health Act was passed, establishing a General Board of Health and allowing each sanitary district to appoint a local board to oversee sewage disposal, water supplies and housing reform (London operated under a separate Metropolitan Commissioner

9 A. Wohl, *Endangered Lives: Public Health in Victorian Britain*, London: J.M. Dent, 1983, p. 133.
10 Altick (see note 5), p. 45.

of Sewers established in the same year). This was followed by a series of Nuisance Removal Acts that empowered local authorities to deal with excrement and refuse accumulation, as well as industrial waste and pollution. Unfortunately, the effectiveness of such Acts was limited by the fact that they were largely permissive rather than mandatory; in other words, they *allowed* local authorities to carry out improvements but did not *demand* that they do so. There were thus notable local discrepancies in their implementation. The situation improved somewhat with the 1866 Sanitary Act, which could force local authorities to carry out vital sewage work and supply water. As the historian Anthony Wohl informs us, however, 'enforcement through legal processes was difficult and expensive, and rarely contemplated or used'.[11] Thus it was the 1872 Public Health Act, demanding that each district appoint and empower a Medical Officer of Health, that marked a decisive step forward.

For the middle classes, who placed cleanliness next to Godliness, the threat represented by the urban masses was as much moral and social as it was physical. The working classes' acceptance of overcrowded and unsanitary living conditions was read not as a realistic attitude of resignation but, rather, as a sign of an innately depraved and animalistic nature. Constructed in these terms, this sector of the population was perceived to require (especially during the turbulent 1830s and 1840s) a system of strict policing and surveillance. Hence between the years of 1829 and 1856, the old system of parish constables was gradually replaced by a professional police force whose very presence was designed to prevent crime while maintaining proper standards of public behaviour (see 'On Duty with Inspector Field', p. 38). Of course this response must be seen in light of a more general anxiety about social stability. As the historian David Taylor suggests, crime 'took on a significance that went beyond its immediate impact. It was invested with new importance as the problems of modernisation became more apparent and as uncertainty increased.'[12]

Thus the middle-class response to the plight of the working classes was informed by two contradictory constructions. The first viewed the working classes as victims of an intolerable environment and advocated social reform, while the second saw them as a threat (both moral and physical) that necessitated strict policing. Both of these constructions informed Dickens's outlook and the resulting contradictions can be seen most clearly in his treatment of the homeless Jo. On the one hand, Dickens is clearly outraged at a society that ignores his plight: dying of fever and abandoned to the streets of London. Yet on the other, Inspector Bucket, determined to extract information from the poor child, is allowed to hound him with impunity (see Key Passages, pp. 131 and 143).

11 Wohl (see note 9), p. 113.
12 D. Taylor, *The New Police in Nineteenth–Century England: Crime, Conflict and Control*, Manchester: Manchester University Press, 1997, pp. 16–17.

Chancery Court

At the heart of *Bleak House* is the protracted and, ultimately, unresolved case of Jarndyce and Jarndyce. As we are told in Chapter 2, the case is 'about a will' and thus it fell under the jurisdiction of the Court of Chancery (for a discussion of Chancery, see D.A. Miller, p. 81; and Schor, p. 93). Established during the reign of Richard II (1377–99), the Court of Chancery differed from the Courts of Common Law in several respects. While the former dealt with cases involving wills, trusts and legacies, as well as guardianship, adoption and marriage, the latter was responsible for criminal cases such as theft or murder. Another key distinction between the two is that while the Common Law Courts called upon witnesses to give oral testimony in front of a judge and jury, the Court of Chancery did away with juries altogether and accepted only written evidence in the form of affidavits, which were then read aloud in Court by the lawyers. Thus while suitors like the novel's Richard Carstone and Miss Flite regularly attend the Court's proceedings, they are never called upon to speak. More importantly, unlike the Courts of Common Law, where judgments were bound by a rigid set of legal statutes, the Court of Chancery was conceived on the principle of equity; that is, on the principles of 'justness' or 'fairness'. In practice, this meant that the Lord Chancellor – the presiding judge – held sole discretionary power to rule on the individual merits of each case. For this reason, it was felt that Chancery was more just than its counterpart and many suitors turned to the Lord Chancellor and his Court when they believed that common law had failed to provide them with adequate relief.

By the mid-nineteenth century, however, the Court of Chancery had evolved into a notoriously inefficient and expensive system that was governed by a set of needlessly complex procedures (many of which were maintained simply to generate income for various Court officials and employees). For example, any party involved in a suit needed to maintain both a solicitor and a barrister whose financial interests lay in the indefinite perpetuation of the suit. In addition, each stage of the complex procedures demanded by the Court entailed yet another delay, as well as additional fees and expenses. Plaintiffs and defendants were also responsible for the cost of producing and copying the reams of documents related to the case (hence the need for law-copiers such as Nemo, the father of Esther Summerson). Throughout this entire process, the property or monies in question remained inaccessible to the suitors in order to ensure that all Court costs could be met. Thus, in *Bleak House*, Richard's hopes of receiving any portion of the Jarndyce estate are dashed when it is discovered that the entire estate has been consumed in costs and the case comes to an abrupt end (see Key Passages, p. 149). In light of this situation, it is hardly surprising that the need for legal reform had become one of the most pressing issues of the day (see Cole, p. 34 and Butt and Tillotson, p. 62). In 1852 Parliament finally responded to this demand by passing the Chancery Reform Act. Further reforms followed in 1854, 1858, 1862 and 1873.

It is worth noting that Dickens had first-hand experience of the plight faced by Chancery suitors. In 1844 he launched a suit against five publishers for breach of copyright when they published pirated editions of *A Christmas Carol*. Although the Court decided in his favour, the costs he incurred were greater than the damages awarded. Faced with further acts of piracy in 1846 he determined, like John Jarndyce of *Bleak House*, never to involve himself with Chancery again, stating that:

> 'it is better to suffer a great wrong than to have recourse to the much greater wrong of the law. I shall not easily forget the expense and anxiety, and horrible injustice of the *Carol* case, wherein, in asserting the plainest right on earth, I was really treated as if I were the robber, instead of the robbed. I know of nothing that could come, even of a successful action, which would be worth the mental trouble and disturbance it would cost.'[13]

The Literary Context

There can be no doubt that the age of Dickens was also the great age of the novel. Cutting across class and gender lines, novels became an omnipresent element of Victorian life. As the novelist Anthony Trollope observed in 1870: 'Novels are in the hands of us all; from the Prime Minister down to the last-appointed scullery maid. We have them in our library, our drawing-rooms, our bed-rooms, our kitchens – and in our nurseries.'[14] Yet in many ways, the origins of this genre were as humble as those of Dickens himself. In the early decades of the century, the novel was considered to be a young, upstart genre, ephemeral by its very nature. Artistically inferior to poetry, it was dubbed morally questionable by the rising tide of Evangelicals (see **p. 12**) and dismissed as mere entertainment and a waste of time by the Utilitarians, whose socio-economic philosophy was based on the principles of 'usefulness' and self-interest established by the economist Jeremy Bentham (1748–1832). Despite such concerns, novel reading was becoming an increasingly popular pastime with the general public. Growing literacy rates and the increase of leisure time associated with industrialisation and urbanisation; cheaper and faster printing processes resulting from technological advances; and the establishment of lending libraries like Mudie's (1842) (where, for an annual fee of a guinea, subscribers were able to borrow all the latest fiction), all helped to contribute to the growing dominance of the genre. By mid-century, the ascendancy of the novel was indisputable and it was widely accepted as a legitimate art form, one worthy of serious critical attention.

The novel's rise to critical respectability (as opposed to popularity) was closely tied to the rise of domestic realism, the genre most obviously associated with the

---

13 C. Dickens, letter to John Forster, cited in W.S. Holdsworth, *Charles Dickens as a Legal Historian*, New Haven, Conn.: Yale University Press, 1929, p. 80. For a more detailed discussion of Chancery Court, see Holdsworth, pp. 79–115.

14 A. Trollope, 'On English Prose Fiction as a Rational Amusement' [1870], cited in David (see Introduction, note 3), p. 1.

novels of George Eliot (author of *Adam Bede* (1859), *The Mill on the Floss* (1860) and *Middlemarch* (1872)) and Anthony Trollope (whose works include *The Warden* (1855) and *Barchester Towers* (1857)). Never constituting a coherent school or theory, realism was more of a general attitude regarding the relationship between art and reality. As is suggested by its very vocabulary – mirror, portrait, *daguerreotype*,[15] transcript, etc. – the ultimate aim of realism was to produce an accurate, faithful and natural representation of the external world. To achieve this, its advocates recommended that novelists limit themselves to depicting ordinary individuals and day-to-day events within a recognisable social and material context. Furthermore, in order not to draw attention to the novel's inherent and inevitable artificiality – it was, after all, an artistic construct rather than a 'slice of life' – the novelist's language and style should be as unobtrusive and transparent as possible. By adopting such stratagems, the realists hoped to blur the boundaries between art and life, making their readers forget that they were reading a work of fiction and accept, at least temporarily, the novelistic universe as their own. By constructing their works so carefully that they appeared to be completely unconstructed, the realists aspired to the paradoxical ideal of allowing artifice to masquerade as nature. By the 1850s, realism was *the* standard against which *all* novels were judged and evaluated. Quite simply, the more realistic they were, the better they were. In the words of one reviewer, 'A novel is good in proportion to its truth to nature; no matter where the scene is laid, or what the characters may be.'[16]

Arguably the single most important factor in the rise of realism was the rise of the middle classes themselves (the leisured wives and daughters of the middle-class family constituted the single largest market for novels, and were thus in a position to influence its development). I have already suggested that the middle classes were a relatively new phenomenon and were struggling to create a coherent sense of their own identity. The realists stepped in to meet this need by taking as their subject matter not the fantastic elements of romance or the gothic but, rather, the everyday lives and values of middle-class individuals and their society. By reading these accounts, the reader learned what it was to be a member of the middle class; they were offered a model to emulate and a code of behaviour to internalise.

Quite clearly, however, Dickens did not see himself as a realist: his assertion in the Preface to *Bleak House* – 'I have purposely dwelt upon the romantic side of familiar things' – explicitly sets him apart from his realistic counterparts. This much should already be obvious to anyone who has read the opening paragraph, with its introduction of a 'Megalosaurus, forty feet long or so, waddling like an elephantine lizard up Holborn Hill' (see Key Passages, **p. 106**). In fact, as is suggested by passages such as that describing the discovery of Krook's charred remains after he spontaneously combusts (see Key Passages, **p. 134**), Dickens's style is actually much closer to that associated with fantasy, fairytales and the

---

15 An early form of photography developed by Louis Daguerre in 1837.
16 '*Adam Bede*', *Edinburgh Review*, 110, July 1859, p. 223.

grotesque (see Schwarzbach, **p. 75**). Moreover, such non-naturalistic genres are deliberately employed as part of a conscious critique of the prevailing tendency towards realism and the scientific or rationalist spirit that informed it. As Dickens suggests:

> 'It does not seem to me to be enough to say of any description that it is the exact truth. . . . The exact truth should be there; but the merit or art in the narrator is the manner of stating the truth. . . . In these times, when the tendency is to be frightfully literal and catalogue-like – to make the thing, in short, a sum in reduction that any miserable creature can do in that way – I have an idea (really founded on the love of what I profess), that the very holding of popular literature through a kind of popular dark age, may depend on such fanciful treatment.'[17]

While advocating a 'fanciful' rather than a realistic treatment, Dickens never went so far as to disavow the relationship between art and life. Rather than severing the tie between them, he wished only to alter it, replacing a slavish fidelity to detail with what he termed a 'fantastic fidelity'.[18] The resulting picture might appear exaggerated or distorted, but by focussing on 'the romantic side of familiar things', it opened the eyes of all those who were 'purposely blind',[19] forcing them to confront and engage with what they would rather ignore (see, for example, Snagsby's reaction to the slum district Tom-all-Alone's, **p. 132**).

A Reminder

Bleak House was the most topical of novels. As Butt and Tillotson suggest, it was 'a fable for 1852' and 'a tract for the times'.[20] Dickens was a social critic who used his fiction as a platform not only to engage with the issues of his day, but also, by offering a direct and explicit critique, to call for remedial action. While it is obviously impossible to recapture fully the atmosphere in which *Bleak House* was conceived, we should never assume that it was produced, or consumed, within a vacuum. Both author and reader were (and are) firmly embedded in a specific social and material environment. For this reason, it is essential to bear in mind the issues raised in both the foregoing comments and the sources below when engaging with the novel.

17 Cited in Forster (see note 3), p. 563.
18 Cited in Forster (see note 3), p. 562.
19 C. Dickens, 'To Working Men' [1854], reprinted in D. Pascoe (ed.), *Charles Dickens: Selected Journalism 1850–1870*, Harmondsworth: Penguin, 1997, p. 467.
20 J. Butt and K. Tillotson, *Dickens at Work* [1957], 2nd edn, London: Methuen, 1982, pp. 179, 200.

Chronology

Bullet points are used to denote events in Dickens's life, and asterisks to denote historical and literary events. For an exhaustive list of Dickens's publications, both major and minor, the reader is referred to Paul Schlicke (ed.), *Oxford Reader's Companion to Dickens*, Oxford: Oxford University Press, 2000. Those interested in Dickens's life should see Peter Ackroyd, *Dickens*, London: Sinclair-Stevenson, 1990.

1812
- Charles Dickens born 7 February in Portsmouth
* Napoleon invades Russia; USA declares war on Britain

1813
- Family move to Southsea
* Jane Austen, *Pride and Prejudice*

1814
* England invades France; George Stephenson's steam locomotive; Jane Austen, *Mansfield Park*; Walter Scott, *Waverley*; William Wordsworth, *The Excursion*

1815
- Family move to London; Catherine Hogarth (CD's wife) born
* Battle of Waterloo (Wellington's defeat of France); Corn Laws passed (restricting the import of foreign grain)

1817
- Family move to Chatham
* Samuel Taylor Coleridge, *Biographia Literaria*; death of Jane Austen

1819
* Peterloo Massacre (when 60,000 people congregated in Manchester to hear a radical speaker, the militia killed 10–15 members of the crowd and hun-

dreds more were injured); Walter Scott, *Ivanhoe*; birth of George Eliot (Mary Ann Evans)

1821
- CD first attends school

1822
- Family returns to London; CD's education discontinued

1823
- Fanny (sister) becomes a boarder at Royal Academy of Music; Elizabeth (Dickens's mother) opens a day school which fails
* Mechanics' Institutes established in London and Glasgow (night-schools for working-class adults)

1824
- CD sent to work in Warren's Blacking Factory; John Dickens (father) arrested for debt and imprisoned in Marshalsea (February–May); CD in lodgings

1825
- John Dickens retires with pension; CD leaves Warren's and resumes education
* First passenger railway line

1826
- John Dickens works as parliamentary correspondent for *The British Press*

1827
- Family evicted from home for non-payment of rates; CD leaves school and becomes a solicitor's clerk

1828
- John Dickens reporting for *The Morning Herald*

1829
- CD teaches himself shorthand and works as a freelance reporter at Doctor's Commons
* Catholic Emancipation Act (allowing Catholics to hold a public office); Metropolitan Police Act (introducing a preventative police force)

1830
- CD reading at British Museum; first serious romance with Maria Beadnell
* Death of George IV; accession of William IV; July Revolutions in France; Sir Charles Lyell, *Principles of Geology* (3 vols, 1830–3)

1831

- CD becomes a reporter for the *Mirror of Parliament*
* Cholera epidemic (to 1832); Temporary Board of Health established to address issues of public health

1832

- CD becomes a parliamentary reporter for the *True Sun*; CD misses audition at Covent Garden Theatre due to illness
* First Reform Act (which doubled the electorate by extending the vote to those who owned or rented property worth £10 per year); Royal Commission on the Poor Law (producing national statistics on matters of public health); J.P. Kay, *The Moral and Physical Conditions of the Working Classes*; Alfred Tennyson, *Poems*

1833

- Relationship with Maria Beadnell broken off; 'A Dinner at Poplar Walk' in *The Monthly Magazine* (first published story)
* British Factory Act (forbidding children under 9 from working in mills and limiting the hours of those between the ages of nine and thirteen); Oxford Movement (asserting the authority of the Church over the state) begins with *Tracts for the Times*; abolition of slavery in British Empire; Thomas Carlyle, *Sartor Resartus* (–1834)

1834

- CD becomes staff reporter for the *Morning Chronicle* which publishes several sketches and stories; meets Catherine Hogarth; moves to Furnival's Inn
* Poor Law Amendment Act (establishing workhouses); Houses of Parliament burnt down

1835

- 'Sketches of London'; 'Scenes and Characters'; CD engaged to Catherine Hogarth
* Municipal Corporations Act (allowing towns to organise a paid police force)

1836

- *Pickwick Papers* (serialised March 1836–November 1837); various sketches and stories published; *Sketches by Boz*; CD's plays *The Strange Gentleman* and *The Village Coquettes* produced at St James's Theatre; CD assumes editorship of *Bentley's Miscellany*; marries Catherine Hogarth; leaves *The Morning Chronicle*; meets John Forster; *Sketches by Boz, Second Series*
* Chartist Movement begins (a working-class political movement)

1837

- *Oliver Twist* (serialised February 1837–April 1839); birth of Charles

Culliford Boz Dickens; family move to 48 Doughty Street (now Dickens House Museum); production of Dickens's short play *Is She His Wife?* at St James's Theatre; death of Mary Hogarth (CD's sister-in-law); first trip to the Continent

*   Death of William IV; accession of Victoria; smallpox epidemic (–1840); introduction of birth, marriage and death certificates; Thomas Carlyle, *The History of the French Revolution*

1838

*   *Nicholas Nickleby* (serialised March 1838–September 1839); *Sketches of Young Gentlemen*; *Memoirs of Joseph Grimaldi*; birth of Mary Dickens
*   Anti-Corn Law League founded; The People's Charter published by The Working Men's Association (demanding universal male suffrage, secret ballots, the payment of parliamentary members, the elimination of property qualifications for members, equal electoral districts, and annual elections); steamship service between England and US established

1839

*   *The Loving Ballad of Lord Bateman*; CD resigns as editor of *Bentley's Miscellany*; birth of Kate Macready Dickens; family move to Devonshire Terrace
*   Chartist riots; Rural Constabulary Act (allowing counties to form their own constabularies); Infants' Custody Act (allowing mothers custody of children under 7); L.J.M. Daguerre patents photographic technique

1840

*   *The Old Curiosity Shop* (serialised April 1840–February 1841); *Sketches of Young Couples*; introduction of CD's weekly journal *Master Humphrey's Clock*
*   Victoria and Albert marry; *Report from the Select Committee on the Health of Towns* (exploring issues of public health in large towns and cities); introduction of the penny post; invention of the telegraph

1841

*   *Barnaby Rudge* (serialised February–November 1841); birth of Walter Landor Dickens; CD refuses invitation to stand for Parliament
*   Robert Peel becomes Prime Minister; Niger Expedition

1842

*   CD and Catherine visit America; *American Notes*
*   Second Chartist Petition rejected; Detective Branch established in London; Mines Act (forbidding women and children under ten from working in mines); Copyright Act; Edwin Chadwick, *An Inquiry into the Sanitary Condition of the Labouring Population of Great Britain*

1843
- *Martin Chuzzlewit* (serialised January 1843–July 1844); *A Christmas Carol*
* Thomas Carlyle, *Past and Present*; William Wordsworth becomes Poet Laureate

1844
- Birth of Francis Jeffrey Dickens; CD moves from Chapman and Hall to Bradbury and Evans (publishers); family in Genoa; *The Chimes*
* Factory Act (limiting the hours of work for women and children); Ragged Schools Union founded (providing basic education to the poorest children); Benjamin Disraeli, *Coningsby*

1845
- CD and Catherine in Italy; CD forms Amateur Players to perform *Every Man in His Humour*; birth of Alfred D'Orsay Tennyson Dickens; *The Cricket on the Hearth*
* Friedrich Engels, *The Condition of the English Working Class* (translated into English in 1887); Benjamin Disraeli, *Sybil*; Irish Famine (–1847)

1846
- *Dombey and Son* (serialised October 1846–April 1848); CD edits *Daily News* (resigns 17 days later); *Pictures from Italy*; family in Lausanne and Paris; *The Battle of Life*
* Corn Laws repealed; Nuisance Removal and Diseases Prevention Act (empowering local authorities to make sanitary improvements); Railway boom begins

1847
- Birth of Sydney Smith Haldimand Dickens; Amateur Players tour with *Every Man in His Humour*; CD undertakes management of Urania Cottage
* Ten Hours Act (limiting women and children to a ten-hour working day); Metropolitan Sanitary Commission established; Anne Brontë, *Agnes Grey*; Charlotte Brontë, *Jane Eyre*; Emily Brontë, *Wuthering Heights*; William Makepeace Thackeray, *Vanity Fair* (–1848)

1848
- Amateur Players on tour; death of sister Fanny; *The Haunted Man*
* Revolutions in Europe; cholera epidemic (–1849); Public Health Act (establishing a General Board of Health, allowing local Boards of Health to be established and the appointment of Medical Officers of Health); City Sewers Act (limited to London, which operated independently of the Public Health Act); Karl Marx and Friedrich Engels, *Communist Manifesto* (translated into English in 1888); Pre-Raphaelite Brotherhood established; collapse of Chartism; Elizabeth Gaskell, *Mary Barton*; William Makepeace Thackeray, *Pendennis* (–1850)

1849

- *David Copperfield* (serialised May 1849–November 1850); birth of Henry Fielding Dickens
* Livingstone explores Africa; Henry Mayhew, *London Labour and the London Poor* in *The Morning Chronicle*; Charlotte Brontë, *Shirley*

1850

- CD launches and edits his weekly periodical *Household Words*; birth of Dora Annie Dickens; CD and Edward Bulwer-Lytton found the Guild of Literature and Art
* Roman Catholic hierarchy restored (extending the rights and powers of the Catholic Church in line with those of Catholic countries); Metropolitan Interments Act (closing the old London churchyards); Public Libraries Act (allowing local authorities to set up public lending libraries); Charles Kingsley, *Alton Locke*; William Wordsworth, *The Prelude*; Alfred Tennyson, *In Memoriam*

1851

- Catherine ill; death of Dora and John Dickens (father); Amateur Players perform for Queen Victoria; family move to Tavistock Square
* Great Exhibition in Crystal Palace, London; Shaftesbury Acts (enabling local authorities to buy land in order to build working-class housing); Window Tax repealed; Herman Melville, *Moby-Dick*; Harriet Beecher Stowe, *Uncle Tom's Cabin*

1852

- *Bleak House* (serialised March 1852–September 1853); birth of Edward Bulwer Lytton Dickens; *A Child's History of England*, vol. 1; Amateur Players on tour; first of many family holidays in Boulogne
* Death of Wellington; Museum of Ornamental Art opens (re-named Victoria and Albert Museum in 1889); William Makepeace Thackeray, *Henry Esmond*

1853

- Trips to Boulogne and Italy; *A Child's History of England*, vol. 2; CD's first public reading (undertaken to raise money for one of his many causes)
* Outbreak of cholera (–1854); compulsory vaccination against smallpox; Charlotte Brontë, *Villette*

1854

- *A Child's History of England*, vol. 3 (serialised January 1851–December 1853); *Hard Times* (serialised April–August 1854); trip to Boulogne
* Crimean War (–1856); British Medical Association founded; Coventry Patmore, *The Angel in the House* (–1863); Elizabeth Gaskell, *North and South* (serialised 1854–5 in *Household Words*)

1855
- *Little Dorrit* (serialised December 1855–June 1857); reunion with Maria Beadnell (CD's first love); CD becomes member of Administrative Reform Association; *The Lighthouse* performed at Tavistock House; family in Paris
* David Livingstone discovers Victoria Falls; Stamp Duty repealed (lowering the price of newspapers); Metropolitan Board of Works established to provide sewers; death of Charlotte Brontë; Anthony Trollope, *The Warden*

1856
- CD buys Gad's Hill Place; family return to England
* Police Act (demanding that all authorities establish police forces); Gustave Flaubert, *Madame Bovary*

1857
- *The Frozen Deep* performed at Tavistock House; CD meets Ellen Ternan; *The Lazy Tour of Two Idle Apprentices* (co-written with Wilkie Collins and serialised October in *Household Words*)
* Indian Mutiny; Matrimonial Causes Act (granting women the right to a divorce on the grounds of adultery plus cruelty, desertion or rape); Charlotte Brontë, *The Professor*; William Makepeace Thackeray, *The Virginians*; Anthony Trollope, *Barchester Towers*; George Eliot, *Scenes from Clerical Life*; Elizabeth Gaskell, *The Life of Charlotte Brontë*; Elizabeth Barrett Browning, *Aurora Leigh*

1858
- *Reprinted Pieces* (from *Household Words*); first public reading tour for profit; CD and Catherine separate
* Suppression of Indian Mutiny; East India Company abolished; London sewage system started (–1865)

1859
- *Household Words* concluded and *All the Year Round* launched; *A Tale of Two Cities* (serialised April–November); second reading tour
* Reform Bill defeated; Charles Darwin, *On the Origin of Species*; John Stuart Mill, *On Liberty*; Samuel Smiles, *Self-Help*; George Eliot, *Adam Bede*; Wilkie Collins, *The Woman in White* (serialised 1859–60 in *All the Year Round*)

1860
- *Great Expectations* (serialised December 1860–August 1861); *The Uncommercial Traveller* (series 1)
* First practical internal combustion engine invented by Jean-Joseph Etienne Lenoir; George Eliot, *The Mill on the Floss*

1861
- Public readings in London and third reading tour

*   American Civil War (–1865); death of Prince Albert; George Eliot, *Silas Marner*

1862

- Public readings in London
*   Albert Memorial built; George Eliot, *Romola*; Christina Rossetti, *Goblin Market*; John Stuart Mill, *Utilitarianism*

1863

- Readings continue in London; a series of readings in Paris (for charity); death of Walter (son) and Elizabeth Dickens (mother)
*   London's underground railway under way; Nuisance Removal Act; death of William Makepeace Thackeray

1864

- *Our Mutual Friend* (serialised May 1864–November 1865)
*   First Trades' Union Conference; Herbert Spencer, *Principles of Biology*; Leo Tolstoy, *War and Peace*; Contagious Diseases Act (allowing a policeman to stop any woman suspected of being a prostitute and force her to undergo medical examination); Louis Pasteur states his germ theory of disease

1865

- CD and Ellen Ternan involved in Staplehurst railway crash; *The Uncommercial Traveller* (2nd series)
*   Lincoln assassinated; slavery abolished in USA; John Ruskin, *Sesame and Lilies*; Lewis Carroll, *Alice in Wonderland*

1866

- Readings in London and several other cities
*   Government resigns after Reform Bill is defeated; outbreak of cholera (–1867); Dr Barnardo opens first home for destitute children; Sanitary Act (making certain health reforms compulsory rather then voluntary); George Eliot, *Felix Holt*; Fyodor Dostoevsky, *Crime and Punishment*

1867

- Reading tour of England and Ireland; American reading tour; first signs of deteriorating health; *No Thoroughfare* (co-written with Collins)
*   Second Reform Act (extending the franchise to all men who owned or rented properties in towns and increasing the representation of large cities); Karl Marx, *Das Kapital* (translated into English in 1887)

1868

- 'George Silverman's Explanation'; 'A Holiday Romance'; CD returns to England and begins farewell reading tour (–1869)
*   Royal Commission on Sanitary Administration appointed; Wilkie Collins, *The Moonstone*

1869
- First public reading of Nancy's murder (from *Oliver Twist*); reading tour cut short due to illness
* Suez Canal opens; Dmitri Mendeleev's periodic table; Matthew Arnold, *Culture and Anarchy*; John Stuart Mill, *On the Subjection of Women*

1870
- Readings in London; audience with Queen Victoria; CD dies 9 June and is buried in Poets' Corner, Westminster Abbey; *Edwin Drood* left incomplete (serialised April–September)
* First Elementary Education Act in England and Wales (establishing compulsory elementary education); Married Women's Property Act (allowing married women to own money and property in their own names)

Contemporary Documents

From **Thomas Carlyle, *Past and Present*** (1843), ed. Richard Altick, New York: New York University Press, 1977, from Book III, Chapter 2, 'Gospel of Mammonism', pp. 150–1

Thomas Carlyle (1795–1881) was one of the most important historians and social critics of his day. A fierce opponent of *laissez-faire* economics and utilitarianism (see Contextual Overview, **pp. 16** and **19**), his writings attack the increasingly mechanised, commercial and alienated world of industrial Britain. Although he belonged to no particular denomination, Carlyle was, in certain ways, a deeply religious individual who believed in Christian duty and community. The language and diction of the following extract is biblical and, at times, reminiscent of the prophetic tone of the Old Testament (it is the same tone adopted by the third-person narrator of *Bleak House* following the death of Jo, the crossing-sweeper; see Key Passages, **p. 143**). Like Jesus, Carlyle employs a parable – a short narrative designed to teach a religious lesson through analogy – to convey his message. The story of the Irish widow who infects her neighbours with typhus (a highly contagious disease transmitted through the faeces of lice and fleas) offers the reader two models of relation: those of community (based on compassion and human sympathy) and those of contagion. This opposition between community and contagion is also a central theme in *Bleak House*. In a world where so many characters deny their 'connexion' (Chapter 16) to others (and the responsibility this 'connexion' entails), it is left to Jo to remind them of this fact by infecting Esther with a disease that is itself the product of social neglect (see Contextual Overview, **p. 16** and 'Speech to the Metropolitan Sanitary Association', **p. 36**). Dickens was a fervent admirer of Carlyle and, as Paul Schlicke points out, the latter's 'practical ethics' anticipate Esther's emphasis on helping those around her (see, for example, Key Passages, **p. 122**).[1]

---

1 P. Schlicke, *Oxford Reader's Companion to Dickens*, Oxford: Oxford University Press, 2000, p. 68.

One of Dr. Alison's Scotch facts struck us much.[2] A poor Irish Widow, her husband having died in one of the Lanes of Edinburgh, went forth with her three children, bare of all resource, to solicit help from the Charitable Establishments of the City. At this Charitable Establishment and then at that she was refused; referred from one to the other, helped by none; – till she had exhausted them all; till her strength and her heart failed her: she sank down in typhus-fever; died, and infected her Lane with fever, so that 'seventeen other persons' died of fever there in consequence. The humane Physician asks thereupon, as with a heart too full for speaking, Would it not have been *economy* to help this poor Widow? She took typhus-fever, and killed seventeen of you! – Very curious. The forlorn Irish Widow applies to her fellow-creatures, as if saying, "Behold I am sinking, bare of help: ye must help me! I am your sister, bone of your bone;[3] one God made us: ye must help me!" They answer, "No; impossible: thou art no sister of ours." But she proves her sisterhood; her typhus-fever kills *them*: they actually were her brothers, though denying it! Had man ever to go lower for a proof?

For, as indeed was very natural in such case, all government of the Poor by the Rich has long ago been give over to Supply-and-demand, Laissez-faire and such like, and universally declared to be 'impossible.' "You are no sister of ours; what shadow of proof is there? Here are our parchments, our padlocks, proving indisputably our money-safes to be *ours*, and you to have no business with them. Depart! It is impossible" – Nay, what wouldst thou thyself have us do? Cry indignant readers. Nothing, my friends, – till you have got a soul for yourselves again. Till then all things are 'impossible.' [. . .] Nothing is left but that she prove her sisterhood by dying, and infecting you with typhus. Seventeen of you lying dead will not deny such proof that she *was* flesh of your flesh;[4] and perhaps some of the living may lay it to heart.

From **Hector Gavin, *Sanitary Ramblings: Being Sketches and Illustrations of Bethnal Green*** (1848), London: Frank Cass & Co. Ltd., 1971, pp. 22–3

Hector Gavin (1815–55) was a lecturer in forensic medicine at Charing Cross Hospital and a member of the Health of Towns Association. Established in 1844, this Association played an important role in publicising the need for housing reform. In the course of his investigations, Gavin undertook house-to-house surveys of many working-class neighbourhoods. *Sanitary Ramblings* documents what he encountered in Bethnal Green, a notorious slum district in East London. Gavin's description of 'Beckford Row' sheds light on Dickens's description of both the brickmaker's cottage and Tom-all-Alone's (see Key Passages

---

2 [Carlyle's note.] *Observations on the Management of the Poor in Scotland*: By William Pulteney Alison, M.D. (Edinburgh, 1840).
3 Genesis 2.23.
4 Another reference to Genesis 2.23.

pp. 120 and 127) and, more generally, the urgent need for wholesale sanitary reform (see Contextual Overview, p. 15 and 'Speech to the Metropolitan Sanitary Association', p. 36). Like all social investigators, Gavin must achieve a balance between authenticity (his readers must believe that he is offering an accurate account) and good taste (so as not to offend). The result is a mixture of factual and euphemistic statements (e.g. 'soil' for all manner of rubbish, including excrement) typical of the social reportage of the time.

This extract refers to three of the most common sources of fever (a catch-all term for a number of diseases, including typhus, cholera and smallpox): the lack of sewers or any other means of waste disposal, overcrowding and the absence of accessible, clean water. When a privy overflowed – a common occurrence after a heavy rain – its decomposing contents became a breeding ground for disease. In addition, this material seeped through the surrounding soil – and even through the floors and walls of the houses – contaminating any nearby water supply. In such a situation, cleanliness was absolutely essential to health yet water (tainted as it was) was in short supply. Those who were able to collect it during its sporadic hours of supply would still need to carry it some distance back to their houses. Those who missed the appointed hours (or were too exhausted to fetch it) were forced to use the stagnant remains from the barrel, or water butt, described by Gavin. Thus it is hardly surprising that many working-class people could not achieve, or maintain, the degree of cleanliness expected by the middle classes. These unsanitary conditions were further compounded by the overcrowding that characterised so many urban districts. Gavin's report of an entire family living, eating and sleeping in a single room was not unusual. As these houses were usually poorly ventilated, the resulting quality of air could actually be deadly. For the Victorians, however, the implications of overcrowding were moral as well as physical: an entire family sleeping in a single room – often a single bed – was an affront to middle-class notions of decency (see Contextual Overview, p. 12).

BECKFORD-ROW, 14. – A narrow confined row of 16 houses with small plots in front. On the south side, they form the northern half of the houses in Alfred-row. The half houses which are in Beckford-row,[1] consist of 2 rooms, one above the other, each room being generally occupied by a separate family. The place is *abominably filthy*; the drains from the houses into a kind of central gutter, are choked up. The privies[2] are full, exposed, and overflowing, and the soil covers the front plots, in which heaps of filth are accumulated. [. . .] In 14 weeks, 13 cases of fever occurred, and one case of erysipelas.[3] Eight cases of fever occurred in one

---

1 In other words, they are 'back-to-back' terraces that allow for no ventilation at the back of either house.
2 Open pits dug into the ground that functioned as toilets. In certain districts, it was common for a single privy to serve for more than one house.
3 A highly contagious skin disease associated with blisters and fever.

house. Threee [sic] persons slept in the lower room, five in the upper; two cases occurred in the opposite house, and three a few doors further off. There is only one stand-tap to supply water to these houses. The reservoir to contain the supply which takes place for two hours three times a-week, is a small barrel 21 inches in diameter, and 12 deep.

From **Alfred Whaley Cole, 'The Martyrs of Chancery'**, Household Words (2) 7 December 1850, pp. 250–2

Alfred Cole (1823–96) combined a successful law career with an ongoing interest in literature. He was qualified to practise in both England and South Africa (where he was eventually appointed as a judge) and, in the course of his life, published several novels and collections of sketches and tales. 'The Martyrs of Chancery' was written when Cole was newly qualified and waiting for briefs.[1] Cole's article was published in Dickens's own weekly periodical Household Words (1850–9). Like Bleak House, this magazine was conceived as a topical publication and a vehicle for social reform, as well as entertainment (for the relationship between the two, see Schwarzbach, **p. 74**). As Dickens stated to one of his regular contributors, the novelist Elizabeth Gaskell, its purpose was 'the raising up of those that are down, and the general improvement of our social condition'.[2] As an editor, he was notoriously demanding and insisted on maintaining personal control over the material that appeared in his magazine. Thus there can be no doubt that Dickens not only was familiar with this piece but also endorsed the views that it set forth.

While Bleak House may offer a damning indictment of Chancery, it played no role in instigating legal reform – a fact supported by the date of this article (see Brimley, **p. 58** and Butt and Tillotson, **p. 62**). It is also worth noting that this piece is primarily concerned with the long-term imprisonment that could result from any involvement in a Chancery suit. As John Butt and Kathleen Tillotson point out, in this respect it is more typical of the treatment of Chancery found in Dickens's first novel, Pickwick Papers (1836–7), than of Bleak House, which addresses the inherent flaws within the system itself: inertia, confusion, prohibitive costs, vested interests and, of course, the endless deferral of judgments (see Contextual Overview, **p. 18**).[3] Having acknowledged this point, it is worth pointing out that the ironic tone adopted by the third-person narrator of Bleak House (especially when dealing with Jarndyce and Jarndyce, the suit that blights the lives of so many of the novel's characters) bears a remarkable resemblance to that used in this article (see Key Passages, **p. 107**). Cole's description of a

---

1   A. Lohrli, *Household Words: A Weekly Journal 1850–1859 Conducted by Charles Dickens*, Toronto: University of Toronto Press, 1973, pp. 229–30.
2   Cited in Schlicke (see Carlyle, note 1), p. 284.
3   Butt and Tillotson (see Contextual Overview, note 19), pp. 182–3.

languishing prisoner, moreover, anticipates the wasting effect that Chancery will exercise on Jarndyce's cousin, Richard Carstone, whose fortune and health is destroyed by his involvement in Chancery (see Key Passages, p. 139).

[. . .] A Chancery prisoner is, in fact, a far more hopeless mortal than a convict sentenced to transportation;[4] for the latter knows that, at the expiration of a certain period, he will, in any event, be a free man. The Chancery prisoner has no such certainty; he may, and he frequently does, waste a lifetime in the walls of a gaol, whither he was sent in innocence; because, perchance, he had the ill-luck to be one of the next of kin of some testator who made a will which no one could comprehend or the heir of some intestate[5] who made none. Any other party interested in the estate commences a Chancery suit, which he must defend or be committed to prison for "contempt".[6] A prison is his portion, whatever he does; for, if he answers the bill filed against him, and cannot pay the costs, he is also clapped in gaol for "contempt". Thus, what in ordinary life is but an irrepressible expression of opinion or a small discourtesy, is "in Equity",[7] a high crime punishable with imprisonment – sometimes perpetual. Whoever is pronounced guilty of contempt in a Chancery sense is taken from his family, his profession, or his trade (perhaps his sole means of livelihood), and consigned to a gaol where he must starve, or live on a miserable pittance of three shillings and sixpence a week charitably doled out to him from the county rate.

Disobedience of an order of the Court of Chancery – though that order may command you to pay more money than you ever had, or to hand over property which is not yours and was never in your possession – is contempt of court. No matter how great soever your natural reverence for the time-honoured institutions of your native land: no matter, though you regard the Lord High Chancellor of Great Britain as the most wonderful man upon earth, and his court as the purest fount of Justice, where she sits weighing out justice with a pair of Oertling's balances,[8] you may yet be pronounced to have been guilty of "contempt". For this there is no pardon. You are in the catalogue of the doomed, and are doomed accordingly. [. . .]

It must not, however, be supposed that Chancery never releases its victims. We must be just to the laws of "Equity". There is actually a man now in London whom they have positively let out of prison! They had, however, prolonged his agonies during seventeen years. He was committed for contempt in not paying certain costs, as he had been ordered. He appealed from the order; but until his appeal was heard, he had to remain in durance vile. The Court of Chancery, like all dignified bodies, is never in a hurry; and therefore, from having no great

4   In the first half of the nineteenth century, convicted prisoners could be punished by being transported to penal colonies in Australia, usually for a period of seven years.
5   A person who dies without leaving a will.
6   A person who disobeys an order of a court of law is said to be 'in contempt'.
7   For a discussion of Equity see Contextual Overview, p. 18.
8   A set of precision balances manufactured by the London firm of Oertling.

influence, and a very small stock of money to forward his interest, the poor man could only get his cause finally heard and decided on in December 1849 – seventeen years from the date of his imprisonment. And, after all, the Court decided that the original order was wrong; so that he had been committed for seventeen years *by mistake*!

How familiar to him must have been the fact of that poor, tottering man, creeping along to rest on the bench under the wall yonder. He is very old, but not so old as he looks. He is a poor prisoner and another victim to Chancery. He has long ago forgotten, if he even knew, the particulars of his own case, or the order which sent him to a gaol. He can tell you more of the history of this gloomy place and its defunct brother, the Fleet,[9] than any other man. [. . .] He knows nothing of the world outside – it is dead to him. Relations and friends have long ceased to think of him or perhaps even to know of his existence. [. . .] What has *he* to do with hope? He has been thirty-eight years a Chancery prisoner.

From **Charles Dickens, speech delivered to the Metropolitan Sanitary Association** (London, 10 May 1851) in K.J. Fielding, ed., *The Speeches of Charles Dickens*, Oxford: Clarendon Press, 1970, pp. 128–9

This speech offers a clear and concise account of Dickens's feelings about the need for fundamental sanitary reform. During the 1850s, he became increasingly vocal on this issue and had, in fact, been a speaker at the inaugural meeting of the Metropolitan Sanitary Association the previous year. This concern with public health dates back to 1842 when Dickens received a copy of Edwin Chadwick's *Report on the Sanitary Condition of the Labouring Population of Great Britain* from his brother-in-law, Henry Austen, who worked with Chadwick. A disciple of Bentham (see Contextual Overview, **p. 19**), Chadwick (1800–90) is widely credited with initiating the sanitary reform movement. He firmly believed that the state must intervene in issues of public health and was a tireless campaigner for centralisation in matters of public health. Another key figure mentioned by Dickens is Thomas Southwood Smith (1788–1861). Another Benthamite, Smith was a medical advisor to the Poor Law Commission of 1832 and is best known for establishing a connection between disease and physical environment. In asserting that sanitary improvements must be a priority for all social reformers, Dickens was in line with the majority of public-health workers who linked both immorality and anti-social behaviour to squalid living conditions (for a discussion of these conditions, see Gavin, **p. 32**).

The notion of disease linking suburb to slum surfaces as a prominent theme in *Bleak House* (it also appears in Carlyle, see **p. 31**). The unidentified fever (probably smallpox) that Esther contracts from Jo is only the most obvious example of how contagion brings together a range of disparate characters and

---

9   A debtor's prison demolished in 1844.

environments. It was precisely because the spread of disease could not be contained within slum districts (and therefore constituted a threat to all classes) that Dickens spoke in support of the Board of Health. Established by the 1848 Public Health Act, this Board was empowered to create local boards to regulate drainage, water supply, waste disposal and burial grounds. It thus represented an important step towards centralisation in sanitary and health reform (see Contextual Overview, **p. 16**). In this extract I have eliminated Fielding's footnotes.

[. . .] I have but a few words to say, either on the needfulness of Sanitary Reform, or on the consequent usefulness of the Metropolitan Sanitary Association.

That no one can estimate the amount of mischief which is grown in dirt; that no one can say, here it stops, or there it stops, either in its physical or its moral results, when both begin in the cradle and are not at rest in the obscene grave [*hear, hear*], is now as certain as it is that the air from Gin Lane will be carried, when the wind is Easterly, into May Fair, and that if you once have vigorous pestilence raging furiously in Saint Giles's, no mortal list of Lady Patronesses can keep it out of Almack's.[1] [*Hear, hear.*]

Twelve or fifteen years ago, some of the first valuable reports of Mr. Chadwick and of Dr. Southwood Smith strengthening and much enlarging my previous imperfect knowledge of this truth, made me, in my sphere, earnest in the Sanitary Cause. And I can honestly declare tonight, that all the use I have since made of my eyes—or nose [*laughter*]—that all the information I have since been able to acquire through any of my senses, has strengthened me in the conviction that Searching Sanitary Reform must precede all other social remedies [*cheers*], and that even Education and Religion can do nothing where they are most needed, until the way is paved for their ministrations by Cleanliness and Decency. [*Hear.*] Am I singular in this opinion? You will remember the speech made this night by the Right Reverend Prelate,[2] which no true Sanitary Reformer can have heard without emotion. [*Hear, hear.*] What avails it to send a Missionary to me, a miserable man or woman living in a fœtid Court where every sense bestowed upon me for my delight becomes a torment, and every minute of my life is new mire added to the heap under which I lie degraded? To what natural feeling within me is he to address himself? What ancient chord within me can he hope to touch? Is it my remembrance of my children? It is a remembrance of distortion and decay, scrofula[3] and fever? Would he address himself to my hopes of immortality? I am so surrounded by material filth that my Soul can not rise to the contemplation of an immaterial existence! Or, if I be a miserable child, born and nurtured in

1 Gin Lane and St Giles's were two notorious slum districts while Mayfair was (and is) a fashionable district in London. Anyone who wished to gain entry into the highly fashionable Almack's Assembly Rooms (established in London in 1765 by William Almack) must first have been approved by the all-female committee known as the Lady Patronesses of Almack's.
2 The Bishop of Ripon.
3 Tuberculosis of the neck lymph glands.

the same wretched place, and tempted, in these better times, to the Ragged School,[4] what can the few hours' teaching that I get there do for me, against the noxious, constant, ever-renewed lesson of my whole existence. [*Hear, hear.*] But, give me my first glimpse of Heaven through a little of its light and air—give me water—help me to be clean—lighten this heavy atmosphere in which my spirit droops and I become the indifferent and callous creature that you see me—gently and kindly take the body of my dead relation out of the small room where I grow to be so familiar with the awful change that even *its* sanctity is lost to me—and, Teacher, then I'll hear, you know how willingly, of Him whose thoughts were so much with the Poor, and who had compassion for all human sorrow!

From **Charles Dickens, 'On Duty with Inspector Field'**, *Household Words* (3) 14 June 1851, pp. 265–70

Dickens's legendary admiration for the police and detective branch is in marked contrast to his utter contempt for other government officials and systems (see, for example, his description of the government in Key Passages, **p. 124**). This article was based on an actual expedition that Dickens undertook in 1851 with Charles Field, an Inspector in the Detective Department established by the Commissioners of Metropolitan Police in 1842. Along with two other articles on the same subject that appeared in Dickens's *Household Words*, it played a key role in making both the police and the detectives acceptable, even popular, with the middle-class public. Although Dickens denied that Inspector Field provided the original for *Bleak House*'s Inspector Bucket, there are a number of marked similarities between the two figures.[1] Most obviously, Bucket is endowed with the same penetrating insight, bordering on omniscience, as Field is shown to possess in this article (see Key Passages, **p. 131**). The similarities between this piece and *Bleak House* are not limited to Bucket and Field; Dickens returns to the sense of disbelief inspired by Rats' Castle (a cheap lodging house) in his description of Snagsby's first encounter with the slum district known as Tom-all-Alone's (see Key Passages, **p. 132** and Schwarzbach, **p. 75**). Note, too, the use of the collective pronouns 'we' and 'our', which allow Dickens to partake in Field's power and authority (for a discussion of these issues, see D.A. Miller, **p. 83**). Furthermore, in revealing the hidden side of life in London, Field performs the same function as our novelist.

Inspector Field comes in [. . .] Is Rogers ready? Rogers is ready, strapped and great-coated, with a flaming eye in the middle of his waist, like a deformed Cyclops.[2] Lead on, Rogers, to Rats' Castle!

---

4   Ragged schools offered very basic instruction to deprived children.

---

1   P. Collins, *Dickens and Crime* [1962], 3rd edn, London: Macmillan and St Martin's Press, 1994, pp. 206–7.

2   The one-eyed monster of Greek mythology. Here, Dickens is using the creature as a metaphor for the bull's eye, or lantern, carried by policemen.

How many people may there be in London, who, if we had brought them deviously and blindfold, to this street, fifty paces from the Station House, and within call of Saint Giles's church, would know it for a not remote part of the city in which their lives are passed? How many, who amidst this compound of sickening smells, these heaps of filth, these tumbling houses, with all their vile contents, animate and inanimate, slimily over-flowing into the black road, would believe that they breathe *this* air? How much Red Tape[3] may there be, that could look round on the faces which now hem us in – for our appearance here has caused a rush from all points to a common centre – the lowering foreheads, the sallow cheeks, the brutal eyes, the matted hair, the infected, vermin-haunted heaps of rags – and say, 'I have thought of this. I have not dismissed the thing. I have neither blustered it away, nor frozen it away, nor tied it up and put it away, nor smoothly said pooh, pooh! to it when it has been shown to me?' [. . .]

[. . .] Inspector Field's eye is the roving eye that searches every corner of the cellar as he talks. Inspector Field's hand is the well-known hand that has collared half the people here, and motioned their brothers, sisters, fathers, mothers, male and female friends, inexorably to New South Wales.[4] Yet Inspector Field stands in this den, the Sultan of the place. Every thief here cowers before him, like a schoolboy before his schoolmaster. All watch him, all answer when addressed, all laugh at his jokes, all seek to propriate him. This cellar company alone – to say nothing of the crowds surrounding the entrance from the street above, and making the steps shine with eyes – is strong enough to murder us all, and willing enough to do it; but let Inspector Field have a mind to pick out one thief here, and take him; let him produce that ghostly truncheon from his pocket, and say, with his business-air, 'My lad, I want you!' and all Rats' Castle shall be stricken with paralysis, and not a finger move against him, as he fits the handcuffs on! [. . .]

There should be strange dreams here. [. . .] To lie at night, wrapped in the legend of my slinking life; to take the cry that pursues me, waking, to my breast in sleep; to have it staring at me, and clamouring for me, as soon as consciousness returns; to have it for my first-foot on New-Year's day, my Valentine, my Birthday salute, my Christmas greeting, my parting with the old year. STOP THIEF!

And to know that I *must* be stopped, come what will. To know that I am no match for this individual energy and keenness, or this organised and steady system! Come across the street, here, and entering by a little shop, and yard, examine these intricate passages and doors, contrived for escape, flapping and counter-flapping, like the lids of the conjurer's boxes. But what avail they? Who gets in by a nod, and shows their secret working to us? Inspector Field. [. . .]

3 A term for needless bureaucracy.
4 Convicted criminals were transported to New South Wales in Australia.

From **Charles Dickens, 'Suckling Pigs'**, *Household Words* (4)
8 November 1851, pp. 145–6

As Michael Slater points out, the title of this article refers to an earlier
piece from *Household Words* entitled 'Whole Hogs' (23 August 1851), 'in which
Dickens had attacked fanatical "whole hog" extremism in such matters as temperance, pacificism and vegetarianism. Bloomerism, is seen as potentially
extremist but as yet only a "suckling pig".'[1] Bloomerism, in turn, refers to
Amelia Jenks Bloomer (1818–94), an American pioneer in the Temperance and
women's rights movements. In order to facilitate easier movement, she advocated the adoption of shorter skirts with full trousers that became known as
'bloomers' but this term (along with 'bloomerism') was also used as a deroga-
tory label for those who fought for women's rights.

'Suckling Pigs' bears directly on the portrayal of Esther and Mrs Jellyby in
Bleak House, where these two characters are used to represent a 'proper' and
an 'improper' femininity (see Contextual Overview, **p. 13** and Key Passages,
pp. 113 and **119**). Dickens clearly subscribed to the separate spheres doctrine
that placed the middle-class woman firmly within a home that, if properly man-
aged, provided a haven and retreat for her male counterpart. As he suggests in a
letter to the philanthropist Angela Burdett Coutts, 'every home in all this land
. . . [is] . . . a World, in which a woman's course of influence and action is marked
out by Heaven'.[2] Misguided women, like Mrs Jellyby, who 'must go in to be a
public character', do so only at the expense of their home and family. In essence,
the argument put forth by the fictional Mr Bellows of this article directly anticipates Mr Jellyby's warning to his daughter Caddy, on the eve of her wedding, to
'Never have a mission' (Chapter 30).

[. . .] In a word, if there were anything that we could dispense with in Mrs.
Bellows above all other things, we believe it would be a Mission. We should put
the question thus to Mrs. Bellows. 'Apple of our eye, we will freely admit your
inalienable right to step out of your domestic path into any phase of public
appearance and palaver that pleases you best; but we doubt the wisdom of such a
sally. Beloved one, does your sex seek influence in the civilised world? Surely it
possesses influence therein to no mean extent, and has possessed it since the
civilised world was. Should we love our Julia (assuming, for the sake of argument,
the Christian name of Mrs. Bellows to be Julia), – should we love our Julia better,
if she were a Member of Parliament, a Parochial Guardian, a High Sheriff, a
Grand Juror, or a woman distinguished for her able conduct in the chair?[3] Do we
not, on the contrary, rather seek in the society of our Julia, a haven of refuge from
Members of Parliament, Parochial Guardians, High Sheriffs, Grand Jurors, and

---

1   M. Slater, *Dickens and Women*, London: J.M. Dent, 1983, p. 437, footnote 19.
2   Cited in Slater (see note 1), p. 310.
3   Various examples of public offices and posts.

able chairmen? Is not the home-voice of our Julia as the song of a bird, after considerable bow-wowing out of doors? And is our Julia certain that she has a small table and water-bottle Mission round the corner, when here are nine (say, for the sake of argument, nine) little Bellowses to mend, or mar, at home? [. . .]

And it is a similar feature in this little pig, that even if Mrs. Bellows chooses to become, of her own free will and liking, a Bloomer, that won't do. She must agitate, agitate, agitate. She must take to the little table and water-bottle. She must go in to be a public character. She must work away at a Mission. It is not enough to do right for right's sake. There can be no satisfaction for Mrs. Bellows, in satisfying her mind after due reflection that the thing she contemplates is right, and therefore ought to be done, and so in calmly and quietly doing it, conscious that therein she sets a righteous example which never can in the nature of things be lost and thrown away. Mrs. Bellows has no business to be self-dependent, and to preserve a quiet little avenue of her own in the world, begirt with her own influences and duties. She must discharge herself of a vast amount of words, she must enlist into an Army composed entirely of Trumpeters, she must come (with the Misses Bellows) into a resounding Spartan[4] Hall for the purpose. [. . .]

---

4   Relating to the ancient Greek city of Sparta and suggesting austerity.

2

Interpretations

Critical History

Today it is widely accepted that *Bleak House* is one of the most significant pieces of writing produced by the Victorian period. Generating a flurry of critical activity in recent years, its place alongside the accepted greats – *Jane Eyre*, *Middlemarch*, etc. – has never been as assured. Yet the novel's reputation was not always so secure. From the very first reviews which nominated *Bleak House* as either the best or the worst of Dickens's works – or, more confusingly, the best *and* the worst – the critical reception of this novel has been unusually changeable and contradictory. In the words of John Forster:

> Some are in raptures over one part, some over another, and some very particular fellows are carping at every part. The judgements on *Bleak House* are, in short, as various as judgements are apt to be upon a man whose failings it is thought a subtle test of criticism to discover, for the very reason that all the world admires and likes him, and his books are bought and read by everybody.[1]

In the intervening century and a half, *Bleak House* has continued to provide fertile ground for the critics and their judgements remain as varied as Forster suggests. Social and historical changes inevitably altered the ways in which the novel was received while the changing nature of the critical landscape, together with the advent of new methodologies, led to a proliferation of readings undreamt of by earlier generations of critics. In the end, perhaps it is only appropriate that a novel as profuse and multifarious as *Bleak House* should have evoked such a wide variety of responses. In the pages that follow, I will outline the major trends and developments that characterise the complex critical history of *Bleak House*.

---

1   J. Forster, review of *Bleak House*, *The Examiner*, 8 October 1853, p. 643.

The Contemporary Reaction

By the time the first monthly instalment of *Bleak House* appeared in March 1852, Dickens was arguably the most famous novelist of his time. Having achieved in 1836 a modest success with his journalistic collection *Sketches by Boz*, his meteoric rise to fame began with *Pickwick Papers* later in the same year. At its height, *Pickwick Papers* was selling 40,000 copies of each number[2] and its phenomenal success secured Dickens a flurry of new offers and opportunities. Thus established as a humorous novelist with a keen eye for detail and an ability to create memorable characters, Dickens went on to pen another seven novels between 1837 and 1852, as well as a number of Christmas stories and a host of non-fictional writings. While growing ever more popular with the general public, Dickens did not emerge unscathed from the critical arena. Indeed, as Forster's comment suggests, Dickens's popularity seemed to irk the critics, provoking accusations that he was writing too much and too quickly in order to meet the public demand and, as a result, was bound to come tumbling down from his pedestal. Without entering into a discussion of the reception of individual novels, it is worth noting that it is during this period that we first encounter the two charges – a tendency towards exaggeration and a basic inability to construct a plot – that were to plague Dickens throughout his career and feature prominently in contemporary discussions of *Bleak House*.

To understand such charges of exaggeration, we need to remember that mid-century criticism was dominated by the demand for realism (see Contextual Overview, p. 20). Evaluated according to its tenets, it is hardly surprising that a novel like *Bleak House* was found to be lacking. When critics demanded whether this novel – which opens with a description of a dinosaur walking up Holborn Hill – was 'representative of experience' or 'true to life', the answer was a resounding 'no'. As a result, even the most favourable of the contemporary reviews are littered with accusations of exaggeration, distortion and improbability (see, for example, Chorley, p. 56). The predominance of such terms as 'unnatural', 'false', 'impossible', 'unreal', etc., testifies to the critical sway held by the realists. Throughout the 1850s and 1860s there were repeated calls for Dickens to cast his novels 'under the broad open sky of nature, instead of in the most brilliant palace of art'.[3]

Another issue that dominated novel criticism at mid-century was the need for organic unity. The demand that all parts of a novel be related and subordinated to an over-reaching whole elevated the novelist from a mere entertainer to a dedicated artist by emphasising the discipline and control needed to achieve it. Subplots and extraneous episodes or characters were deemed to have no place in a well-constructed novel and were read as a sign of shoddy workmanship. Not surprisingly, a novel as teeming with incident and character as *Bleak House* was

2   Schlicke (see Carlyle, note 1), p. 455.
3   H. Martineau, *Autobiography* [1877], cited in G.H. Ford, *Dickens and His Readers: Aspects of Novel-Criticism Since 1836*, New York: W.W. Norton, 1965, p. 130.

inevitably criticised for being poorly constructed and lacking a coherent plot. The reviewer for *Bentley's Miscellany* was only voicing the general consensus when he complained: 'We feel that the story has not been carefully constructed, [. . .] The want of art is apparent, if we look only at the entire work' (see **p. 61**).

In part, the perceived 'want of art' in *Bleak House* may be attributed to the fact that its critics seemingly did not understand how to read it. In a crucial passage from Chapter 16, the narrator demands, 'What connexion can there have been between many people in the innumerable histories of this world, who, from opposite sides of great gulfs, have, nevertheless, been very curiously brought together!' (see Key Passages, **p. 126**). As J. Hillis Miller eventually went on to suggest, this passage is actually a directive to the reader, urging them to actively search for and establish 'connexions' between the various elements in the novel (see **p. 67**). Unfortunately, the hint was lost upon the majority of Dickens's contemporary reviewers who largely failed to recognise the vast and intricate web of 'connexions' that render *Bleak House* one of the most tightly constructed novels of the period. Needless to say, such views have not been upheld by modern critics and, as we shall see, explorations of the novel's thematic unity represent a significant trend in its more recent critical history.

What Dickens was seen to lack as a constructor of plots, he more than made up for as a creator of characters. The early reviewers of *Bleak House* were generally in agreement that 'Delineation of character [was] his *forte*' and assertions that 'as the creator of distinct types of humanity, he stands second only to Shakespeare'[4] were actually quite commonplace. Despite the lavish praise implied by such comparisons, the critics were not slow in registering certain objections. The most serious of these was part and parcel of the prevailing sway of realism. Realism demanded the depiction of ordinary men and women, the kind of individuals one might actually expect to meet. Such characters must have a fully developed inner life and be consistent in their behaviour and actions. Dickens, in contrast, was seen to rely on external tics or turns of phrase in his characterisation and, instead of creating what we might now call well-rounded characters, had a tendency to produce mere caricatures. He had, moreover, an unhealthy predilection for what H.F. Chorley described as 'eccentrics, Bedlamites,[5] ill-directed and disproportioned people' (see **p. 56**). As a result, many of the novel's characters were judged to be both exaggerated and unnatural.

Because of her central role in the novel and the prominent position she assumes in twentieth-century criticism (see extracts by Langland, **p. 84**; Dever, **p. 88**; and Schor, **p. 93**), it is worth pointing out that Esther Summerson was one of the characters routinely deemed unnatural. The critics' dislike of Esther stemmed not so much from her characterisation itself (although a number of them found this embodiment of feminine virtue surprisingly annoying) as from the contradictions created by her dual role as character *and* narrator. The product of this unhappy combination was, according to James Augustine Stothert, a 'self-forgetting young

4 Anonymous review of *Bleak House*, *Putnam's Magazine*, 2, November 1853, p. 558.
5 England's most famous madhouse, Bethlem Hospital (established 1247), was commonly known as 'Bedlam' and its inhabitants as 'Bedlamites'.

lady, who notes in her journal every thing that a self-forgetting mind would not note'.[6] Inconsistent and hence unnatural, Esther was in clear violation of the realistic norms of characterisation.

As characters were continually judged by how 'life-like' they were, perhaps it was only inevitable that readers should come to view them not as literary constructs, but as living and breathing people. As the reviewer for *Putnam's Magazine* suggests, the characters of *Bleak House* are 'distinct and striking individuals, who are remembered and alluded to as real personages'.[7] At its most naive, the discussion then turned upon whether individual characters constituted an agreeable addition to the reader's circle of friends and acquaintances or whether, on the contrary, they were deemed offensive. In the words of the *Westminster Review*, there are 'some people with whom we are not glad to have met' and whether they gained access to the middle-class home via the front door or the pages of a novel was quite irrelevant.[8]

The reception of other characters, especially the nonconformist preacher, Reverand Chadband, and Mrs Jellyby, was subject to the political or religious views held by the individual reviewer. Thus the *Illustrated London News* described Mrs Jellyby – who devotes so much time to her 'duties' as a philanthropist that she neglects her own home and children – as 'an admirable effort' and claimed that, 'for the sake of hundreds of families, she deserves to be at length brought out into the clear light, that people may see and feel what is the true value of such a wife, mother, and woman'.[9] On the other hand, this same character provoked nothing but disgust from John Stuart Mill, a staunch defender of women's rights and future author of *On the Subjection of Women* (1869). For Mill, not only does Dickens have 'the vulgar impudence in this thing to ridicule rights of women. It is done in the very vulgarest way – just the style in which vulgar men used to ridicule "learned ladies" as neglecting their children and household etc.'[10] Finally, we should note that critics were virtually unanimous in asserting that Dickens had violated the boundaries of good taste in making Harold Skimpole a clearly recognisable portrait of the contemporary poet and essayist Leigh Hunt.

Another element of the novel that concerned contemporary critics was its critique of Chancery Court (see Contextual Overview, p. 18). In 1858 Walter Bagehot (an important Victorian political writer) was one of the first to accuse Dickens of 'sentimental radicalism':[11]

Nothing can be easier than to make a case, as we may say, against any particular system, by pointing out with emphatic caricature its

6 J. Stothert, 'Living Novelists', *The Rambler*, new series 1, January 1854, p. 43.
7 *Putnam's Magazine* (see note 4), p. 562.
8 Anonymous review of *Bleak House*, *Westminster Review* [1853], reprinted in A.E. Dyson (ed.), *Dickens: Bleak House. A Selection of Critical Essays*, Basingstoke: Macmillan, 1969, p. 70.
9 Anonymous review of *Bleak House*, *Illustrated London News*, 22, 24 September 1853, p. 247.
10 J.S. Mill, letter to Harriet Taylor [1854], reprinted in P. Collins (ed.), *Dickens: The Critical Heritage*, London: Routledge & Kegan Paul, 1971, p. 298.
11 W. Bagehot, 'Charles Dickens', *National Review* [1858], reprinted in S. Wall (ed.), *Charles Dickens: A Critical Anthology*, Harmondsworth: Penguin, 1970, p. 136.

inevitable miscarriages and by pointing out nothing else. Those who so address us may assume a tone of philanthropy, and for ever exult that they are not so unfeeling as other men are; but the real tendency of their exhortations is to make men dissatisfied with their inevitable condition, and what is worse, to make them fancy that its irremediable evils can be remedied, and indulge in a succession of vague strivings and restless changes.[12]

Part of the problem was that Dickens, never credited with a great intellect, was seen to lack the requisite knowledge and expertise to engage in the really serious issues of the day. In the words of one reviewer, 'He is not a man of *thought*.'[13] Dickens's attack on Chancery was, moreover, simply too late. *Bleak House* made it clear that Chancery suits were slow and expensive and that the whole system was in desperate need of reform. Yet as a range of critics were quick to point out, 'all this we knew before, and the whole country knew' (see **p. 61**). It is now widely accepted that Dickens was no prophet; as a social critic he spoke with, rather than ahead of, his age. As Butt and Tillotson demonstrate, the novel's critique of Chancery would have been familiar to any reader of *The Times* echoing, as it does, a series of articles published in 1851 (see **p. 62** and Cole, **p. 34**). Yet the topicality of Dickens's subject should not distract us from the originality of its treatment. According to F.S. Schwarzbach (see **p. 75**), Dickens's success as a reformer stemmed from his ability to make readers see what was going on all around them through fresh eyes, a process of defamiliarisation achieved through an unusual yet strategic combination of realistic and fantastic elements. And thus, as a critic for the *Eclectic Review* suggests, 'if the theme be not altogether a new one, there is a freshness about our author's manner of setting it forth which is as good as novelty'.[14]

Although Dickens had originally made his reputation as a humorous novelist, by 1853 he was already well known as a social critic. Yet prior to *Bleak House*, such criticism tended to be offset by humour and, moreover, was largely limited to particularised and remediable evils. With its more sustained critique of the ubiquitous and systemic abuse perpetuated by Chancery, this novel was seen to represent something altogether darker. Commenting on this change in tone and emphasis, *Bentley's Miscellany* notes that '[t]here is nothing, indeed, more remarkable in "Bleak House" than the almost entire absence of humour. In this story the grotesque and contemptible have taken the place of the humorous' (see **p. 60**).

Reaction, Decline and Reassessment

There is no question that the critical reputation of *Bleak House*, and indeed Dickens's entire corpus, suffered a severe decline in the years following his death

---

12 Bagehot (see note 11), p. 139.
13 Stothert (see note 6), p. 43.
14 Anonymous review of *Bleak House*, *Eclectic Review*, 6, December 1853, p. 667.

in 1870. Several interrelated factors help to account for such a change. Throughout the 1870s and 1880s, critical tastes were changing and developing in new directions, directions best met not by Dickens, but by a very different type of writer such as the Russian novelist Ivan Turgenev (1818–83) and, closer to home, George Eliot (1819–80) or Thomas Hardy (1840–1928). What this new breed of novelists had in common was a more sophisticated understanding of the complex inner lives of their characters, combined with a new degree of intellectual seriousness; qualities designed to meet the increasingly mature and sophisticated taste of the cultivated reader. Placed beside them, Dickens appeared to be a decidedly superficial, even naive, writer. Once castigated for the absence of humour in his later works, he was now accused of lacking the requisite seriousness of a proper novelist.

Further developments in the 1890s, a period of artistic experimentation associated with such figures as Henry James, Joseph Conrad and a host of other European authors, did little to redeem Dickens's reputation. Quite simply, it was felt that the novel had come of age, and it was now time to relegate Dickens to its distant and outgrown childhood. Be that as it may, each decade following his death saw sales of his novels increase, suggesting that he continued to be read and enjoyed by the general public.[15] Moreover, the last decades of the century saw a growing critical appreciation of his work on both the Continent and in Russia, where he was admired by two of the most important novelists of the period, Leo Tolstoy (1828–1910) and Fyodor Dostoevsky (1821–81). Nor was Dickens without his critical supporters at home. Confining ourselves to the critical fortunes of *Bleak House*, it is possible to identify two readings which played a decisive role in its rehabilitation: the 1937 Foreword to *Great Expectations* by the staunch socialist and playwright George Bernard Shaw, and Edmund Wilson's groundbreaking 1941 essay 'Dickens: the Two Scrooges'.

In direct opposition to the well-established view that Dickens belonged to the political vanguard and 'never went ahead of his public', Shaw argued that the mature Dickens was, unbeknownst to himself, a 'revolutionist' comparable to Marx.[16] And while there is no doubt that certain of Shaw's statements exaggerate and even distort the nature and extent of Dickens's radicalism, this piece was pivotal in re-asserting Dickens's importance as a social critic and reformer. Like Shaw, Wilson saw Dickens as an individual fundamentally at odds with his time. As he suggests, 'Of all the great Victorian writers, he was probably the most antagonistic to the Victorian age itself.'[17] Unlike Shaw, however, Wilson's focus is psychological rather than political reading the corpus as an expression of, and attempt to come to terms with, a number of traumatic episodes within Dickens's own life (the blacking factory, his failed marriage, etc.). Although recent developments in critical theory have called into question such a simple (even simplistic) understanding of the relationship between author and text, Wilson's essay

---

15 Ford (see note 3), pp. 171–2.
16 G.B. Shaw, Foreword to *Great Expectations* [1937], reprinted in Wall (see note 11), p. 285.
17 E. Wilson, 'Dickens: the Two Scrooges', *The Wound and the Bow: Seven Studies in Literature*, Cambridge: Houghton Mifflin Company, 1941, p. 29.

remains an insightful exploration of Dickens's development as an artist. Concentrating on the symbolic dimension of his writing, Wilson detects certain patterns and motifs that, while lending the earlier novels a previously denied degree of coherence, also cast a darker shadow across his supposed optimism and humour. All in all, the Dickens who emerges from Wilson's essay is a figure of complexity, both as an individual and as an artist.

Both within Dickens's own lifetime and subsequently, the critical preference had always been for his earlier humorous or sentimental works. Shaw and Wilson's essays helped to re-direct the critical spotlight onto the later and darker masterpieces that begin with *Bleak House*. But, more importantly, they claimed for Dickens the status of a serious artist and demanded he be read as such.

> [T]he people who like to talk about the symbols of Kafka and Mann and Joyce[18] have been discouraged from looking for anything of the kind in Dickens, and usually have not read him, at least with mature minds. But even when we do know Dickens, we may be surprised to return to him and find in him a symbolism of a more complicated reference and a deeper implication than these metaphors that hang as emblems over the door. The Russians themselves, in this respect, appear to have learned from Dickens.[19]

Seemingly, the problem lay not with Dickens, whose writing was childish, but with those who read him in a childish manner.

Dickens in the Twentieth Century

Before proceeding to more recent developments in the critical history of *Bleak House*, we need to acknowledge two significant mid-twentieth-century trends that built upon yet ultimately challenged the positions put forward by Shaw and Wilson. The first of these is historical in orientation and originates with Humphrey House's *The Dickens World* (1941). In this analysis he aims to show 'the connexion between what Dickens wrote and the times in which he wrote it'.[20] Following House's lead, a number of critics (most notably John Butt and Kathleen Tillotson – see p. 62 – and Philip Collins) began to relate the novels not only to the social and material context in which they were produced and consumed, but also to Dickens's letters, speeches and journalism. Like Shaw,

---

18 In stories such as 'The Metamorphosis' (1915) and *The Trial* (1925), Franz Kafka (1883–1924) offered a distinctively modern representation of the effects of alienation and anxiety on the psyche; the German novelist Thomas Mann (1875–1955) is best known for works such as *Buddenbrooks* (1901) and *Death in Venice* (1913); one of the key figures of modernism, James Joyce (1882–1941) experimented with both language and style in his most famous works, *Ulysses* (1922) and *Finnegans Wake* (1939).
19 Wilson (see note 17), pp. 37–8. At this point in time, Russian novelists had considerable cultural prestige and were seen as leading innovators of the genre.
20 H. House, *The Dickens World* [1941], 2nd edn., London: Oxford University Press, 1965, p. 14.

those who adopted an historical approach were primarily interested in Dickens as a social critic and in the nature and extent of his radicalism. Yet the conclusions they reached – that Dickens's allegiances ultimately lay with his predominantly middle-class readership – provided a necessary corrective to Shaw's rather grandiose claims.

Equally important, such readings equip the twentieth-century reader with a wealth of contextual information. In refusing to treat Dickens's novels as if they were produced in a temporal and social vacuum, this tradition of historical investigation added a new and necessary dimension to Dickensian criticism. Yet it is not without its own inherent limitations. As the critic Pam Morris astutely observes, all such critics are 'arguing within a common, realist perception of fictional art. What they share is the assumption that the aim of a novelist is to present an accurate reflection of his or her world.'[21] They must be seen, therefore, as a continuation of, rather than a departure from, a much older critical tradition, one that, as we have already seen, is of limited use when dealing with a non-naturalistic writer like Dickens.

The second trend to dominate mid-twentieth-century responses to *Bleak House* assumes an altogether different direction from the first. Eschewing all interest in questions relating to author and context, it concentrates on the text itself, which is viewed not as a social document, but as a timeless work of art. Concerned primarily with issues of form, structure, unity and complexity, such readings were part and parcel of the New Criticism that dominated the critical scene from the early 1940s through to the mid-1960s. While maintaining Wilson's interest in the complex symbolism of the novel, they refute all psychologising tendencies as 'a refusal, or an inability, to read the novels as literature'.[22] The significance of such symbolic or thematic readings is that, in re-visiting the question of form that preoccupied critics of the 1850s, they affected a complete reversal of the charge that *Bleak House* suffers from 'an absolute want of construction' (see **p. 58**). For instance, where Dickens's contemporaries deemed certain characters irrelevant, the New Critics recognised that 'each plays a part in a complex whole and stands in relation to a total theme'.[23] And where the former perceived only a 'want of art' and denied Dickens the stature of a serious artist, the latter consistently emphasise his technical mastery and the degree of artistic control exercised over his material.

Recent Developments

The advent of post-structuralism (broadly defined as the critique of all centres, grounds or foundations) in the late 1960s not only sent shockwaves through the critical scene at large, it also effected nothing short of a revolution in Dickensian studies. Viewed primarily as self-conscious and, above all, linguistic constructs

21 P. Morris, *Bleak House: Open Guides to Literature*, Milton Keynes: Open University Press, 1991, p. 50.
22 F.R. and Q.D. Leavis, *Dickens the Novelist*, Harmondsworth: Pelican Books, 1972, p. 15.
23 Leavis (see note 22), p. 238.

(e.g. objects which exist only in and as language), Dickens's texts suddenly seemed distinctly and, for some, disturbingly modern. Indeed, they became virtually unrecognisable to an earlier generation of critics who expressed concern about 'the way [Dickens's] books have been made to reflect the pressures and perplexities of the twentieth century rather than the realities of the nineteenth'.[24]

It is quite clear why the flurry of critical activity generated by J. Hillis Miller's 'Interpretation in *Bleak House*' – the first significant post-structuralist reading of Dickens – was so disconcerting to the critical establishment. Quite simply, it overturned the assumptions held sacred by both dominant trends within mid-century criticism of *Bleak House*. Unlike the thematic readings, which emphasised the novel's unity and tightly controlled structure, the post-structuralists insisted that *Bleak House* was an inherently contradictory text, one characterised by a plurality that refused to be synthesised into a single, overarching meaning: 'Like the case of Jarndyce and Jarndyce it remains unfinished at its end, a tissue of loose ends and questions rather than of neatly resolved patterns' (see **p. 70**). Yet these 'loose ends and questions' are read not as so many flaws and imperfections but as a series of fissures that open the text to new and multiple interpretations. Highly suggestive and entirely productive, such disruptions to the text's unity confirm, for the post-structuralists, its continued critical and literary relevance.

This seemingly perverse emphasis on the indeterminacy and plurality of *Bleak House* is, in large part, attributable to the post-structuralists' understanding of language. For many traditional literary critics, including the realists, language should ideally be a transparent medium whose primary purpose is to refer to an extra-textual universe (i.e. one that exists independently of language). According to the adherents of this view, Dickens's language is both exaggerated and excessive and each rhetorical flourish, like a smudge on a window, merely interferes with the reader's ability to gain access to the reality behind it. In contrast, post-structuralism views language as an infinite and inescapable system of signs which refer to, and only gain meaning from, other signs. As a result, meaning is never stable but is always on the move, dispersed throughout the entire language system. This is a difficult concept to grasp and you may find the following analogy helpful. When you look up a signifier in the dictionary, the word 'apple' for example, you don't find a final or definitive meaning. All you see are more signifiers ('edible', 'fruit', etc.) and looking up these signifiers, you find more again and so on, *ad infinitum*. As a result, meaning is always on the move and, hence, postponed or deferred. Thus any attempt to assign a single, definitive meaning to this, or any other text, is rendered futile. In short, we live in a decentred universe, a world without ground or foundation in which we search for answers and sureties that continually elude us.

For those who hold such views, the appeal of *Bleak House* is obvious. With 'this solicitor instructing and this counsel appearing for A, and that solicitor instructing and that counsel appearing for B; and so on through the whole alphabet' (see Key Passages, **p. 119**), Chancery Court becomes the perfect analogue of

24 A.G. Hill, review from *Critical Quarterly* [no publication date], cited in A.E. Dyson (ed.), *Dickens: Modern Judgments*, Basingstoke: Macmillan, 1968, p. 27.

the endless deferrals and referrals of meaning within the language system. Furthermore, like the language system it mirrors so closely, Chancery is both omnipresent and inescapable, while all concerned are forced to inhabit what might only be described as a world devoid of a centre where their desire for resolution and meaning is destined to remain unfulfilled (think of Richard Carstone or Miss Flite). Finally, having severed the sign from its extra-textual referent (the actual object in the real world), post-structuralists are better able to appreciate the linguistic exuberance that characterises this novel. Indeed, in passages such as that describing the political rivalry of Boodle and Coodle (see Key Passages, **p. 124**), Dickens shows so little regard for the referential value of signs and so much pleasure in the materiality of language itself that he is justifiably labelled a protomodernist whose stylistic experimentation anticipates that of James Joyce.

Of course, this tendency to sever sign from referent also calls into question the assumptions behind traditional historical readings of the text. As we have seen, critics from Chorley to Butt and Tillotson have queried whether *Bleak House* offers an accurate representation of the external world. In contrast, certain post-structuralists (especially those who, like Hillis Miller, are most closely associated with the deconstructive readings of the French philosopher Jacques Derrida) concentrate solely on issues of textuality and its destabilising effects on interpretation. Furthermore, because such theorists view language as a purely self-referential system – in which each word 'takes its meaning not from something outside words, but from other words' (see **p. 70**) – they are able to eschew the question of history altogether.

Reacting against the ahistoricism of such textual readings are the new historicists who refuse to divorce questions of textuality from those of history. Yet, unlike traditional historical critics, new historicists insist that history itself is textualised (in other words, every aspect of our lives and our pasts is mediated through language). Thus there is no extra-textual reality to capture and historical documents are themselves treated as yet another form of representation. Entirely typical of such an approach is D.A. Miller's 'Discipline in Different Voices' (**p. 81**), which insists on viewing Chancery Court as a site of institutional power rather than a site of proliferating texts. Like many new historicists, Miller's work bears the obvious imprint of Michel Foucault (a highly influential French post-structuralist), especially in its preoccupation with the novel's representations of power and surveillance; representations that are themselves read through and against the competing ideological discourses of the period. These issues are also at the heart of the extract by Elizabeth Langland (**p. 84**). In contrast to Miller, however, Langland foregrounds questions relating to gender in order to explore the middle-class home as the site of power and the formation of class identity. Like Miller and Langland, Hilary Schor (**p. 93**) is interested in the very real and material practices that inform Dickens's novel. Yet in her reading, this emphasis on materiality is complemented by an interest in textuality and narrative form. Bridging the work of Hillis Miller and D.A. Miller, Schor's reading represents an important new development in the novel's critical history.

Finally, we must note that a number of significant readings have been generated by ongoing developments in feminist and/or psychoanalytic theories. Such readings tend to concentrate on the character of Esther Summerson and the ways in which her subjectivity is constructed in the course of her narrative. For post-structuralists, the term 'subject' replaces the more dated concept of the 'individual'. The latter suggests a coherent, unique and autonomous entity that is captured most obviously in the statement of the Enlightenment philosopher René Descartes, 'I think, therefore I am.' This statement presupposes that we are all free to think whatever we wish and to determine who and what we are. In contrast, the notion of the subject foregrounds the fact that we are all subject *to* various external and internal forces. Factors such as our education and our upbringing as well as constructions of gender and class all help to *construct* us into the subjects that we are. Furthermore, internal divisions between the conscious and unconscious aspects of our psyche produce additional fractures. The result is a subject both contradictory and contingent, both unstable and always in process (see, for example, Key Passages, **p. 135**). It is worth noting, finally, that language plays a pivotal role in the construction of a subject. Not only are we born into a language system that pre-dates us, we are all *products* of this system. As the post-structuralist critic Catherine Belsey suggests: 'In order to speak the child is compelled to differentiate; to speak of itself it has to distinguish "I" from "you." In order to formulate its needs the child learns to identity with the first person singular pronoun, and this identification constitutes the basis of subjectivity.'[25] In other words, it is through language that we begin to grasp the difference between self and other – between 'what-is-me' and 'what-is-not-me' – a distinction essential to our ability to conceive of ourselves. As we shall see in the extract by Caroline Dever (**p. 88**), the concept of the subject sheds new light on both Esther and her narrative.

---

25 C. Belsey, 'Constructing the Subject: Deconstructing the Text' [1985], reprinted in R.C. Davis and R. Schleifier (eds), *Contemporary Literary Criticism*, 3rd edn, New York and London: Longman, 1994, p. 357.

Early Critical Reception

From **[Henry Fothergill Chorley], unsigned review of *Bleak House* in the *Athenaeum*,** 17 September 1853, p. 1087

Henry Chorley (1808–72) was a regular reviewer for the weekly literary periodical the *Athenaeum* and, from the mid-1850s onwards, a close friend of Dickens. In offering qualified praise for *Bleak House*, Chorley's review is entirely typical of the initial critical response to the novel. Like many of his peers, he judged *Bleak House* as a work of realism (see Contextual Overview, **p. 20** and Critical History, **p. 46**) and inevitably found it lacking. Dickens's tendency towards exaggeration, seen most obviously in his preference for the grotesque over the typical or ordinary, was seen to damage the novel's ability to offer a faithful representation of the world. Also typical is Chorley's obvious distaste for certain characters who are deemed unfit subjects for literature. What is unusual about this review is Chorley's praise for the novel's construction. He was one of the few contemporary reviewers to recognise just how tightly this novel is structured, with every character playing a material part in the mystery.

[. . .] There is progress in art to be praised in this book – and there is progress in exaggeration to be deprecated. At its commencement the impression made is strange. Were its opening pages in anywise accepted as representing the world we live in, the reader might be excused for feeling as though he belonged to some orb where eccentrics, Bedlamites,[1] ill-directed and disproportioned people were the only inhabitants. Esther Summerson, the narrator, is, in her surpassingly sweet way, little less like ordinary persons than are Krook and Skimpole. [. . .] Granting the simple heroine of Mr Dickens to possess the immediate power of the daguerreotype[2] in noting at once the minutest singularities of so many exceptional people – granting her, further, in its fullest extent, the instantaneous influence for good in word and in deed which she exercises over every person with whom she is

1 See Critical History, note 5.
2 See Contextual Overview, note 15.

brought into contact – it surely befalls few such angels of experience, simplicity and overflowing kindness to enter Life through the gate of usefulness down a highway lined with figures so strange as the above. The excuse of Esther's creator, we suppose, lies in the supposed necessity of catching his public at the outset, by exhibiting a rare set of figures in readiness for the coming harlequinade.[3] But in *Bleak House* they stand in one another's way; [. . .]

This resolution to startle, besides being bad in itself, leads the novelist, even though he have of the richest *cornucopia* of humours at his disposal, into two faults, – both of which may be seriously objected against *Bleak House*. First, from noticing mere peculiarities, he is beguiled into a cruel consideration of physical defects – from the unnatural workings of the mind, the step to the painful agonies of the body is a short one. [. . .] The death of Krook – attacked as an impossible catastrophe, and defended by our novelist on medical testimony – would be false and repugnant in point of Art, even if it were scientifically true. We would not willingly look into fiction for the phenomena of *elephantiasis*,[4] or for the hopeless writings of those who suffer and perish annually in the slow sharp pains of cancer. [. . .]

Thus much recorded as regards the progress in exaggerations which we conceive *Bleak House* to exhibit – we now turn to the admirable things which this last tale by Mr Dickens contains. And first, though he has been thereby led away from his great Chancery case further than may have been his original intention, we must signalize the whole machinery by which Lady Dedlock's private history is gradually brought to day – as admirable in point of fictitious construction – an important advance on anything that we recollect in our author's previous works. Not a point is missed – not a person left without part or share in the gradual disclosure – not a pin dropped that is not to be picked up for help or for harm to somebody. The great catastrophe is, after all, determined as much by the distant jealousy of Mrs Snagsby, the fretful law-stationer's wife, as by the more intimate vengeance of the discarded lady's maid. Capital, too – of an excellence which no contemporary could reach – is the manner in which Mr Bucket the detective officer is worked into the very centre and core of the mystery, until we become almost agreed with Sir Leicester Dedlock in looking on him as a superior being in right of his cool resource and wondrous knowledge. [. . .]

In his own particular walk – apart from the exaggerations complained of, and the personalities against which many have protested – Mr Dickens has rarely, if ever, been happier than in *Bleak House*. [. . .] Perhaps among all the waifs and strays, the beggars and the outcasts, in behalf of whose humanity our author has again and again appealed to a world too apt to forget their existence, he has never produced anything more rueful, more pitiable, more complete than poor Jo. The dying scene, with its terrible moral and impetuous protest, Mr Dickens has nowhere in all his works excelled. The book would live on the strength alone of that one sketch from the swarming life around us. [. . .]

3 A popular form of seventeenth- and eighteenth-century pantomime based on the adventures of the comic servant Harlequin.
4 A parasitic infection that causes enlargement of the limbs or genitals.

From **[George Brimley], unsigned review of** *Bleak House* **in the**
Spectator (26) 24 September 1853, pp. 923–4

George Brimley (1819–57) was the Librarian of Trinity College, Cambridge,
from 1845 to his death in 1857. A prolific essayist, he regularly contributed
literary reviews to both the *Spectator* and *Fraser's Magazine*. His comments on
Bleak House are a prime example of the ways in which many contemporary
critics were seemingly blind to the intricate web of connections that hold the
novel together (see, for example, Key Passages, p. 126). Also of note is Brimley's
dismissal of Dickens's critique of Chancery suits as 'stale and commonplace'
(see Contextual Overview, p. 18 and Butt and Tillotson, p. 62). The final
paragraph acknowledges the qualities for which Dickens was best known, but
relegates him to the status of a mere entertainer rather than a serious artist. In
so doing, Brimley upheld the prevailing critical view that Dickens's novels
appealed to the heart rather than the head of his readers.

[. . .] *Bleak House* is, even more than any of its predecessors, chargeable with not
simply faults, but absolute want of construction. A novelist may invent an
extravagant or an uninteresting plot – may fail to balance his masses, to distribute
his light and shade – may prevent his story from marching, by episode and discur-
sion: but Mr Dickens discards plot, while he persists in adopting a form for his
thoughts to which plot is essential, and where the absence of a coherent story is
fatal to continuous interest. In *Bleak House*, the series of incidents which form the
outward life of the actors and talkers has no close and necessary connexion; nor
have they that higher interest that attaches to circumstances which powerfully aid
in modifying and developing the original elements of human character. The great
Chancery suit of Jarndyce and Jarndyce, which serves to introduce a crowd of
persons as suitors, lawyers, law-writers, law-stationers, and general spectators
of Chancery business, has positively not the smallest influence on the character of
any one person concerned; nor has it any interest of itself. Mr Richard Carstone is
not made reckless and unsteady by his interest in the great suit, but simply
expends his recklessness and unsteadiness on it, as he would on something else if
it were non-existent. This great suit is lugged in by the head and shoulders, and
kept prominently before the reader, solely to give Mr Dickens the opportunity
of indulging in stale and commonplace satire upon the length and expense of
Chancery proceedings, and exercises absolutely no influence on the characters
and destinies of any one person connected to it. The centre of the arch has nothing
to do in keeping the arch together. [. . .]

If Mr Dickens were now for the first time before the public, we should have
found our space fully occupied in drawing attention to his wit, his invention, his
eye for common life, for common men and women, for the everyday aspect of
streets and houses, his tendency to delineate the affections and the humours
rather than the passions of mankind; and his defects would have served but to
shade and modify the praises that flow forth willingly at the appearance among us
of a true and original genius. And had his genius gone on growing and maturing,

clearing itself of extravagance, acquiring art by study and reflection, it would not be easy to limit the admiration and homage he might by this time have won from his countrymen. As it is, he must be content with the praise of amusing the idle hours of the greatest number of readers; not, we may hope, without improvement to their hearts, but certainly without profoundly affecting their intellects or deeply stirring their emotions.

From a review of *Bleak House* in the *Illustrated London News* (22) 24 September 1853, p. 247

Like Brimley (**p. 58**), this anonymous reviewer argues that *Bleak House* is poorly constructed and lacks a coherent plot. These flaws are then directly linked to the novel's failure as a work of realism. The demand that novels be 'faithful in their analogies, strict in their proportions, and scrupulously object-like in their tendency and settlement' reminds us of the criteria by which literature was judged at mid-century (see Contextual Overview, **p. 20**). Interestingly, the charge that *Bleak House* lacks closure is an issue that dominates more recent, post-structuralist readings of the novel (see, for example, Hillis Miller, **p. 70** and D.A. Miller, **p. 82**). For these critics, however, this lack of resolution is seen as one of the novel's greatest strengths.

[. . .] *Bleak House* has one grand defect, while exhibiting every quality of its author's undoubted genius. People want some story in a work of fiction; and not only is the desire for a story perfectly natural and perfectly reasonable [. . .] but it is, in an artistic sense, one of the essential elements of all good prose works of this nature. Now, most unfortunately, Mr Dickens fails in the construction of a plot. This is the very point in which he has generally been weakest. No man, we are confident, could tell a story better, if he had but a story to tell. We suspect that he is not at all unconscious of his own deficiency; for, in *Bleak House* especially – and, we might add, in many of his other novels – he resorts to a thousand artifices to excite curiosity; and lo! there is nothing about which we need have been curious – there is no explanation, by which, when our curiosity has been excited, it will be gratified or satisfied. [. . .] And this marked characteristic of Mr Dickens's story-telling is no slight or trivial blemish. So far as the intrinsic congruities and self-evident laws of fictitious writing demand of the narrator a sort of artistic honesty, from which he may depart without being a bad man, but from which he cannot depart without being (in that at least) a bad author – so far, we say, Mr Dickens violates, to his own injury, one of the obligations which he has undertaken to respect. We are speaking here of an offence which the Germans would call an aesthetic immorality. Of course, it is evident that all the immoralities and all the moralities of the mimic world of fiction are but shadows; that the writer is in that world bound, not under pain of guilt, but under pain of nonsense; that his culpabilities affect him not as a member of society, in a personal sense, but as a citizen of the lettered republic, and a citizen whose usefulness, instructiveness, and value are to be estimated; and that, while his materials are permitted to be untrue literally, they are required to be both true and suggestive allegorically – faithful in their analogies, strict in their proportions, and scrupulously object-like in their tendency and settlement. Now, a story-teller professing to offer you a representation of real life, yet unable to construct a good plot, is under a disadvantage which we need not enlarge upon.

From a review of Bleak House in Bentley's Miscellany (34) October 1853, pp. 372–4

A number of common complaints surface in this review. Not only is Bleak House seen to be characterised by exaggeration, it lacks organic unity and it is populated with all manner of extraneous characters who are judged to be both 'unnatural' and 'unpleasant'. It is now universally acknowledged that Bleak House marks the beginning of a darker, more sophisticated period within Dickens's career and this transition from humour to 'pathos' was a matter of some consternation for contemporary critics and readers alike (see Critical History, p. 49). In limiting his praise for certain 'detached passages', this reviewer was in line with the judgement of many of his peers.

[. . .] "Bleak House" is, in some respects, the worst of Mr. Dickens' fictions, but, in many more, it is the best.

It is the worst, inasmuch as in no other work is the tendency to disagreeable exaggeration so conspicuous as in this. There are a great number of *dramatis personae* moving about in this story, some of them exercising no perceptible influence upon its action or in any way contributing to the catastrophe of the piece. They disappear from the scene, give no sign, and when we come to look back upon our transient acquaintance with them, we begin to suspect that the story would have profited more by "their room than by their company." Now such characters are only serviceable in fiction, when they represent a class, and something is gained in morality, if nothing to art. When, on the other hand, they are exaggerated exceptions, and represent nothing which we have ever seen, or heard, or dreamt of, we cannot but regard them as mere excrescences which we should like to see pruned away. [. . .] [I]s it, we ask, within the rightful domain of true art to make the unnatural in character thus predominate over the natural? In "Bleak House," for every one natural character we could name half a dozen unnatural ones; for every pleasant personage, half a dozen painful ones. [. . .]

There is nothing, indeed, more remarkable in "Bleak House" than the almost entire absence of humour. In this story the grotesque and the contemptible have taken the place of the humorous. There are some passages in the history of Mr. Guppy which raise a smile, but beyond these we really do not remember anything provocative of even a transient feeling of hilarity. It would seem, however, that in proportion as Mr. Dickens has ceased to be, what he was once believed to be only, a humorous writer, he has been warmed into a pathetic one.

The pathos of "Bleak House" is as superior to that of "David Copperfield," as "David Copperfield" was, in this respect, superior to any of the author's former productions. There are passages, indeed, in it which nothing can excel.

The chief merit of "Bleak House" lies, indeed, in these detached passages. There are *parts* which, without hesitation, may be pronounced more powerful and more tender than anything that Dickens ever wrote – but the whole is disappointing. We feel that the story has not been carefully constructed, and that the undue elaboration of minor and unimportant characters crowding the canvas, and blocking up the space at the author's command, has compelled such a slurring over of required explanations towards the end of the story, that the reader lays down the last number of the series scarcely believing that he is not to hear anything more. The want of art is apparent, if we look only at the entire work.

From **a review of Bleak House in Bentley's Monthly Review**, October 1853, p. 227

Of particular interest are this reviewer's comments about Dickens's critique of Chancery Court (see Contextual Overview, **p. 18**). As he rightly points out, the flaws that Dickens identified were already well known to the general public (see Butt and Tillotson, **p. 62**). The suggestion that Dickens lacked the necessary intellectual tools to engage with such a weighty issue re-enforces the construction of the author as a mere entertainer of the masses.

But we have said that Mr. Dickens always writes *with a purpose* now. And what is the task he has set before him in "Bleak House?" No less a one than the exposure of the infamies of Chancery. A great theme and a difficult one. Not difficult in one sense – for it is easy to attack and to abuse any system, and especially one which is confessedly most faulty. But an author who sets out with the intention of running a tilt against any institution, either of our constitution or of society, should first take care to understand his subject. We do not think that Mr Dickens displays this knowledge in "Bleak House." That Chancery Suits were long and expensive; that people got very weary of them; were occasionally imprisoned in respect of them; and that reform was needed somewhere: all this we knew before, and the whole country knew. But if Mr. Dickens wished to effect any good in this matter, why did he not point out the *roots* of the particular evils he complains of, and suggest remedies? The answer will probably be – how can he, a layman (though a "student for the bar," by the way)[1] understand the subject? Exactly so: then until he *does* understand it, to what practical purpose do his blows, dealt in the dark, serve?

Heartily, most heartily, do we wish for "Chancery Reform" – some reform there has been, but more is still needed: however, we really do not think that "Bleak House" will aid in obtaining that desideratum. The aim is good and honest, no doubt; but it is futile.

1   Dickens worked as a solicitor's clerk for much of 1827–8.

Modern Criticism

From **John Butt and Kathleen Tillotson, *Dickens at Work*** (1957), second edition, London and New York: Methuen & Co., 1982, from Chapter 7, 'The Topicality of *Bleak House*', pp. 183–7

The Chancery suit of Jarndyce and Jarndyce lies at the heart of *Bleak House*. From the very first chapter, Dickens took great pains to establish both its centrality and pervasiveness. Yet because his rendering of this case is so obviously symbolic, even fantastic, it is all too easy for readers today to forget that Dickens's critique of Chancery Court was firmly based in the material reality of his day (see Cole, **p. 34** and Contextual Overview, **p. 18**). Indeed, as Butt and Tillotson demonstrate, the substance, if not the style, of Dickens's attack mirrors the ongoing discussion of Chancery reform that occurred within *The Times* throughout 1851. Quoting extensively from that discussion, this piece substantiates the claims made by contemporary reviewers that, even at the time of publication, Dickens's critique of Chancery was outdated (see Brimley, **p. 58** and *Bentley's Monthly Review*, **p. 61**).

Dickens at Work played an important role in shaping the current understanding of Dickens as a social critic. Following their detailed historical investigations, it is now largely accepted that, as a reformer, Dickens spoke with, rather than ahead of, his age. The treatment and representation of Chancery, as well as its overall place within *Bleak House*, are issues that surface repeatedly in twentieth-century interpretations of the text. Butt and Tillotson's historical reading provides the necessary background for the more abstract treatments that we shall encounter below (see Hillis Miller, **p. 65**; D.A. Miller, **p. 81**; and Schor, **p. 93**).

[. . .] What had directed Dickens's attention to the Court of Chancery in 1851 was the interest which everyone was taking in chancery that year. The reader of *The Times* who opened his newspaper on 1 January would have noticed a leading article on the subject, in the course of which the writer remarked:

We believe that the time is rapidly approaching when the public neces-
sities and the public will must triumph over the *inertia* of an antiquated
jurisprudence and the obstacles raised by personal or professional interest . . . the community suffers . . . from a confused mass of laws, from
costly and dilatory procedure, and from an inadequate number of
Judges . . . This opinion has now become so strong and universal in the
country that active measures for the reform of the law . . . are becoming
the test by which a large proportion of the Liberal party are disposed to
try the sincerity and the capacity of their present leaders. We could
crowd our columns day after day with the remonstrances which are
addressed to ourselves, especially with reference to the present state of
the Court of Chancery.

[. . .] In *The Times* of 24 December 1850, there had been an even stronger protest,
and once again the complaint has a familiar ring:[1]

If a house be seen in a peculiarly dilapidated condition, the beholder at
once exclaims, "Surely that property must be in Chancery;" and the
exclamation very correctly expresses the popular opinion as to the effect
of legal proceedings generally upon all property which unluckily
becomes the subject of litigation in any shape . . . Success and defeat are
alike fatal to litigants.

and again, later in the same article,

the lingering and expectant suitors waste their lives as well as their
substance in vain hopes, and death robs them of their wished-for triumph, if ruin have not already rendered it impossible.

Richard Carstone, Miss Flite, and Gridley,[2] as well as Tom-all-Alone's can there
be seen casting their shadows before. [. . .]

Thus in December and January alone the columns of *The Times* contain most
of the charges in Dickens's indictment of chancery. There was more to come. A
new session of Parliament was opened early in February, and in the course of the
Queen's speech it was predicted that the administration of justice in the several
departments of law and equity would 'doubtless receive serious attention'. The
announcement was welcomed; but a week later *The Times* had already heard
rumours that legislation might be delayed till the end of the session, although 'the
state of the Court of Chancery is an evil . . . of extreme magnitude'. The rumour
proved to be correct. [. . .] A revised bill was not ready until the middle of June at
almost the last possible moment before the end of the Parliamentary session.
Though the bill was welcomed by Lord Brougham as 'a step—not a great or a long

---

1   In Chapter 8, Jarndyce attributes the deplorable state of Tom-all-Alone's to the fact that it is 'in
    Chancery'.
2   The angry suitor from Shropshire who tells his story in Chapter 15.

step, but still a step—in the right direction',[3] and though it passed all its readings before Parliament was prorogued in August,[4] criticism was by no means silenced. *The Times*, which was describing the feeling of the public as 'one of angry and restless impatience',[5] permitted itself to adopt a more sardonic approach to the question. A clever young leader-writer, Robert Lowe,[6] later to become Chancellor of the Exchequer, discovered a chancery suit which had been introduced as long ago as 1815:

> Thirty-six years [he commented] are something in the life of a man, of a nation, of a dynasty, or even of a planet, but in the history of a Chancery suit they are a brief interval . . . a mere decent pause in the slow and stately march by which parties proceed to what, by a fine irony, we are in the habit of calling "equitable relief." When this old suit was new, the counsel who have succeeded to its management were probably babes in arms, and the judge before whom it is heard a truant schoolboy. Since the parties first applied to this dilatory tribunal for the determination of their rights three Monarchs have succeeded to the aged Prince in whose reign it was commenced . . . The occupant of every throne in Europe, and every prominent office in the English church and State, has been changed, but still the inexorable Chancery suit holds on its way, permanent in the midst of never-ending change, the only immutable thing in an era of restless transition . . .

And he continues, in words which bring Richard Carstone to mind:

> It is usual to speak of lawsuits as embittering the lives of those who embark in them; but such an expression does but little justice to the hereditary curse which a suit in equity on the present system hands down to the children who are to inherit it. We leave our suits to our children just as we bequeath to them too often our mental peculiarities and bodily infirmities. The little plaintiffs and defendants grow up for the benefit of Chancery; and she adopts them as naturally as they succeed to us. (14 June.)

Bleak House was not begun until the end of November, though Dickens's letters show that as early as 7 September his 'new book [was] waiting to be born'.[7] By that date, Russell's[8] Chancery Reform Act was a month old; but the public was still critical. Throughout those weeks when the new story was 'whirling through'

---

3   [Butt and Tillotson's note.] *The Times*, 15 July.
4   When the meetings of the House are discontinued for the summer vacation.
5   [Butt and Tillotson's note.] *Ibid.*, 4 July.
6   [Butt and Tillotson's note.] *The History of The Times 1841–1884* (London, 1939), II 130.
7   [Butt and Tillotson's note.] *Letters*, II 341. The first reference to the new novel is even earlier: on 17 Aug. he had written to Miss Coutts, 'I begin to be pondering afar off, a new book' (*Coutts Letters*, p. 184).
8   John Russell (1792–1878) was Prime Minister 1846–52 and again in 1865.

Dickens's mind,[9] *The Times* kept hammering at the inadequacies of legal education, and at the eminent members of the legal profession who were thwarting legal reform. The opening of the law courts on 3 November had provided one more occasion for insisting that 'not one whiff of wholesome fresh air has been let into the Court of Chancery and its purlieus'.

Thus Dickens's indictment of chancery was more than merely topical. It followed in almost every respect the charges already levelled in the columns of *The Times*. In both we read of houses in chancery and wards in chancery, of dilatory and costly procedure, of wasted lives, and of legal obstructionists. [. . .]

From **J. Hillis Miller, 'Interpretation in *Bleak House*'** (1971), reprinted in *Victorian Subjects*, Durham, N.C.: Duke University Press, 1991, pp. 182–8, 194–7

J. Hillis Miller is a key figure within deconstructive theory: an important branch of post-structuralism that reads texts against themselves, identifying moments where the language of a text undermines or problematises its meaning (for a discussion of the relationship between language and meaning, see Critical History, **p. 53**). At the heart of Miller's argument is the belief that *Bleak House* is primarily a novel about interpretation, about the need to create meaning and the ultimate impossibility of doing so. Hence it is populated with characters that spend their lives trying to decipher written documents, often in vain. Similarly, he postulates it is a novel that demands the reader play an active role in searching for and establishing the connections, analogies and recurrences that draw together the multitude of disparate characters and events. Furthermore, it is only through their relation to each other, rather than to some extra-textual reality, that the various elements of the novel become meaningful at all. The irrelevance of the referent is, according to Miller, foregrounded by Dickens's rhetorical exuberance. This pleasure in the materiality of language privileges the signifier (spoken or written word) over the signified (the mental image it suggests) and thus emphasises the novel's status as artifice. Thus *Bleak House* seemingly anticipates a view of language and meaning articulated by post-structuralists more than a hundred years after its publication. Once language is perceived in this manner – as an infinite relay of signifiers – the possibility of arriving at a stable and definitive meaning disappears. This is borne out within the novel by both the large number of unsuccessful detectives and its lack of resolution and closure.

It would be difficult to overestimate the impact that this essay had on subsequent readings of *Bleak House*. By alerting its readers to the ways in which a post-structuralist approach illuminates the novel, especially its treatment of language, Miller initiated a host of readings that viewed *Bleak House* as a distinctly modern (even postmodern) text. Thirty years on from the publication of

9   [Butt and Tillotson's note.] *Letters*, II 349.

this influential reading of Dickens's novel, Miller re-visited it in 'Decisive Moments in *Bleak House*'.[1] Acknowledging that textual readings have, to some extent, given way to more contextual and materialist approaches to the novel (such as those by D.A. Miller, **p. 81**; Langland, **p. 84**; and Schor, **p. 93**), Miller explores the role and implication of the novel's performative statements – speech acts that make something happen, such as 'I promise' or 'I pronounce you man and wife' – as well as how the novel as a whole may be considered as performative. By directing his attention to how language can effect material change in the world, this essay may be seen to bridge the gap between textual and materialist readings of *Bleak House*.

[. . .] The reader of *Bleak House* is confronted with a document which he must piece together, scrutinize, interrogate, at every turn – in short, interpret – in order to understand. Perhaps the most obvious way in which he is led to do this is the presentation, at the beginning of the novel, of a series of disconnected places and personages – the Court of the Chancery, Chesney Wold, Esther Summerson as a child, the Jellyby household and so on. Though the relations among these are withheld from the reader, he assumes that they will turn out to be connected. He makes this assumption according to his acceptance of a figure close to synecdoche,[2] metonymy. Metonymy presupposes a similarity or causality between things presented as contiguous and thereby makes story-telling possible. The reader is encouraged to consider these contiguous items to be in one way or another analogous and to interrogate them for such analogies. Metaphor and metonymy together make up the deep grammatical armature by which the reader of *Bleak House* is led to make a whole out of discontinuous parts. At the beginning of the second chapter, for example, when the narrator shifts "as the crow flies" from the Court of Chancery to Chesney Wold, he observes that both are alike in being "things of precedent and usage," and the similarity between Krook[3] and the Lord Chancellor is affirmed in detail by Krook himself:

> You see I have so many things here . . . of so many kinds, and all, as the neighbours think (but *they* know nothing), wasting away and going to rack and ruin, that that's why they have given me and my place a christening. And I have so many old parchmentses and papers in my stock. And I have a liking for rust and must and cobwebs. And all's fish that comes to my net. And I can't abear to part with anything I once lay hold of . . . or to alter anything, or to have any sweeping, nor scouring, nor cleaning, nor repairing going on about me. That's the way I've got the ill name of Chancery. (Chapter 5)

---

1 Miller's essay may be found in J.O. Jordan (ed.), *The Cambridge Companion to Charles Dickens*, Cambridge: Cambridge University Press, 2001, pp. 49–63.
2 An example of figurative language in which a part stands for the whole (e.g. the crown for the monarch).
3 The landlord of both Nemo (Esther's father) and Miss Flite, Krook is the victim of spontaneous combustion (see Key Passages, **p. 132**).

Such passages give the reader hints as to the right way to read *Bleak House*. The novel must be understood according to correspondences within the text between one character and another, one scene and another, one figurative expression and another. If Krook is like the Lord Chancellor, the various Chancery suitors – Miss Flite, Gridley, Tom Jarndyce and Richard Carstone – are all alike; there are similarities between Tulkinghorn, Conversation Kenge and Vholes;[4] Tom-all-Alone's and Bleak House were both in Chancery; Esther's doll is duplicated with a difference by the brickmaker's baby, by the keeper's child at Chesney Wold and by Esther herself. Once the reader has been alerted to look for such relationships she discovers that the novel is a complex fabric of recurrences. Characters, scenes, themes and metaphors return in proliferating resemblances. Each character serves as an emblem of other similar characters. Each is to be understood in terms of his reference to others like him. The reader is invited to perform a constant interpretative dance or lateral movement of cross-reference as she makes her way through the text. Each scene or character shimmers before her eyes as she makes these connections. [. . .]

Though many of the connections in this elaborate structure of analogies are made explicitly in the text, many are left for the reader to see for himself. One valuable bit of evidence that Dickens took conscious pains to prepare these correspondences is given in his plan for Chapter 16.[5] In this chapter Lady Dedlock gets Jo to take her to see the paupers' graveyard where her lover lies buried. Jo points through the iron gate at the spot, and Lady Dedlock asks if it is "consecrated ground." Dickens' notes show that he was aware, and perhaps intended the reader to be aware, of the similarity between Jo's gesture of pointing and the gesture of the pointing Allegory on Mr Tulkinghorn's ceiling. The latter is mentioned in passing earlier in the chapter and of course is made much of at the time of Tulkinghorn's murder. "Jo – ," says the note for this chapter, "shadowing forth of Lady Dedlock in the churchyard. / Pointing hand of allegory – consecrated ground / 'Is it Blessed?' " The two gestures of pointing are alike, as is suggested by the similarity of pose in the illustrations of both by "Phiz" for the first edition: "Consecrated ground" and "A new meaning in the Roman." Both are examples of that procedure of indication which is the basic structural principle of *Bleak House*. This procedure is "allegorical" in the strict sense. It speaks of one thing by speaking of another, as Dickens defines the Court of Chancery by talking about a rag and bottle shop. Everywhere in *Bleak House* the reader encounters examples of this technique of "pointing" whereby one thing stands for another, is a sign for another, indicates another, can be understood only in terms of another, or named only by the name of another. The reader must thread her way through the labyrinth of such connections in order to succeed in her interpretation and solve the mystery of *Bleak House*.

The situation of many characters in the novel is exactly like that of its writer or reader. So many people in this novel are engaged in writing or in studying

4 Conversation Kenge is John Jarndyce's lawyer while the unscrupulous Vholes acts for Richard Carstone (see Cohen, **p. 78** and Key Passages, **p. 139**).
5 [Miller's note.] See p. 940, Penguin edition. [Miller is referring to the 1971 Penguin edition of *Bleak House* edited by N. Page.]

documents, in attempting to decipher what one chapter-title calls "Signs and Tokens," in learning to read or write, in hiding documents or in seeking them out, there are so many references to letters, wills, parchments and scraps of paper, that the interpretation of signs or of texts may be said to be the fundamental theme of the novel. [. . .]

Not to put too fine a point upon it, as Mr Snagsby would say, what is the meaning of all this hermeneutical and archival activity?[6] The reader of the novel must go beyond surface appearances to the deeper coherence of which these surfaces are the dispersed signs. In the same way, many of the characters are cryptographers. They attempt to fit details together to make a pattern revealing some hidden secret. Like Krook they must put "J" and "a" and so on together to spell "Jarndyce." They want to identify the buried truth which is the substance behind all the shadowy signs with which they are surrounded, as Richard Carstone believes that there "is – is – must be somewhere" "truth and justice" in the case of Jarndyce and Jarndyce (Chapter 37). Two motives impel these readers of signs. Like Richard, Gridley or even, in spite of herself, Esther, they may want to find out secrets about themselves. Each seeks his unrevealed place in the system of which he is a part. To find out how I am related to others will be to find out who I am, for I am defined by my connections, familial or legal. Esther *is* the illegitimate daughter of Lady Dedlock and Captain Hawdon. Richard *is*, or perhaps is not, a rightful heir to the Jarndyce fortune. Other characters – Mr Tulkinghorn, Guppy, Grandfather Smallweed, Hortense, Mrs Snagsby[7] or Inspector Bucket – want to find out secrets about others. Their motive is the search for power. To find out the hidden place of another in the system is to be able to manipulate him, to dominate him, and of course to make money out of him. [. . .]

The remarkable fact is that these interpreters for the most part are failures. Sometimes their interpretations are false, fictional patterns thrown over the surface of things like a mirage without relation to any deeper truth. Sometimes authentic secrets are discovered but are found out too late or in the wrong way to be of any use to their discoverers. *Bleak House* is full of unsuccessful detectives. The "plan of his own" which Sir Leicester constructs does not save him from the revelation that will shatter his proud complacency. Mrs Snagsby is ludicrously mistaken in her idea that her husband has been unfaithful and is the father of Jo. Krook dies before he finds anything of value in his papers, and even Grandfather Smallweed makes little out of his discovery. Guppy finds out Lady Dedlock's secret, but it does not win him Esther's hand. Gridley dies without resolving his suit. The case of Jarndyce and Jarndyce is used up in costs before the revelation of the newly-discovered will which might have brought it to a close. Even Tulkinghorn and Bucket, the two most clairvoyant and persistent detectives in the novel, are failures. Tulkinghorn is murdered just before he is going to make

6   Originally restricted to the interpretation of the Bible, hermeneutics now denotes the theory of interpretation in general.
7   Grandfather Smallweed is a moneylander who attempts to bribe Sir Leicester Dedlock; Hortense is Lady Dedlock's French maid and the murderer of Tulkinghorn; Mrs Snagsby is the wife of Mr Snagsby, the law stationer.

use of the secret he has discovered about Lady Dedlock. Bucket, in spite of the fact that "the velocity and certainty of [his] interpretation . . . is little short of miraculous" (Chapter 56), does not save Lady Dedlock. The masterly intuition which leads him to see that she has changed clothes with the brickmaker's wife (another lateral displacement) gets Esther to her mother just too late. They find her "cold and dead" on the steps of Nemo's graveyard. Moreover, the novel is deliberately constructed by Dickens in a way calculated to make the reader a bad detective. Carefully placed clues are designed to lead the reader to believe that either George Rouncewell or Lady Dedlock has murdered Tulkinghorn. Even now, when Dickens' strewing of false clues may seem amateur in comparison with the sophisticated puzzles in modern mystery stories, some readers, one may imagine, are inveigled into thinking that Lady Dedlock is a murderess. [. . .]

The somber suggestion toward which many elements of the novel lead, like points converging from different directions on a single spot, is that the guilty party is not any person or persons, not correctable evil in any institution. The villain is the act of interpretation itself, the naming which assimilates the particular into a system, giving it a definition and a value, incorporating it into a whole. If this is the case, then in spite of Dickens' generous rage against injustice, selfishness and procrastination, the evil he so brilliantly identifies is irremediable. It is inseparable from language and from the organization of men into society. [. . .]

Bleak House itself has exactly the same structure as the society it exposes. It too assimilates everything it touches into a system of meaning. In the novel each phrase is alienated from itself and made into a sign of some other phrase. If the case of Jarndyce and Jarndyce is a "masterly fiction" (Chapter 3), and if many characters in the novel spend their time reading or writing, Bleak House is a masterly fiction too, and Dickens too spent his time, like Mrs Jellyby, covering paper with ink, his eye fixed not on his immediate surroundings but on an imaginary world. The novel too has a temporal structure without proper origin, present, or end. It too is made up of an incessant movement of reference in which each element leads to other elements in a constant displacement of meaning. Bleak House is properly allegorical, according to a definition of allegory as a temporal system of cross references among signs rather than as a spatial pattern of correspondence between signs and referents. Most people in the novel live without understanding their plight. The novel, on the other hand, gives the reader the information necessary to understand why the characters suffer, and at the same time the power to understand that the novel is fiction rather than mimesis.[8] The novel calls attention to its own procedures and confesses to its own rhetoric, not only, for example, in the onomastic system of metaphorical names already discussed, but also in the insistent metaphors employed throughout.[9]

8   *Mimesis*, the Greek word for imitation, is the basis of realism. The point that Miller is making is that *Bleak House* self-consciously foregrounds its own fictionality or artificiality.
9   *Onomastics* is the study of proper names. Miller is referring to Dickens's tendency to give his characters metaphorical names. For example, Esther Summerson (summer sun) brings light to those around her while Sir Leicester Dedlock (dead lock) is trapped in an outmoded (dead) aristocracy. Such names constitute yet another example of how Dickens draws attention to the overt fictionality of *Bleak House*.

Each character in *Bleak House* is not only named in metaphor but speaks according to his own private system of metaphors. Moreover, he is spoken of by the narrators in metaphors which recur. Nor are these metaphors allowed to remain "buried." In one way or another they are brought into the open. Their figurative quality is insisted upon. In this way the reader has constantly before him one version of the interpretative act whereby nothing is separately itself, but can be named only in its relation to some other thing. Dickens is master of an artificial style which makes its artifice obvious. Among the innumerable examples of this the following contains the linguistic texture of the novel in miniature: "The Mercuries, exhausted by looking out of the window, are reposing in the hall; and hang their heavy heads, the gorgeous creatures, like overblown sun-flowers. Like them too, they seem to run to a deal of seed in their tags and trimmings" (Chapter 48). The nominal metaphor (Mercuries) has been used throughout to label the Dedlock footmen. To this is here added a second figure, a metaphor of a meta-phor. These Mercuries are like gorgeous sunflowers. To name them in this way has a double effect. It invites the reader to think of real footmen being described by the narrator in ornately witty language. This language names them as some-thing other than themselves, but it also calls attention to its own wit, uncovers it by playing with it and extending it. The reader knows it is "just a figure of speech." The footmen are not Mercuries, nor are they sunflowers. These are ways of talking about them which bring them vividly before the reader and express the narrator's ironic scorn for aristocratic display. At the same time, the figures and figures within figures remind the reader that there are no real footmen in the novel. The Mercuries have only a linguistic existence. They exist as metaphors, and the reader can reach them only through Dickens' figurative language. This is true for all the characters and events in the novel. The fabric of Dickens' style is woven of words in which each takes its meaning not from something outside words, but from other words. The footmen are to be understood only in terms of Mercury, Mercury only in terms of sunflowers. This way of establishing fictional reality matches the kind of existence the characters in the novel have. They too are helpless parts of a structure based on words. [. . .]

Bleak House is a powerful book, an extraordinary work of Dickens' creative power. It is also to some degree a painful book. The pain lies partly in its prevail-ing darkness or bleakness, its presentation of so many admirably comic creations who are at the same time distorted, grotesque, twisted (Krook, Grandfather Smallweed, Mrs Jellyby, Chadband,[10] Guppy, Miss Flite – what a crew!). It is painful also because of its self-contradictions. Like the case of Jarndyce and Jarndyce it remains unfinished at its end, a tissue of loose ends and questions rather than of neatly resolved patterns. As in all Dickens' work, there is at the center of *Bleak House* a tension between belief in some extra-human source of value, a stable center outside the shadows of the human game, and on the other hand the shade of a suspicion that there may be no such center, that all systems of interpretation may be fictions. [. . .]

10 A hypocritical preacher.

From **Harvey P. Sucksmith, 'Sir Leicester Dedlock, Wat Tyler, and the Chartists: The Role of the Ironmaster in** *Bleak House'*, *Dickens Studies Annual* (4) 1975, pp. 123–5, 130

While Dickens was not slow to condemn the limitations and inequities of his own society, he did not entertain any nostalgic illusions about England's past. In this article, Sucksmith locates Dickens's sympathies firmly on the side of progress and innovation rather than the established but outmoded models of the past. These two positions – the modern and the antiquated – are represented by Rouncewell (the Northern Ironmaster) and Sir Leicester Dedlock respectively (see Key Passages, **p. 117**). In part, this piece is a response to the historical critic Trevor Blount, who argued that 'we are intended to take a highly critical view of the Ironmaster' (127). In contrast, Sucksmith stresses Dickens's admiration for the values represented by this character. As a member of the manufacturing classes, Rouncewell represents a new construction of masculinity based on energy, initiative and pride in hard work (for a discussion of gender, see Contextual Overview, **p. 13**). Even more interesting, however, is Rouncewell's significantly named son, Watt. Recalling both Wat Tylor, the leader of the Peasants' Revolt of 1381, and James Watt, the Scottish inventor, this character embodies all of the various threats – social and political – to the landed interests here represented by Dedlock. One of the most significant of these threats was Chartism, a political movement named after The People's Charter which demanded: universal male suffrage; annual parliaments; equal electoral districts; no property qualifications for Members of Parliament; secret ballots; and payment of Members of Parliament. Demanding political reform, the Chartists presented petitions to Parliament in 1839, 1842 and 1848. All were rejected and the movement effectively came to an end in 1848. Elsewhere in his article, Sucksmith refers to a number of articles that appeared in *The Times* in 1848 that repeatedly refer to Isaac Jefferson, a Chartist leader, by his nickname of 'Wat Tyler'. Thus Sucksmith is able to make a connection between this name and the Chartist movement.

In his treatment of such issues, Sucksmith argues, Dickens assumes a decidedly radical stance. In demonstrating how Dickens engaged with contemporary class issues, this article represents yet another confirmation of the topicality of *Bleak House*. Emphasising Dickens's political radicalism, it also offers an alternative reading to that of Butt and Tillotson above. In this extract, I have cut Sucksmith's footnotes.

As we might expect, whenever Dickens refers to Wat Tyler in *Bleak House* after Chapter ii, he continues to do so in connection with Sir Leicester Dedlock and the attitudes he represents, that is, Wat Tyler is presented, with satirical irony, as the Dedlock concept of the social threat against its position. Thus, Wat Tyler is linked by a characteristically bold and brilliant stroke of valid humorous imagination both with the class of inventors and industrial capitalists, represented by the Ironmaster, and with the Chartist workers. [...] The deliberate fusing of inventors, industrialists, Chartist workers at torchlight demonstrations, and the Wat Tyler image is not an instance of *gross* caricature on Dickens' part. The Dedlock protest is that of the Tory landed aristocracy and interest against all the social and political forces unleashed by the Industrial Revolution. [. . .]

Moreover, far from oversimplifying the social situation, Dickens' satire takes accurate note of its complexity. Thus, we know from social historians and biographers that the industrial capitalists of the eighteenth and early nineteenth centuries came very largely from either the yeoman class or from artisans,[1] often inventors, like James Watt, George Stephenson, Samuel Crompton, James Hargreaves, Richard Arkwright, and John Brown.[2] The Lancashire proverb, "From clogs to clogs [*sic*] in three generations," certainly bears this out. [. . .] Indeed, Dickens accurately describes the progress of the working-class artisan, with a talent for invention, both in Daniel Doyce's case in *Little Dorrit* (188–89) and that of the Ironmaster in *Bleak House*: " 'I have been,' proceeds the visitor [Mr. Rouncewell], in a modest clear way, 'an apprentice, and a workman, I have lived on workman's wages, years and years, and beyond a certain point have had to educate myself. My wife was a foreman's daughter, and plainly brought up' " (Chapter 28).[3] [. . .]

If we still think it strange that Sir Leicester should identify the Ironmaster with Chartist demonstrators, we must remember that, although the Chartists failed because they enjoyed little middle-class support, the Reform Bill of 1832 did not finally establish a Britain in which the middle classes immediately assumed paramountcy over the landed aristocracy nor by 1846 when Free Trade won its victory over the Corn Laws is this wholly true.[4] On the contrary, in mid-Victorian Britain, the old aristocracy and upper levels of the middle class, as W. L. Burn has shown, continued to exercise enormous power and influence, hence the aptness and topicality of Dickens' attack on Sir Leicester.[5] [. . .] [T]he continued parliamentary struggle between the radical manufacturers and the Tory landed aristocracy for political power is carefully reflected in *Bleak House* in the clash between the electioneering interests of Sir Leicester and the Ironmaster. There can be little doubt, here, to which side Dickens directs our sympathy for, while Sir Leicester is shown involved in bribery and wild reactionary abuse and

---

1 A yeoman possessed a small landed estate while an artisan was a skilled manual worker.
2 Watt and Stephenson both played an important role in the development of the steam engine; Crompton, Hargreaves and Arkwright all helped to automate the weaving process; John Brown invented the steel spring buffer for railway wagons.
3 As readers will obviously be using a variety of editions of *Bleak House*, I have replaced page references with chapter references throughout all the extracts in this chapter.
4 The 1832 Reform Act extended the electorate by enfranchising 40 shilling freeholders (those who owned property worth 40 shillings per year); 10 pound copyholders (those who held a three generation lease on property worth £10 per year); and 50 pound leaseholders (those who leased property worth £50 per year). The Corn Laws of 1815 (amended in 1828) kept the price of grain artificially inflated to the point where many working-class people could not afford to buy bread. They were repealed in 1846 and free trade flourished.
5 Sucksmith is referring to W.L. Burn, *The Age of Equipoise: A Study of the Mid-Victorian Generation*, London: Allen & Unwin, 1964, pp. 304–20.

recriminations, the Ironmaster and his son, Watt, are shown throughout in a calm, intelligent, and rational light all the more impressive since our view of them is conveyed through the eyes of Tulkinghorn:[6] "He is a very good speaker. Plain and emphatic. He made a damaging effect, and has great influence. In the business part of the proceedings he carried all before him . . . And he was much assisted . . . by his son" (Chapter 40). If it is contended that Dickens gives an unfair representative picture of the manufacturing and the aristocratic contenders in a contemporary parliamentary election, then that very unfairness would only demonstrate further where Dickens' sympathies lie. Sir Leicester had already commended the propriety of Rouncewell in not standing for Parliament himself, but his reaction on learning that Rouncewell and his son have intervened in the election against Sir Leicester's party is that "the floodgates of society are burst open, and the waters have—a—obliterated the landmarks of the framework of the cohesion by which things are held together!" (Chapter 40). [. . .]

In so far as *Bleak House* is concerned with the "Condition of England" question,[7] Sir Leicester, for all his saving graces, is at the center of social and political deadlock. Positive social energy must necessarily manifest itself, therefore, as a kind of rebellion against an excessively static status quo, either in the destructive forms of Chartism or through the constructive experiment of a modern industrial society freed not from responsibility and humanity but from the restrictiveness of the aristocratic view of class, social mobility, and progress, a rigid and perpetual dividedness. [. . .]

From **F.S. Schwarzbach, *Dickens and the City***, London: The Athlone Press, 1979, from Chapter 6, '*Bleak House*: Homes for the Homeless', pp. 120–5, 127

This extract from *Dickens and the City* should be read in conjunction with that of Butt and Tillotson presented above. While they emphasised that Dickens's critique mirrored the ongoing discussion of the day, what emerges from Schwarzbach's discussion is the recognition that, while the subject matter of Dickens's social critique was neither original nor contentious, the techniques he adopted to represent these subjects are both. Dickens's claim, made in the Preface to *Bleak House*, to have 'dwelt upon the romantic side of familiar things' constitutes the starting point for Schwarzbach's reading. He relates this statement to Dickens's general thoughts regarding the role of literature and the relationship between art and reality as well as the style of *Bleak House* itself. Dickens was always the champion of imagination and fancy, believing they had an important role to play in an increasingly mechanistic society. Yet as

---

6   The Dedlocks' menacing lawyer.
7   The phrase coined by Carlyle (see **p. 31**) to suggest the state of increased interest generated by class tensions in the 1840s.

Schwarzbach reminds us, their role was not limited to entertaining the masses: they could also be put to good use in the fight for social reform. Dickens believed that many of his contemporaries were blind to the injustices and inequities that surrounded them, that they simply ignored what they would rather not see. Concentrating on the images of mud that dominate the opening number of Bleak House (see Key Passages, **p. 104**), Schwarzbach demonstrates how Dickens's style defamiliarised the everyday world, rendering the familiar strange. Through this carefully achieved tension between the romantic and the familiar, the concrete and the fantastic, Dickens forced his readers to see and acknowledge unpleasant and unwelcome truths (Key Passages, **p. 132** offers a good example of this technique).

Both contemporary and more recent critics have argued that Dickens's non-naturalistic style detracted from both the realism and social criticism of Bleak House (see, for example, Illustrated London News, **p. 59**). By insisting on the ways in which Dickens's style allowed him to 'rescue reality from obscurity', Schwarzbach's reading functions as a necessary corrective to such views.

[. . .] 'In *Bleak House*, I have purposely dwelt upon the romantic side of familiar things.' This statement has always been puzzling, for it is not really clear what 'romantic' might refer to in a novel about the law and death, nor what 'familiar' might refer to in a novel in which it is said it would not be strange to encounter a dinosaur on a public street. Nevertheless, I think we can ascertain what Dickens was pointing toward. In fact, one of the difficulties is that he seems to have meant two quite different things.[1]

Part of his meaning is involved in his growing conviction that the imaginative, entertaining—i.e. 'romantic'—aspect of literature was one important means of combating what he had earlier called the 'mental starvation' of the working classes. The value of literature as entertainment was under strong attack in mid-Victorian England, both from earnest Evangelicals who called it immoral, and latter-day Utilitarians, who thought it insufficiently serious.[2] Throughout his career, Dickens had considered fiction to have the dual functions of amusement and instruction, but in the early 1850s, with the establishment of *Household Words*, he became especially concerned to stress the value of entertainment *per se*.[3] 'A Preliminary Word', the announcement heading the first issue of the magazine, proclaimed it would contain 'knowledge' but still not be bound 'to grim realities'. It would show instead 'that in all familiar things, even in those that are repellant on the surface, there is Romance enough, if we will find out' ([*Household Words*], 30 March 1850; [*Miscellanies Pieces*], 167–9).

---

1 [Schwarzbach's note.] In the discussion below I am indebted to two valuable studies of Victorian critical thought and practice, Richard Stang, *The Theory of the Novel in England, 1850–1870* (New York: Columbia University Press, 1959), and Kenneth Graham, *English Criticism of the Novel, 1865–1900* (Oxford: Clarendon, 1965).
2 See Contextual Overview, pp. **12** and **19**.
3 [Schwarzbach's note.] See Harry Stone, 'Dickens and the Uses of Literature', *Dickensian*, 69 (1973), 139–47, for a fuller discussion of this question.

This theme of the remark, the importance of the imagination and the value of fancy and romance, later would develop as the central message of *Hard Times*. But the statement also suggests another meaning, involving the nature of the relationship between art and reality. In this statement, Dickens was trying to express a belief that certain aspects of the real world had become remote to our sensibilities, and that it was the role of art to make us aware of them. Somehow, we had come into the position of not fully knowing what the world we live in is actually like; it was the function of art and the duty of the artist to change this. What we were not seeing, Dickens told his readers, were those things around us that indicated the gravity of the fundamental social problems and how little was being done to solve them. Whatever was ugly was being ignored: if important aspects of the social reality were ugly, they simply would not be allowed to exist. [. . .]

[. . .] Dickens, from the time of *Oliver Twist*, had always felt it a duty to acquaint his reading public with unpleasant but serious social problems, revelations of harsh fact impossible to believe, yet true.[4] But in *Bleak House*, we are no longer dealing with specific problems, but a society which is problematical—in fact, it is the city itself which has become the problem.[5] And it is a problem so complex, so convoluted, and so very unpleasant, that only through extreme measures can the novelist compel his audience to confront it. This was the second motive for presenting the romantic side of familiar things—to force readers to see a truth far stranger and far more horrifying than any possible fiction.

This intention is evident from the very first words of the novel. [. . .] The details of the descriptions are concrete: the weather, the places, the people and animals, even the fog and the mud, are all commonplace and to a Londoner of 1851, part of his everyday experience. Yet the overall effect of the passage is one of estrangement: the individual components are ordinary but they are so coloured by the strange atmosphere of the passage that they are transmuted into an alien cosmos. The mud threatens to dissolve everyone or everything that touches it; smoke becomes a threatening rain of blackness, blotting out the sun; fog isolates people from the city around them as if each were in separate balloons. The odd syntax heightens the dislocating effect. Before us as we read, these ordinary objects are being endowed with striking new meanings. The familiar elements of the London cityscape have been assembled into a terrifying atmosphere of darkness and stagnation.

The opening pages of the novel represent the beginning of a deliberate campaign by Dickens to force his audience to see and understand the hidden, problematic nature of their familiar environment. So far, the effect is one only of strangeness. But as the novel progresses, the problems of sanitation and disease will be seen to make up the substance of the hidden connections that exist in this

---

4 *Oliver Twist* was serialised 1837–9.
5 [Schwarbach's note.] See Alexander Welsh, *The City of Dickens* (Oxford: Clarendon, 1971), 16–32, for a discussion of the growing perception of the city as problem in nineteenth-century literature.

bewildering urban scene. We can begin to approach Dickens' meaning by examining some of the important elements of the opening passages, beginning with the mud.

The mud of mid-century London was, after all, quite different from the harmless if messy stuff children today make into pies. It was compounded of loose soil to be sure, but also of a great deal more, including soot and ashes and street litter, and the fecal matter of the legion horses on whom all transport in London depended. In addition, many sewers (such as they were) were completely open, and in rainy weather would simply overflow into the streets. Dogs, cattle in transit either to Smithfield or through the town (many dairies were still inside the city), and many people as well as used the public streets as a privy, but then even most privies were simply holes in the ground with drainage into ditches or another part of the street. (London was still a good fifteen years away from having an effective drainage system.) The mud must at times have been nothing less than liquid ordure.

Millions of people who walked through it daily, it seems, in some important sense were unaware of this simple fact. Though at every street corner, a waif like Jo might be standing, waiting to sweep a relatively clean path through the mud (perhaps six inches deep at the centre of the road according to one estimate) for well dressed pedestrians, somehow the fact of his existence or that of the mud itself was not 'real'. Jo swept the mud, but beyond his sweeping he could be ignored. Even so, occasionally women still wore pattens, elevated wooden outer shoes, to traverse the streets, to keep their feet out of the mud. The boot scrapers one still sees outside older London houses and public buildings are additional indications of the condition of the streets, yet rarely does one find them mentioned in the literature of the period.

This insensitivity, then, is what Dickens felt he must assault—the sensibility of an audience cut off from their perceptions of the actual world in which they lived. One of the great mysteries of the Victorian period is how stark realities such as this needed to be 'discovered' by people who could hardly avoid daily contact with them. Yet such discoveries nevertheless were frequent: how often in Victorian letters, diaries, articles or novels do we come across the horrified confession, 'I had not known such things existed'? In *Bleak House*, Dickens even provides us with a classic and no doubt typical instance of this experience, that of Mr Snagsby, who is taken out on a tour of Tom-all-Alone's by Inspector Bucket. He finds there 'such smells and sights that he, who has lived in London all his life, can scarce believe his senses' (Chapter 22). And in the end, he does disbelieve his senses, becoming 'doubtful of the reality of the streets through which he goes' (Chapter 22). It is the 'romance' of *Bleak House* which makes the necessary connections for him and for the reader: Jo, the crossing sweeper whose existence society refuses to acknowledge, spreads the infectious disease engendered by the foul material in which he must work and live. [. . .]

The technique is that of the novel as a whole. The familiar things—closely observed, carefully described—form the basis whence proceed by incontrovertable logic their 'romantic', visionary, ultimately even apocalyptic, aspects. Nothing, in the end, no matter how fantastic, seems out of place: as Forster wrote, 'Nothing is introduced at random, everything tends to the catastrophe, the various lines of the plot converge and fit to its centre, and to the larger interest all the rest is irresistibly drawn' (*Life* [*of Charles Dickens*], II, 114). The final result is to rescue reality from obscurity.[6]

From **Jane R. Cohen,** *Charles Dickens and His Original Illustrators,* Columbus, Ohio: Ohio State University Press, 1980, from Chapter 4, 'Dickens and His Principal Illustrator', pp. 107–12

Today's readers are not accustomed to finding illustrations within a 'serious' work of literature. There is therefore a danger that, not recognising the pivotal role that they played in many nineteenth-century novels, such illustrations will be viewed as extraneous, even distracting, additions to the text. Concentrating on a number of individual plates, Cohen's discussion provides a useful reminder that Hablot Browne's (1815–82) illustrations for *Bleak House* not only complemented Dickens's text, they actually helped to develop and re-enforce its key themes. The importance that Dickens accorded to the novel's illustrations is indicated by the care with which he supervised Browne's work. Although Browne (better known as 'Phiz') had been Dickens's principal illustrator since the mid-1830s, Dickens still insisted on approving his preliminary sketches and demanding appropriate amendments.

Of particular interest is Cohen's discussion of the illustration that graces the novel's wrapper. The amount of detail included in this plate suggests that Dickens, contrary to contemporary opinion, had planned the overall structure of *Bleak House* very carefully. Also of interest are Cohen's comments about the 'dark plates' that dominate the second half of the novel. These were achieved by ruling the metal plate with a number of fine lines in order to produce a marked contrast between light and shadow. As Cohen suggests, this technique was particularly well suited to capture the increasingly sombre tone of the novel. Throughout this extract, I have cut Cohen's footnotes. Four of the illustrations that she discusses are included in this Sourcebook but I strongly recommend that you take the time to consider each one she refers to.

6   [Schwarzbach's note.] A great number of the novel's particulars have been linked closely to 'real', that is to say actual, people and events. See John Butt, *Dickens at Work* (London: Methuen, 1957), pp. 176–200, and '*Bleak House* Once More', *Critical Quarterly*, 1 (1959), pp. 302–7; K.J. Fielding and Alec Brice, '*Bleak House* and the Graveyard', in Robert B. Partlow, ed., *Dickens the Craftsman* (Carbondale, Ill.: Southern Illinois University Press, 1970), pp. 115–39; numerous studies by Trevor Blount, including 'The Graveyard Symbolism of *Bleak House* in the Context of 1850', *Review of English Studies*, N.S. 14 (1963), pp. 370–8, 'The Importance of Place in *Bleak House*', *Dickensian*, 61 (1965), pp. 140–9, and 'Dickens and Mr. Krook's Spontaneous Combustion', *Dickens Studies Annual*, 1 (1970), pp. 183–211; and Anne Smith, 'The Ironmaster in *Bleak House*', *Essays in Criticism*, 21 (1971), pp. 159–69.

[. . .] Dickens planned his most ambitious narrative, which even T. S. Eliot praised as his "finest piece of construction,"[1] with unusual care. The new blue *Bleak House* wrapper [see Figure 1, p. 4], compared to the one for *Copperfield* in the usual green, shows that Browne was better apprised of the story's direction and spirit. Returning to a simpler paneled border of a kind he had not used since *Martin Chuzzlewit*,[2] the artist picked actual characters and episodes from the narrative, which is structured by the interminable lawsuit of Jarndyce *vs.* Jarndyce. Chancery clearly dominates the cover, as it does society, irresponsibly dwarfing individuals it supposedly services. Across the wrapper top, as Butt and Tillotson have described, Browne unfolds an allegorical game of blindman's buff in which the Lord Chancellor, judges, and lawyers, all blindfolded, pursue witnesses for fun and litigants for cost, tripping over the woolsack and mace in the perverted process.[3] In the lower corners, this kind of inhumane sport is further amplified by two scenes, one of a judge looking on bemused while two barristers play chess with clients as chessmen, and another of their colleagues opposite similarly misusing clients for their games of battledore and shuttlecock. A picture of Bleak House itself occupies the center panel, at the bottom of which stands John Jarndyce in despair, besieged by specious philanthropists. The acid satire and grim subjects of Browne's wrapper perfectly anticipate the tone and targets of the narrative to come.

Throughout *Copperfield*, Browne reflected Dickens's exuberance in an abundance of unsolicited graphic details; in *Bleak House*, his touches reflect the author's bitterness. But whereas the details for *Copperfield* usually lend range and depth to the first-person narrative, those for *Bleak House* often return to the more superficial satirical level of his work for earlier books. This time, however, in keeping with the narrative, they satirize institutions and their representatives rather than individuals and their actions. On the wall facing Jarndyce and his guests inside 'The little church in the park' (Chapter 18), for example, the artist places a memorial to a judge as if to imply the futility of escape from Chancery even on the Sabbath or in death—though the bird perched irreverently on the magistrate's stone wig adds salutary humor. Elsewhere in the narrative, not only does religion prove indifferent to institutional evils, but clergy, like Chadband, whose pose during his pitiless lecture to Jo caricatures that of the saint pictured behind them, perpetuate them (Chapter 25). Similarly, officers of the law pervert their function as the artifacts in Vholes's office repeatedly make clear (Chapter 39). As the attorney enmeshes Richard more and more inescapably in the Jarndyce case, Browne's details—the legend of the fox and grapes carved in his mantle,[4] the portrait of a nearsighted judge above, the wolves' heads below, the ironically labeled cartons stacked to the right, the butterfly net leaning against the wall, the spider web with trapped flies on the ceiling corner, the cat watching for the mouse behind the desk, the overturned wastebasket disclosing an

---

1   Cohen is referring to Eliot's article 'Wilkie Collins and Dickens', *Times Literary Supplement*, 4 August 1927, p. 525.
2   *Martin Chuzzlewit* was serialised in 1843–4.
3   Cohen is referring to Butt and Tillotson (see Contextual Overview, note 20), p. 195.
4   'It is easy to despise what you cannot get.'

advertisement for "fool's cap," the book opened to a plan of a maze, and the mass of tangled string next to it—all comment on his dubious brand of legal aid [see Figure 4, p. 140]. [. . .]

At their best, Browne's illustrations had always complemented Dickens's texts. With apparently inexhaustible ingenuity, the artist continued correlating his visual structures and techniques with the author's changing ones. The dark plates not only reflect the novel's prevailing somber tone and atmosphere, but the oppressive dominance of the setting—both weather and structures—over the characters, an inordinate number of whom die in the story's course. As both Steig and Harvey have pointed out, of the ten dark plates in *Bleak House*, six have no human figures at all: of the four that do, only one figure is clearly discernible: and, moreover, the absence of people is not an inevitable result of the technique or of Browne's use of it, as is clear from the dark plates the artist executed for other authors.[5] The insignificance of the characters in the artist's plates sensitively reflects their insignificance in the author's narrative, which depicts a society whose institutions dwarf, isolate, and too often destroy members. As Dickens increasingly abandoned his usual satiric devices, finding them insufficient to portray his society, so Browne gradually had to dispense with the traditional methods and subjects of graphic satire.

The dark plates, depicting the settings associated with the aristocratic Dedlocks, Tulkinghorn, their attorney, and the slum orphan, Jo, link these characters graphically as Dickens links them narratively. Utilizing light and shadow more conventionally than structure and artifact, Browne ingeniously relates Jo to all of society in his portrayal of Tom-all-Alone's (Chapter 46), whose name nearly supplied the book's title [see Figure 3, p. 128]. A garbage-filled passage leads out past a sign for a pawnshop [. . .] and ends abruptly in a graveyard, which promises the only escape. Little reassurance is implicit in the gray church tower which, like religion itself in *Bleak House*, coldly and impassively overlooks the environs, typical of impoverished London streets of the time. [. . .]

Linked graphically as well as narratively to Tom-all-Alone's is remote Chesney Wold, whose aristocratic inhabitants and environs provide the subjects of over half the total number of dark plates. Browne's exploitation of the striking light and shadow contrasts of this technique deliberately parallel Dickens's verbal devices (including the titles of the illustrations) for portraying Chesney Wold and its owners, especially Lady Dedlock. Though Browne's means are conventional, his deployment of them is sophisticated. From the first, the author leans heavily on the symbolic potential of shadow to anticipate how Lady Dedlock's adultery will affect Chesney Wold and the declining way of life it represents. He describes her portrait, which Guppy's obsessive interest has fixed in the reader's mind (Chapter 7), in these terms: "Athwart the picture of my lady, over the great chimney-piece, [the cold sunlight] throws a broad bend sinister of light that strikes down crookedly into the earth, and seems to rend it" (Chapter 12). In his dark plate, entitled

---

5   Cohen is referring to J.R. Harvey, *Victorian Novelists and their Illustrators*, New York: New York University Press, pp. 151–2 and M. Steig, 'Dickens, Hablot Browne, and the Tradition of English Caricature', *Criticism*, 11, Summer 1969, p. 229 and 'Structure and the Grotesque in Dickens: *Dombey and Son*, *Bleak House*', *Centennial Review*, 14, Summer 1970, p. 326.

'Sunset in the long Drawing-room at Chesney Wold,' [see Figure 2, p. 92] as Harvey has discussed, Browne graphically reflects the theme of light and shadow, which is used to highlight the few permitted aesthetic objects that are dramatically as well as visually essential (Chapter 40).[6] In the center of the room, in the darkest shadow relieved only by flecks of light, stands a sculptured maternal figure attending a small cherub. At the upper left corner, face averted from the tender pair as well as from the sunlit portrait opposite of a young girl, is the portrait of Lady Dedlock. The artifacts, all linked by light, suggest what events will prove true—that Lady Dedlock turned away from her maternal duties and abandoned her illegitimate daughter to preserve her aristocratic station. But the effect of her misconduct, like the gathering shadow, here touching her pictured skirt like a stain, threatens to overwhelm her as Dickens suggests in the accompanying text. "And now, upon my lady's picture over the great chimney-piece, a weird shade falls from some odd tree, that turns it pale, and flutters it, and looks as if a great arm held a veil or hood, watching an opportunity to draw it over her" (Chapter 40).

The next dark plate that features Lady Dedlock—in person this time—is entitled 'Shadow' (Chapter 53), and indeed Dickens uses more and more shadow in describing her, so that she gradually becomes equated with it. The illustration does more than afford a technical and titular contrast with the preceding scene, 'Light,' in which Esther Summerson, Lady Dedlock's selfless daughter, comforts the newly married Ada (Chapter 51). In the dark plate, shadow acts as a protagonist in the implicit psychological drama, enveloping the entire staircase at Chesney Wold and all but the head and shoulders of Lady Dedlock as she mounts it. It almost blankets the maternal scene on the landing, from which her ladyship, as before, averts her head. In contrast to Edith Dombey's encounter with Florence on the stairway ([Dombey and Son], Chapter 47), a scene that invites comparison with this one, there is no acknowledged responsibility to a child to give this woman pause. Her attention is drawn instead to the area of light near the "MURDER-REWARD" poster, a reference to the recent death of the family lawyer, Mr. Tulkinghorn, as blunt as that of the figure of Allegory in the preceding dark plate (Chapter 48).

The next two dark plates are more exciting and mysterious. Paired by title and original placement as well as by technique, as Harvey has shown, they capitalize on the confusion created by Lady Dedlock's use of the brickmaker's wife to conceal her movements.[7] The fact that the figure in 'The Night' (Chapter 57) does not turn out to be her ladyship increases the ambiguity surrounding the collapsed figure in 'The Morning' (Chapter 59). Perhaps it is Jenny, as Esther initially believes; perhaps the woman is not dead, but merely ill or asleep. After the text reveals the secret, the plate, though losing its mystery (which the double meaning of its title had reinforced), remains a moving portrayal of the fate of Lady Dedlock, her face averted in death as it had been in life. The last dark plate, as is appropriate in a story in which nine deaths occur, is a picture of the Dedlock mausoleum (Chapter 66). Esther's concluding epilogue only partly fulfills the

---

6   Cohen is referring to Harvey (see note 5), pp. 155–7.
7   Cohen is referring to Harvey (see note 5), pp. 153–4.

implicit promise of the scene's brighter horizon. By adding irreverent demons to the margins of his sketch for this scene, Browne may have sought comic relief from Dickens's unabated pessimism through *Bleak House*. [. . .]

From **D.A. Miller, *The Novel and the Police***, Berkeley, Calif.: University of California Press, 1988, from Chapter 3, 'Discipline in Different Voices: Bureaucracy, Police, Family, and *Bleak House*', pp. 66–9, 73–5

This essay was, in part, written as a rejoinder to that of Hillis Miller (**p. 65**). As a new historicist, D.A. Miller objects to the ways in which Hillis Miller treats the novel as a purely linguistic structure ('an allegory of meaning'), thereby divorcing it from history (for a brief introduction to new historicism, see Critical History, **p. 54**). In contrast, he insists on viewing Chancery Court as a real institutional system firmly grounded in a network of material practices (as does Schor, **p. 93**). According to this reading, the deferrals associated with Chancery are not a product of textuality but, rather, a self-serving practice designed to prolong and extend its proceedings in order to generate profit. According to Miller, Chancery Court exercises, maintains and extends its power precisely through its refusal to limit its boundaries or offer definitive interpretations of its own cases.

One consequence of Chancery's ability to resist interpretation is a desire for an alternative system that satisfies the needs denied by the former. This alternative system, Miller argues, is represented by the detective story that comes to dominate *Bleak House*. In contrast to Chancery Court, the detective story is limited (a defined struggle between the criminal, the victim and the detective), efficient and productive of meaning (the murderer is identified and the mystery is solved). Yet as Miller goes on to conclude, Chancery Court and the detective story are actually complementary rather than opposing practices. In fulfilling the needs generated by Chancery, the detective story helps to render it acceptable and thus prolongs and legitimises its power.

D.A. Miller's new historicist reading of *Bleak House* is indicative of how interest in Dickens has been regenerated by recent developments in critical theory. Following Miller's lead, the representation and treatment of power have become key issues within current interpretations of Dickens's work. In this extract, I have cut Miller's footnotes.

[. . .] Of all the mysteries that will crop up in *Bleak House*, not the least instructive concerns the curious formal torsion whereby a novel dealing with a civil suit becomes a murder mystery, and whereby the themes of power and social control are passed accordingly from the abyssal filiations of the law into the capable hands of the detective police. By what kinds of logic or necessity is the law thus turned over to the police, and the civil suit turned into the criminal case? For if Jarndyce and Jarndyce provides the ground from which mysteries and the consequent detections originate, it is certainly not because the suit is itself a mystery. In one way, it is so illegible that we don't even have a sense, as we should with a mystery, of what needs to be explained or, more important, of what might constitute either the clues or the cruxes of such an explanation. In another, the suit may be read fully and at leisure: in the reams of dusty warrants, in the tens of thousands of Chancery-folio pages, in the battery of blue bags with their heavy charges of paper—in all the archival litter that has accumulated over the dead letter of the original will. Dickens's presentation offers either too little or else too much to amount to mystery. Besides, nothing about the suit is secret or hidden, unless we count the second will found late in the novel, and this hardly brings us closer to a judgment. All that is ever unavailable is the dead legator's intentions.

It would be seriously misleading, however, on the basis of this exception, to deconstruct the suit into an allegory of interpretation as that which, confronting the absence of an immediate meaning effected by the very nature of the sign or text, must unfold as an interminable proliferation of readings. For one thing, if the suit can be thought to give expression to such difficulties of interpretation, this is because, more than merely finding them acceptable, it goes out of its way to manufacture them; and no response would serve Chancery or the logic of its law better than to see this manufacture as inhering in the nature of "textuality" rather than belonging to an institutional practice that seeks to implant and sanction its own technical procedures. For another, it seems willful to see the work of inter- pretation occurring in what is far more obviously and actually the profitable busi- ness of deferring it indefinitely. With its endless referrals, relays, remands, its ecologically terrifying production of papers, minutes, memoranda, Dickens's bur- eaucracy works positively to elude the project of interpretation that nominally guides it. [. . .] Esther properly recognizes how "ridiculous" it is to speak of a Chancery suit as "in progress," since the term implies a linear directedness that, while fully suitable to the project that subtends Esther's own narration (indica- tively begun under the title of "A Progress"), must be wholly absent from a case that, typically, "seemed to die out of its own vapidity, without coming, or being by anybody expected to come, to any result" (Chapter 24). Moreover, to see that, in Chancery, the process of decision and interpretation is diverted is also to see that it is diverted *into* Chancery, as an apparatus. It is diverted, in other words, into the work of establishing the very channels for its diversion: channels by means of which a legal establishment is ramified, its points of contact multiplied, and routes of circulation organized for the subjects who are thus recruited under its power.

Yet Chancery can never dispense with the judgments that it also never dispenses. Though the project of interpretation is virtually annulled in the workings of its formalism ("the lantern that has no light in it"), the *promise* of interpretation, as that which initiates and facilitates this formalism, remains absolutely necessary. At the theoretical level of ideology, the promise functions to confer legitimacy on Chancery proceedings: as even poor crazed Miss Flyte [*sic*], in her confusion of the Last Judgment with the long-delayed judgment in her own case, is capable of revealing, the legal system must appeal for its legitimacy to transcendent concepts of truth, justice, meaning, and ending, even when its actual work will be to hold these concepts in profitable abeyance or to redefine and contain them as functions of its own operations. And at the practical and technical level of such operations, the promise of judgment becomes the lure of advertising, extended by venalities such as Vholes to promote the purchase and exercise of their services.

Perhaps the most interesting effect of all produced by the promise, however, considerably exceeds these theoretical and practical functions. If Chancery exploits the logic of a promise by perpetually maintaining it as *no more than such*, then the suit must obviously produce as much frustration as hopefulness. Accordingly, one consequence of a system that, as it engenders an interpretative project, deprives it of all the requirements for its accomplishment is the desire for an interpretative project that would *not* be so balked. [. . .] What such a desire effectively seeks, therefore, is a reduced model of the untotalizable system and a legible version of the undecidable suit. What such a desire calls for, in short, both as a concept and as a fact, is the detective story.

The detective story gives obscurity a name and a local habitation: in that highly specific "mystery" whose ultimate uncovering motivates an equally specific program of detection. If the Chancery system includes everything but settles nothing, then one way in which it differs from the detective story is that the latter is, precisely, a *story*: sufficiently selective to allow for the emergence of a narrative and properly committed, once one has emerged, to bringing it to completion. In relation to an organization so complex that it often tempts its subjects to misunderstand it as chaos, the detective story realizes the possibility of an easily comprehensible version of order. And in the face—or facelessness—of a system where it is generally impossible to assign responsibility for its workings to any single person or group of persons, where even the process of victimization seems capricious, the detective story performs a drastic simplification of power as well. For unlike Chancery, the detective story is fully prepared to affirm the efficacy and priority of personal agency, be it that of the criminal figures who do the work of concealment or that of the detective figures who undo it. [. . .]

[. . .] The novel's shift in focus from the Court of Chancery to the Detective Police encompasses a number of concomitant shifts, which all operate in the direction of this simplification: from civil law and questions of liability to criminal law and less merely legal questions of guilt; from trivial legal hairsplitting to the urgency of the fact, beyond such disputing, of murder; from a cause with countless parties represented by countless attorneys in an anonymous system, to a case essentially reduced to two personal duels, between the criminal and his victim and between the criminal and the detective; from long, slow, to all appearances utterly inefficient procedures to swift and productive ones; and finally, from an institution that cannot justify its power to one that, for all the above reasons, quite persuasively can. It is as though every complaint that could be made about the one institution had been redressed in the organization of the other, so that one might even argue, on the basis of Dickens's notorious willingness to serve as a propagandist for the New Police,[1] that the excruciating *longueurs* of Chancery existed mainly to create the market for Mr. Bucket's expeditious *coups*.[2] Along these lines, one might even want to read, in the police

---

1 See headnote to 'On Duty with Inspector Field', p. 38.
2 *Longueur* denotes length while 'un coup' is a quick blow and suggests speed and efficiency.

activity that develops over the dead body of the law ("or Mr. Tulkinghorn, one of its trustiest representatives" [Chapter 22]), Dickens's exhilarated announcement of the agencies and practices of social discipline that, claiming to be merely supplementing the law, will come in large part to supplant it. Yet to the extent that we stress, in the evident archaism of Chancery, the emergence of a new kind of bureaucratic organization, and in the blatantly modern Detective Police (instituted only ten years before the novel began to appear), a harkening back to a traditional and familiar model of power, then we need to retain the possibility that Dickens's New Police still polices, substantively as well as nominally, *for* the law, for the Chancery system, and that, as a representation, it serves a particular ideological function within this system, and not against it. Made so desirable as a sort of institutional "alternative" to Chancery, the police derive their ideological efficacy from providing, within a total system of power, *a representation of the containment of power*. The shift from Chancery to the police dramatically localizes the field, exercise, and agents of power, as well as, of course, justifies such power, which, confined to a case of murder and contained in a Mr. Bucket, occupies what we can now think of as the right side. And when the novel passes from adulatory wonder at the efficiency of the police to sad, resigned acknowledgment of their limits (such as emerges in Hortense's last exchange with Bucket),[3] the circumscription of power, reaching the end to which it always tended, has merely come full circle.

From **Elizabeth Langland, *Nobody's Angels: Middle-Class Women and Domestic Ideology in Victorian Culture***, Ithaca, N.Y.: Cornell University Press, 1995, from Chapter 4, 'Charles Dickens's Angels of Competence', pp. 90–2, 96–7

Elizabeth Langland, like D.A. Miller, is concerned with the representation and exercise of power in *Bleak House*. More specifically, she is interested in the ways in which surveillance and discipline operate within the one sphere that is normally seen as exempt from their operations: the middle-class home. Langland challenges traditional readings of 'the angel in the house' as both powerless and passive, as well as the construction of the domestic sphere as a space separate from, and opposed to, the male-dominated public realm of power (for a discussion of these issues, see Contextual Overview, p. 14). In so doing, she foregrounds the extent to which the nineteenth-century housewife transformed the domestic haven into a site of discipline and surveillance by assuming an active role in the construction and maintenance of class identity.

The following extract is, in part, a rejoinder to the reading of *Bleak House*

---

3 Having been arrested for the murder of Tulkinghorn, Hortense demands whether Bucket can restore the victim to life or make 'a honourable lady' of Sir Leicester's wife (Chapter 54).

offered by D.A. Miller in *The Novel and the Police* (see **p. 81**). Asserting that Miller is 'disturbingly unaware of gender', Langland suggests that his argument is based on 'a radical chauvinism, which can always point to women [. . .] as representatives of that (illusory) "outside" of power operations' (89). In contrast, she reads femininity and the domestic realm as an alternative site of power where Esther Summerson engages in a form of surveillance as effective as the lawyer Tulkinghorn and polices her charges as successfully as Bucket does his. By so doing, Esther helps to consolidate the middle-class sense of identity, teaching the values of thrift, organisation and household management to a range of willing pupils (see, for example, Key Passages, **p. 122**). It has long been accepted that hegemony – the ways in which a dominant group disseminates its values throughout society – works best when invisible (what cannot be seen, cannot be questioned). Taking up this idea in her conclusion, Langland reminds us that the ability of the middle-class woman to exercise power was rendered all the more effective by the pervasive myth that this woman – and the home over which she presided – were, by nature, outside the realm of politics and power.

In addition to illuminating the extract by D.A. Miller, the argument put forth by Langland provides insight into the novel's treatment of gender, the family and class. Stressing the material dimension of identity – that identity is constructed by the real, material conditions of life – it offers an alternative approach to the psychoanalytic reading of Dever (**p. 88**).

[. . .] Dickens's *Bleak House*, read through the prism of gender and the middle-class manager, reveals a struggle for the terms in which meaning and identity are to be constituted. Rather than representing the family as a realm idealistically outside of an institutional and public sphere, Dickens positions the middle-class home as a competing site of power, the province of emerging cultural definitions that seek to supplant the cumbersome behemoths[1] of Chancery and the aristocracy with the detective police and the middle-class, to displace inheritance and tradition with self-reliance and application, to replace external controls with self-discipline. And the guardians of middle-class life and the agents of that discipline are bourgeois women. Mr. Bagnet's[2] mantra—"Discipline must be maintained"— ironically announces a man's subservient position within a culture whose order is established by women. Mr. Bagnet pronounces this mantra preliminary to enforcing his wife's authority to deliver "his" opinion on all matters: "You know me," he tells his friend George, "It's my old girl that advises. She has the head. But I never own to it before her. Discipline must be maintained" (Chapter 27). She, thus, originates "their" opinions and values while he plays out his ideological role

---

1 Someone or something that is unusually large or powerful.
2 Friends of Trooper George (the son of Mrs Rouncewell who is erroneously arrested for the murder of Tulkinghorn), the Bagnets represent one of the few examples of a happy family in the novel.

as "head" of the family. The two together enact a parodic[3] drama of the cultural myth of dominant husband and submissive wife, while testifying to the wife's managerial authority.[4]

Although women's authority is mystified within patriarchal ideologies, another image emerges within a bourgeois class ideology. Once we perceive the way a middle-class wife imposes discipline we can see how the detective police are deliberately linked to the values of home and hearth for their complementary ability to impose order and coherence in the novel's fragmented, enmired world. At the center of this scheme is Esther Summerson. The London "particular"[5]—a metaphor for Chancery—that opens the novel and greets Esther's arrival in the metropolis finds its analogue in the mire of the Jellyby household where she is lodged. Like the lawyers in Chancery, Mrs. Jellyby—one of the parodied philanthropists in the novel—engages in continual correspondences and petitions, none of which produces any resolution. Indeed, the result of the endeavors – the Borioboola-Ghan [sic] King's desire to sell everybody for rum—echoes the slavery to a system produced by Chancery. [. . .]

Successfully imposed domestic order is a form of middle-class colonization much more efficient and far-reaching in its effects than the loudly bruited efforts of the philanthropists. Esther quietly and systematically begins to impose order that, if pursued, will culminate in middle-class comfort and respectability for reformed individuals. Ada remarks to Esther: "You do so much, so unpretendingly! You would make a home out of even this house" (Chapter 4). She efficiently releases Peepy[6] from the prison of railings through which he has wedged his head, takes him into her own custody, subdues him, and cleans him up. In short, she sets him on the road to middle-class industry and allows us to anticipate his metamorphosis into the young man at the end of the novel, "in the Custom House, and doing extremely well" (Chapter 67). Caddy, too, falls under Esther's training and management. Having secured a prospective husband, the bedraggled Miss Jellyby turns to Esther for a four-week training course in household management, three to be conducted at Bleak House and the fourth in London preparing the Jellyby house for the nuptials. They begin with dress and the acquisition of some skill in needlework, at which Caddy "improve[s] rapidly."

---

3   An act of imitation designed to deflate, or parody, its original source.
4   [Langland's note.] [L.] Langbauer [*Women and Romance: the Consolations of Gender in the English Novel*, Ithaca, NY: Cornell University Press, 1990] reads the episode quite differently, arguing that "*Bleak House* indeed presents Mrs Bagnet's seeming autonomy, and even authority, as comic grotesquery, benign because clearly understood as comic, a reversal of (what the novel believes ought to be) women's actual domestic subjection" (149–50). She continues this argument, turning to Esther's narrative as exemplification: "The endlessness of Esther's narrative echoes the way women are characteristically sacrificed to the perpetual enslavement of the everyday: the monotonous and self-perpetuating drudgery performed by slaves of the home like Guster or the Marchioness" (152). But to emphasize only the patriarchal dimensions of the home and overlook the class dimensions, to link Esther's managerial tasks with Guster's menial labor, is to miss a distinction operating consistently throughout the novel. Mrs. Snagsby, who "manages" Guster, sometimes quite brutally, is a vulgar, lower-class example of the more "gentle" Esther.
5   A particularly dense fog.
6   The youngest Jellyby child.

Caddy is "very anxious 'to learn housekeeping,' as she said" (Chapter 30), so Esther relates that "I showed her all my books and methods, and all my fidgety ways. You would have supposed that I was showing her some wonderful inventions, by her study of them; and if you had seen her, whenever I jingled my housekeeping keys, get up and attend me, certainly you might have thought that there never was a greater impostor than I, with a blinder follower than Caddy Jellyby" (Chapter 30). The disclaimer—Esther as impostor—inevitably follows the revelation of a systematic scheme of organization. This requisite modesty about her effects contributes to the mystification of the middle-class woman's management labors. [. . .]

Although the novel points to Esther's achievements, it disguises the nature of her work because to reveal it is to introduce class issues prominently into the home-as-haven. In the novel's conclusion, Esther takes her place by Woodcourt's side, merged in the more shining qualities of her husband. She claims that the people of Yorkshire "like me for his sake, as I do everything I do in life for his sake" (Chapter 67). [. . .] At the end of the novel, Allan Woodcourt's capacity for work correlates with his wife's talent for management. And the disappearance of Esther from view depends on the sleight of hand of that same skillful manager. Esther's final effacement of herself and her effects contributes to the Victorian myth of the idle angel. But that static icon is found only in the figure of Ada Clare, whose single task is to shine "in the miserable corner [of her home with Richard] like a beautiful star" (Chapter 60). The many lives and houses Esther manages leave her no leisure to serve as an elegant light fixture.[7]

One final word on *Bleak House*. Mrs. Jellyby, who has reduced her own home to chaos, becomes an advocate of "the rights of women to sit in Parliament" (Chapter 67). Apparently, Dickens's irony suggests, she intends to wreak havoc on the country if her folly is not stopped. The least talented housekeeper becomes the most vocal feminist. Mrs. Jellyby is joined in her efforts by women like Miss Wisk,[8] whose "mission . . . was to show the world that woman's mission was man's mission; and that the only genuine mission, of both man and woman, was to be always moving declaratory resolutions about things in general at public meetings" (Chapter 30). Miss Wisk angrily informs Esther that "such a mean mission as the domestic mission, was the very last thing to be endured" and that "the idea of woman's mission lying chiefly in the narrow sphere of Home was an outrageous slander on the part of her Tyrant Man" (Chapter 30). These pointed jibes at women who abandon their proper "mission," the home, help to persuade us that the Victorian middle-class home is a very isolated, conventional

---

7 [Langland's note.] Martin Danahay ['Housekeeping and Hegemony in *Bleak House*', *Studies in the Novel*, 23, Winter 1991] is interested in establishing that Esther and middle-class women, in general, do *work* in the home, despite mystifications of that fact. He claims, however, that Esther's "labor is not explicitly recognized as work in the same sense as the tasks performed by the male professionals. This lack of acknowledgement of Esther's labor results directly from the growing separation of women from work in the Victorian period" (418). Danahay reads the gaps in Esther's character "as products of the Victorian gender hierarchy of labor in which women's work could not be acknowledged overtly" (419). He does not examine class issues.

8 A member of Mrs Jellyby's philanthropic circle.

place, indeed—the repository of traditional values. They become part of the mystification.

But the home we have been examining is far from traditional—it is a primary locus for solidifying class identities and establishing a middle-class hegemony by colonizing the "natives" of England. The Victorian idealizations of home as outside of politics, as a refuge from strife, helped to facilitate its operation as a new base for struggle. Such idealizations, in which it is so easy for a public to participate because they feed into stereotypes of women, inevitably work to consolidate upper-middle-class centrality and power, separating the genteel both from the working classes, who serve them, and the lower middle classes, who emulate them.

From **Carolyn Dever, Death and the Mother from Dickens to Freud: Victorian Fiction and the Anxiety of Origins**, Cambridge: Cambridge University Press, 1998, from Chapter 3, 'Broken Mirror, Broken Words: *Bleak House*', pp. 85–9.

Bleak House is full of absent or inadequate mothers: women who, through death, abandonment or neglect, fail to fulfil the maternal ideal (for a discussion of gender, see Contextual Overview, p. 13). Reading psychoanalysis and Victorian narratives through and against each other, Dever explores the effect maternal loss has upon Esther's subjectivity – the ways in which this 'orphan' must struggle to construct a sense of identity – and 'the ambivalent compensatory structures that emerge in the wake of her departure' (xi). In the extract below, she concentrates on two such 'compensatory structures': Donald Winnicott's concept of 'transitional objects' and language itself.

Winnicott (1896–1971) was a prominent member of the British school of psychoanalysis and a leading proponent of object-relations theory. This theory concentrates on the individual's relationship to society; especially the relationship between a child and its mother. In both his writings and his practice, he was interested in how a child uses 'transitional objects' (dolls, blankets, etc.) in the process of constructing an identity. It is important to recognise that babies are not born with an innate sense of selfhood. Unable to distinguish between themselves and the outside world (between 'me' and 'not-me'), they exist in a world without boundaries, a world in which the mother – the first object of love and desire – is a part of them. The difficult and fraught process of constructing an identity is, according to classical psychoanalysis, initiated and dominated by the father, who disrupts the relationship between mother and child. In so doing, he allows the child to differentiate itself from her and begin to see itself as a separate entity. In contrast, Winnicott insists that it is the mother, not the father, who is the crucial figure in the construction of identity. In the first few months of life, the child begins to gain a sense of identity through the image that the mother reflects back to the child through her eyes, voice and touch. In other words, the child sees itself as it is seen by the mother. This strong sense of identification between mother and child is not unproblematic and inevitably poses certain dangers for the child who resents its utter dependence. In order to protect itself, the child must learn to separate itself from the mother. For Winnicott, however, this process of differentiation involves only the mother and the child: the father has no role to play in it. It is also important to understand the importance of what Winnicott calls 'transitional objects' in this process. Such objects help the child to learn about and negotiate between internal and external reality, self and other, illusion and reality. The crucial role played by such objects is made clear in Dever's discussion of Esther's doll. As a substitute for her 'dead' mother, the doll functions like a mirror that reflects an image of Esther back to her, an image that provides the basis of subjectivity (see Key Passages, **p. 111**). As Dever suggests, 'Esther's subjectivity is at this point directly dependent on her ability to construct a self by reading her reflection in the eyes of another.' At the same time, the doll functions as Esther's other (a 'not-me' object) against which she can differentiate herself: an important step towards seeing herself as an autonomous being.

The second 'compensatory structure' discussed by Dever is language itself. As she suggests, there is a 'direct relationship between abandonment and articulation' (81). Building on the work of the prominent American deconstructionist Paul de Man, Dever suggests that in the act of writing her autobiography, Esther writes herself into existence, that she constructs herself as a subject and gains a sense of agency, an ability to act (for a discussion of the relationship between language and subjectivity, see Critical History, **p. 55**). By insisting that articulation precedes existence, this reading calls into question the traditional assumption that ' "life *produces* the autobiography" '. In other words, only when Esther is capable of articulating 'I' does she become an 'I'. This relationship between writing and subjectivity is developed through de Man's discussion of the rhetorical trope of *prosopopeia*. This is a figurative device 'that summons up an absent, dead, or ghostly personage by means of an act of naming'.[1] By giving herself a name and a voice in her narrative, Esther – the child who 'died' at birth – brings herself back from the dead.

The complexity of Dever's argument – suggested by the length of this head-note – is entirely typical of the increasingly sophisticated readings of Dickens made possible by recent developments in literary theory. While such readings may place extra demands on the reader, they represent an important strand within the critical history of the novel. As the child of 'no one' (Chapter 10) who is, at her birth, 'laid aside as dead' (Chapter 36), Esther continually struggles to construct a coherent sense of selfhood (see, for example, Key Passages, **pp. 135–6**). Thus it is hardly surprising that this character and her narrative are

---

1   C. Norris, *Paul De Man: Deconstruction and the Critique of Aesthetic Ideology*, New York and London: Routledge, 1988, pp. xix–xx.

so appealing to those exploring questions related to subjectivity and identity. Dismissed or ignored for far too long, the issues raised by Esther's 'little body' (Chapter 3) have come to dominate recent interpretations of the novel.

[. . .] The issues at stake here – for Esther, for Dickens – are issues of authenticity and agency. In a discussion of the relationship between fiction and auto-biography, Paul de Man attempts to destabilize the assumptions that traditionally inform these generic classifications:

> We assume that life *produces* the autobiography as an act produces its consequences, but can we not suggest, with equal justice, that the auto-biographical project may itself produce and determine the life and that whatever the writer *does* is in fact governed by the technical demands of self-portraiture and thus determined, in all its aspects, by the resources of his medium? And since the mimesis[2] here assumed to be operative is one mode of figuration among others, does the referent[3] determine the figure, or is it the other way round: is the illusion of reference not a correlation of the structure of the figure, that is to say no longer clearly and simply a referent at all but something more akin to a fiction which then, however, in its own turn, acquires a degree of referential productivity?[4]

De Man's analysis problematizes the discretion of the autobiographical mode through a reversal of agency at the site of production. To privilege a mimetic or causal relationship between experience and signification is to do so at the expense of the narrative itself, belying its implications in the production of experience. The extent to which the text has agency in the production of that experience is underscored in Esther's narrative, which is engaged [. . .] in an attempt to deploy this text as a means of rewriting the unsatisfactory tale of her birth and childhood. [. . .]

Significantly, then, the opening of Esther's text functions as both an originary and an historicized moment. Its title, "A Progress," refers to its own internal events, to its commencement *in medias res*[5] in the life of Esther Summerson, and also to its position as the third chapter, not the first, of *Bleak House*. This is a moment which puts into question the status of the originary; although Esther does not respond actively to the events of the previous chapters, the opening of her story is already contingent, already inflected with the markers of an anterior presence. The condition of the narrative is equivalent to the condition of its

---

2   See Hillis Miller, note 8.
3   See Critical History, p. 54.
4   P. De Man, 'Autobiography as De-Facement', in *The Rhetoric of Romanticism*, New York: Columbia University Press, 1984, p. 69.
5   Literally, 'in the middle of things'.

narrator: Esther is seemingly more aware of the past than the present, attempting to read backward in these opening moments to (re)construct a personal history, but frustrated by the fact that the text of her biography is as yet a blank.

Esther's childhood narrative is constructed in the form of an apostrophe[6] to her doll, her best friend: "And so she used to sit propped up in a great arm-chair, with her beautiful complexion and rosy lips, staring at me – or not so much at me, I think, as at nothing – while I busily stitched away, and told her every one of my secrets [Chapter 3]". At this time, of course, Esther "had never, to [her] own mother's knowledge, breathed – had been buried – had never been endowed with life – had never borne a name" [Chapter 36]. Esther, the dead baby, talks with this inanimate, nameless baby about her missing mother, about the mystery of her origins. In object-relations theory, Esther's doll would itself function as a substitute or median mother for her; D. W. Winnicott argues that children use transitional objects such as this doll to compensate for anxieties that accompany the process of differentiation from the mother. Transitional objects function in education about borderlines: as the child's first "not-me" possession, they provide symbolic instruction in the construction and negotiation of self – other relationships.[7] The centrality of the transitional object to Esther's early ability to articulate herself indicates why the presence of a mother, even if it is only temporary, is critical to her self-conscious construction of herself as a speaking subject. When she looks at this doll, she looks simultaneously at herself and at an Other; her ability to articulate the question of origins as a question depends on the artificial appropriation of a mother-object against which she can differentiate.

Esther's doll compensates for the multiply overdetermined markers of absence in her world. As she talks with her doll, she talks with herself, and by talking with her doll she constitutes herself; by means of apostrophe, she creates an Other, she makes an absence (at least provisionally) a presence, and manufactures the conditions for discourse. Esther's subjectivity is at this point directly dependent on her ability to construct a self by reading her reflection in the eyes of another. For it is later revealed that her father is the opium-addicted law-writer of Chancery, known only as "Nemo," which translates as "no one." With uncanny[8] prescience, Esther foregrounds her paternal identity in her discussion with her doll; before she reveals her name, which is only the signifier of her absence, she reveals her signifier of absence: "staring at me – or not so much at me I think, as at nothing [Chapter 3]." For an autobiographical narrator whose own mother believes her dead, the capacity for autobiographical articulation signals a form of agency: if

---

6 A rhetorical trope in which the speaker addresses someone or something that is not there.
7 [Dever's note.] D.W. Winnicott, "Transitional Objects and Transitional Phenomena," in *Playing and Reality* (New York: Routledge, 1971), 1–25. See also Melanie Klein, "Love, Guilt and Reparation," in Melanie Klein and Joan Riviere, *Love, Hate and Reparation* (New York: Norton, 1964).
8 From the German '*unheimlich*', the uncanny denotes the unfamiliar, or strange, as well as the familiar or homely (the qualities associated with its supposed antithesis, the canny, or '*heimlich*'). In his 1919 essay on the subject, Sigmund Freud associates the uncanny with the feeling produced when repressed material re-emerges into consciousness. See S. Freud, 'The Uncanny' [1919], in *Art and Literature*, trans. J. Strachey, The Penguin Freud Library, vol. 14, Harmondsworth: Penguin, 1990, pp. 339–76.

Figure 2 'Sunset in the long Drawing-room at Chesney Wold' (from Chapter 40).

she is capable of articulation, she is capable of existence. For when Esther speaks of herself, she animates the body of that dead baby. Returning to de Man,

> The figure of prosopopeia, the fiction of an apostrophe to an absent, deceased, or voiceless entity . . . posits the possibility of the latter's reply and confers upon it the power of speech. Voice assumes mouth, eye, and finally face, a chain that is manifest in the etymology of the trope's name, *prosopon poiein*, to confer a mask or a face (*prosopon*). Prosopopeia is the trope of autobiography, by which one's name . . . is made as intelligible and memorable as a face.[9]

In the terms of this argument, rhetoric insistently precedes embodiment; the existence of Esther's face relies on her capacity for figuration, for the figurative construction of subjectivity maintained in her encounter with her doll–baby but disrupted in her encounter with her mother.[10] Language is the vehicle by which Esther can create something – herself – out of nothing. [. . .]

From **Hilary M. Schor, *Dickens and the Daughter of the House***, Cambridge: Cambridge University Press, 1999, from Chapter 4, '*Bleak House* and the Dead Mother's Property', pp. 101–4, 110–12

In *Dickens and the Daughter of the House*, Hilary Schor offers us a materialist reading of Dickens's novel. In other words, she reads it in terms of the actual, material conditions of its day and, more specifically, the social and legal position of women and illegitimate children at mid-century. At the same time, however, Schor is also interested in questions relating to textuality; in the novel's multiple narratives and proliferation of documents. In the following extract, she asserts that *Bleak House* offers us two models of inheritance – one of property and one of affection – that seem to correspond to the novel's two narratives. The first of these narratives, that of the semi-omniscient, implicitly male, third-person narrator, tells the story 'of the law, of London, of wills and inheritance and procedure' (102). The second, that of Esther herself, narrates the story of a maternal legacy and a search for origins (an issue also treated by Dever, **p. 90**). At one level, these two narratives appear to be completely distinct for, unlike so many characters in this novel, Esther is 'no party in the suit' (Chapter 3). This distinction is re-enforced by the differing styles adopted by the two narrators. While the voice of the third-person narrator is 'magisterial', Esther is 'modest', 'coy' and 'indirect' (see, for example, Key Passages, **p. 110**). It is precisely these qualities in Esther's narration that have annoyed many critics and readers of *Bleak House*. In recent years, however, advances in psychoanalytic and feminist

---

9 De Man (see note 4), pp. 75–6.
10 When Lady Dedlock requests that Esther henceforth consider her as dead (Chapter 36), she disrupts the newly established relationship between mother and daughter, a relationship that might have formed the basis of Esther's subjectivity.

theories have led to a major re-assessment of Esther as both character and narrator. The feminist critic Valerie Kennedy, for example, has established a connection between Esther's self-denigrating style and the feelings of worthlessness instilled in her as a child by her aunt (see Key Passages, **p. 112**).[1] According to the materialist reading offered by Schor, Esther's 'stylistic quirks' – more specifically her refusal to speculate on her own involvement in the suit – may also be read in terms of the social and legal position of women and illegitimate children at mid-century. Lacking any status or social position, Esther earns and keeps her place only by assuming the role of a dutiful, submissive and self-sacrificing daughter. Yet this social construction of femininity (see Contextual Overview, **p. 13**) is re-enforced by the law. As the bastard child of 'no one' (Nemo), Esther cannot inherit property and thus the best she can hope for is to 'win some love to [her]self' (Chapter 3). As Schor suggests, she would 'not advance too far in her struggles to win love, if she were to ask John Jarndyce if she stands to win any property from the suit' (107).

Complicating the relationship between the two narratives and the models of inheritance they represent, Schor goes on to argue that the two are actually connected through Esther's 'relations': both familial and narratorial. The double sense of the term 'relations' is central to Schor's argument. As we are told in Chapter 2, Lady Dedlock is a party in Jarndyce and Jarndyce and thus, through her 'relations', so is Esther. Yet under English law, Lady Dedlock is unable to leave her daughter any property and hence the only bequest she can make is one of maternal affection, a legacy that is, itself, transmitted through the narratives she relates (the two letters to her child in Chapters 36 and 59). While this female model of inheritance parallels its male counterpart, it also assumes a specifically female form. Instead of being transmitted from father to son (via 'documents, wills, testimonies'), it circulates within the transgressive narratives passed between women.

In Chapter 35, Miss Flite offers a good example of the particular form that female inheritance assumes in the novel. The stories she relates are concerned with secrets, doubles and sexual transgression. Thus they represent an indirect way of re-inscribing the story of Esther's origins back into the narrative – a story that cannot be expressed more directly. It is through such 'relations' that Lady Dedlock's legacy of maternal affection can be passed on to her daughter. At the same time, Miss Flite's story 'returns us to the world of female property', to the laws of coventure that precluded a married woman from entering a legal contract, as well as the angry female plots generated by such powerlessness. In exploring the relationship between narrative and the law, Schor's argument lies somewhere between the textual approach of Hillis Miller and the material approach of D.A. Miller (see **pp. 65** and **81**). By bridging the gap between them, she opens up a new direction for future readings.

---

1   V. Kennedy, 'Bleak House: More Trouble with Esther?', Women's Studies in Literature, 1:4, 1979, pp. 330–47.

[. . .] In *Bleak House*'s split narration [. . .] Esther Summerson, the novel's bastard daughter, seems initially to stand apart from the work of the law plot [. . .]

But Esther's disingenuousness (her position outside the law) is the novel's central trick. As the plot proceeds, we learn that Esther *is*, indirectly, a party in the suit. The seemingly random second chapter, which finds the beautiful and icy Lady Dedlock reading the papers from the Jarndyce suit, and unintentionally starting on recognizing a familiar handwriting, places Lady Dedlock in both the will plot and an adultery plot; the handwriting is that of Esther's absent father, Captain Hawdon, now living, secretly, as "Nemo," the law-writer.[2] Lady Dedlock's insistence on staying in the suit is not her husband's reason, which is that it is a "slow, expensive, British, constitutional kind of thing" but her own: it was the only property that she brought into the marriage. And among the names in the suit, we learn early, are Carstone, Clare, Dedlock, and Barbary – the name of Esther's supposed godmother, in fact, her aunt, Lady Dedlock's sister.[3] *Both* parts of the narration, however circuitously, are "In Chancery," and it is female curiosity about property that brings the connection to light.

The text goes to considerable trouble to mask this double plot of property; Esther, in her narrative, never makes it explicit, though much of the evidence – including that last piece, about the names – appears in her narrative [. . .] Rather, she clings to the division with which the novel begins: that unlike the "Chancery" narration, her narration is personal, is familial, is about powerlessness.[4] Her stylistic quirks, as a narrator, encourage this reading. Esther is modest, she is coy, she is indirect, she has a strong tendency to veer into the parenthetical. Throughout, she expresses only anger that she is "obliged to write all this about myself!" but assures us (and herself) that "my little body will soon fall into the background now" (Chapter 3). She seems to incorporate the worst of female self-presentation in her discourse, and in her relations (of all sorts) to others – the only person to whom she speaks firmly is herself, when admonishing herself to "collect herself,"

---

2 [Schor's note.] For a reading of naming, paternity, and nobody, see Michael Ragussis, *Acts of Naming: The Family Plot in Fiction* (New York: Oxford University Press, 1986), pp. 87–109, and Katherine Cummings, *Telling Tales: The Hysteric's Seduction in Fiction and Theory* (Stanford, Calif.: Stanford University Press, 1991), pp. 191–229.

3 [Schor's note.] The only other person I know to have noticed this is Susan Shatto, in "Lady Dedlock and the Plot of *Bleak House*" in *Dickens Quarterly*, Vol. 5, No. 4, 1988, pp. 185–191. For other interesting essays on Esther, Lady Dedlock, and the will plot, see F.S. Schwarzbach, " 'Deadly Stains': Lady Dedlock's Death," *Dickens Quarterly*, Vol. 4, 1987, pp. 160–165; Michele S. Ware, " 'True Legitimacy': The Myth of the Foundling in *Bleak House*," *Studies in the Novel*, Vol. 22, 1990, pp.1–9; David Holbrook, "Some Plot Inconsistencies in *Bleak House*," *English: The Journal of the English Association*, 39, 1990, pp. 209–214, and Gillian West, "The 'Glaring Fault' in the Structure of *Bleak House*," in *The Dickensian*, Vol. 89, 1993, pp. 36–38. Timothy Peltason, in a fine essay entitled "Esther's Will" (*ELH*, Vol. 59, 1992, pp. 671–691) connects Esther's absence from the suit and her "compulsive self-denial" (671) to a larger problem of will in Dickens's fiction. [. . .]

4 [Schor's note.] Among the many significant readings of Esther's narration, see in particular Alex Zwerdling, "Esther Summerson Rehabilitated," in *Charles Dickens: New Perspectives*, edited by Wendell Stacy Johnson (Englewood Cliffs, NJ: Prentice Hall, 1982), pp. 94–113, and Suzanne Graver, "Writing in a 'Womanly' Way and the Double Vision of *Bleak House*," *Dickens Quarterly*, 4, 1987, pp. 3–15; see also Cummings, *The Hysteric's Seduction*.

"remember herself," to repress emotion or suppress anger. If, as D. A. Miller has noted, Esther keeps her place only by her constant striving to earn it, she also keeps her social place (as ward, as the "person in authority" at Bleak House) by struggling to earn that, and by never questioning it – including the strategic silence she maintains about her family: her origins, her relations, her place within the suit.[5] The "place" she accepts is one that the split narration seems to need as well: it thrives on the contrast between that magisterial (a.k.a. Dickensian) third-person narrator, who dares to address the "lords and gentlemen" of England (572), to speak with Carlylean[6] tenderness to Jo as "thou," to call on the forces of night and apocalypse, that voice of complete authority and Esther's still, small voice – the voice of the least powerful person in the novel who is still capable (as the crossing-sweeper Jo and the diminutive servant Charley[7] are not) of penning a narrative. [. . .]

But we might question Esther's relational and legal powerlessness when we turn back not just to her modes of narration, but to the fact that it is Esther's "relations" that connect the two narratives – both her familial relations and the stories she relates to us. It is her little body, with its annoying refusal to "fall" out of the novel, that connects Chancery and family, and the two models of inheritance the book proposes, the one of property, the other of affection. [. . .]

It is never clear in *Bleak House* what kind of property the daughter could hope to inherit. In this Chancery-infected world, as critics have noted since the book's initial publication, property is figured as a graphic chaos, documents that multiply as meaning slips further and further away.[8] Relationship is figured by the repetitions of names (Jarndyce *and* Jarndyce) and the disintegration of homes: to be "in Chancery" is to be in decay. To be "in Chancery" is also to be entirely in the place of writing: what distinguishes Chancery from other courts is that there is no oral testimony within it; all testimony is in the form of endlessly duplicated pieces of paper, and no suitor is ever without his or her documents, behind which (we must imagine) stand real properties – however decayed, lost, misplaced, misused.[9] And yet, it is in the nature of these documents never to come to anything: much as the suit itself "melts away," dissolving itself in its own costs, so the documents shred and multiply in the "ecologically terrifying" world of

---

5 [Schor's note.] As Miller notes, Esther has an "absolute refusal to be touched by the suit and [it is] the constitution of Bleak House that her refusal enables." "Discipline in Different Voices: Bureaucracy, Police, Family, and *Bleak House*" in *The Novel and the Police* (Berkeley, Calif.: University of California Press, 1988), p. 76.

6 Thomas Carlyle, see p. 31.

7 Esther's illiterate maid.

8 [Schor's note.] The still definitive account of this chaos is J. Hillis Miller's in his introduction to the Penguin edition of *Bleak House* (Harmondsworth: Penguin 1971), pp. 11–34; the definitive response to it is D.A. Miller's. I would place my argument between theirs not in following D.A. Miller's lead in *The Novel and the Police* and reading the linguistic excess as further policing, but in seeing Dickens's linguistic tricks (or Esther's, as deceptive narrator) as leading our eyes away from a serious plot of property, one that underwrites the extravagance of the documentary wars we witness.

9 See Contextual Overview, p. 18.

Chancery.[10] Within the other world of female inheritance, relationship seems to be figured in what I have identified as a more Gothic (and more Byzantine)[11] fashion: wandering women, fractured resemblance (Esther seeing her face in her mother's as "in broken glass" [Chapter 18]), the series of portraits and portrait-like doubles invoked here.[12] But the particular form male property takes in this novel (documents, wills, testimonies) has its parallel in the forms of separate female property: narrative secrets, contagion, resemblance, a bastard line of property.

One final, uncanny[13] return of Esther's mother suggests the relationship of tattered documents and female inheritance. Miss Flite, the Chancery petitioner who carries in her reticule[14] her "documents" (in her case, mere scraps of paper) comes to see Esther after Esther's illness. Miss Flite tells Esther the story of a "lady with a veil inquiring at a cottage" after Esther, and taking with her a handkerchief because it was Esther's (Chapter 35). The lady (whom we recognize by her disguise, one worn earlier when she visits Hawdon's grave, and worn later by Hortense to frame Honoria for Tulkinghorn's murder) is Lady Dedlock, following the trail of her missing daughter; the handkerchief had covered the dead baby of the brickmaker's wife, a dead baby whose presence recreates the presence of the baby Lady Dedlock took for dead (Esther herself) all those years ago. But Miss Flite offers another explanation:

> "in *my* opinion ... she's the Lord Chancellor's wife. He's married, you know. And I understand she leads him a terrible life. Throws his lordship's papers into the fire, my dear, if he won't pay the jeweller!" (Chapter 35)

Miss Flite's anecdote accomplishes something the rest of the novel can only hint at: the destruction of all the documents of Chancery in a blaze of fire, fed by the hands of an angry woman.[15] But the motive she imputes to the Lord Chancellor's wife returns us to the world of female property, reminding us that under the laws that govern marriage, women were incapable of making a binding contract, and a husband bore the responsibility of paying all his wife's debts – including the jeweller's bill. The connection this narrative makes between female allurement,

---

10 [Schor's note.] The phrase is D.A. Miller's (*Novel and the Police*, p. 67).

11 From the Goths (a Germanic tribe that invaded the Roman Empire), the Gothic came to be associated with the irrational, excess and transgression. Byzantine refers to Byzantium, the ancient Greek city established around 660 BC. In terms of style, both Gothic and Byzantine suggest the ornate, colourful and highly rhetorical.

12 Examples would include the portrait by which Guppy discerns the relationship between Esther and Lady Dedlock (Chapter 7); Lady Dedlock disguising herself first as her maid Hortense (Chapter 16) and then as Jenny the brickmaker's wife (Chapter 59); Jo mistaking Esther for Lady Dedlock (Chapter 31); etc.

13 See Dever, note 8.

14 A small bag.

15 [Schor's note.] Robert Newsom has suggested to me that the scene also holds out the possibility that if Lady Dedlock is the Lord Chancellor's wife, Esther must be his daughter – an interesting version of "wards of the court," and Chancery's power to unmake as well as make orphans.

female property, and female anger has its darker relationship to Chancery as well: it is at this moment in the novel that Miss Flite tells her own story of being "drawn into" Chancery, and the story of her father, her brother, and finally her sister, "drawn. Hush! Never ask to what!" (Chapter 35). The sister's destruction, presumably through prostitution, carries us back to that realm of sexual transgression outside the law – and to that transgression that caused Esther's birth, the adultery the novel never narrates, but that Miss Flite alludes to, subtly, in her way of naming Esther: it is she who calls her "my dear Fitz-Jarndyce," invoking the age-old name of bastards in English law.[16]

The tale of the writing of female property (fragmented, charred, impassioned) is one best told, as *Bleak House* is, by a female bastard: it is the story I have been telling here, of Honoria's surprise at seeing her dead lover's handwriting on a legal document; of her interest in protecting "the only property" (Chapter 2) she brings into her marriage (the "piece" that binds her, and binds Esther, into "Jarndyce and Jarndyce"); the story of Esther's different version of the monstrous suit. Within the story Esther is telling, the story figured psychically is the story of the dead mother and the dead child, there is a different story of inheritance: one we can follow only through the fragments, torn documents, the story of resemblance written on the wandering "face" of the female plot. Where it leads is not only a different version of *Bleak House*, but a different version of property altogether: the daughter's quest for her maternal legacy. [. . .]

16 Fitz means 'son of'.

3

Key Passages

Introduction

Even when judged by the standards of its own day, *Bleak House* is an unusually complex novel, a virtuoso performance that reflects the sheer fecundity of Dickens's imagination. Ostensibly dominated by two plots – the Chancery suit of Jarndyce and Jarndyce and the unravelling of Esther Summerson's secret parentage – the novel contains myriad subplots and an impressively large cast of characters. Furthermore, not content to offer a single perspective of the novelistic universe, Dickens undertook the unprecedented step of constructing a double narrative where the responsibility for recounting the story is divided between two markedly different voices. The first is that of a third-person, implicitly male narrator (written in the present tense), while the second consists of Esther's more limited and personal retrospective. Yet such diversity should not suggest disorder. The following summary – necessarily brief and incomplete – cannot do justice to the novel's intricate construction, but the selected passages, which form the bulk of this section, should make the reader aware of the hidden connections and thematic parallels that draw the various characters and events ever more closely together.

The highly symbolic opening centres upon the obscure and pervasive workings of Chancery Court and, more particularly, the case of Jarndyce and Jarndyce, a suit so prolonged and complicated that any notion regarding its original meaning has long since been lost. We are then carried to another outmoded and blighted institution, the aristocratic home of Sir Leicester and Lady Dedlock, who have a small stake in the suit. When their lawyer Tulkinghorn comes to update them on its 'progress', Lady Dedlock catches sight of a legal document, inquires about the handwriting and uncharacteristically faints. At this point the reader is introduced to Esther Summerson who narrates her own history in the most self-deprecating manner. Kept in the dark about her own origins, she is raised by a strict, evangelical aunt who continually alludes to some secret shame.

Upon the death of this aunt, Esther is sent to school by the generous John Jarndyce (a descendant of the original suitor) and six years later is called to London to act as a companion to Ada Clare who, together with her cousin Richard Carstone, is a ward of Court. All three are to live under the protection of Jarndyce at Bleak House. Before leaving London they spend the night at the house of Mrs Jellyby, a philanthropist whose preoccupation with generating documents about the natives of Borrioboola-Gha leads her to neglect her own house and family. They also encounter Miss Flite, the novel's most obvious victim of Chancery, and her landlord Krook. Once ensconced in her new home, Esther proves herself to be a model of 'proper' femininity: managing the household, serving as trusted companion to Jarndyce, and acting as surrogate mother to Richard and Ada.

Determined to investigate Lady Dedlock's unusual behaviour, Tulkinghorn discovers that the document that caused her to faint was written by the poverty-stricken Captain Hawdon (alias Nemo), who is subsequently discovered dead from an opium overdose. With the help of the omnipotent Inspector Bucket, he also determines that a disguised Lady Dedlock paid Jo, a crossing sweeper, to conduct her through Hawdon's environment, including the appalling slum district known as Tom-all-Alone's (unsurprisingly the property is part of the Jarndyce suit). Based on this information he surmises that the two had an illicit affair in the past that produced an illegitimate child. Meanwhile, a parallel investigation has been undertaken by Guppy, a law clerk with amorous intentions towards Esther. Recognising the resemblance between her ladyship and the young 'orphan', he subsequently discovers that Esther's true name is Hawdon and that she was raised by Lady Dedlock's sister. Having informed Lady Dedlock of these facts, he offers to return a bundle of love letters currently in the possession of Krook. Yet before he can hand these over, Krook spontaneously combusts and is reduced to a pile of sticky soot.

At Bleak House, relationships are developing apace. Ada has fallen in love with Richard who, becoming more and more ensnared in Chancery, has developed a vacillating character and is increasingly hostile towards his guardian. Esther too has developed feelings for a young doctor, Allan Woodcourt, but blinded by a sense of worthlessness and her gratitude to Jarndyce, she does her best to repress them.

Since his encounter with Inspector Bucket, Jo (the crossing sweeper) has been 'moved on, and moved on' (Chapter 31) under Tulkinghorn's orders. Having walked from London to St Albans, he is found by Jenny, a brickmaker's wife known to Esther. Hearing about the unfortunate orphan, Esther and her maid Charley pay a visit and find Jo delirious with fever. Brought back to Bleak House to be nursed, he disappears but not before passing the fever on to Charley who, in turn, infects Esther. Convalescing at a friend's estate, a now disfigured Esther encounters Lady Dedlock who confesses that she is her long lost mother but, because of Tulkinghorn's suspicions, they must never meet again. Reconciling herself to her new appearance, Esther relinquishes all hope of a romance with Woodcourt and accepts a marriage proposal from Jarndyce.

In full possession of Lady Dedlock's secret, Tulkinghorn continues to exercise power over her, threatening exposure while also forbidding her to leave. Following an interview with her, Tulkinghorn is shot dead in his chambers and anonymous letters accuse Lady Dedlock of the crime. These accusations, together with the belief that her husband has been made aware of her past, lead Lady Dedlock to run away. Inspector Bucket has indeed informed Sir Leicester about her illicit liaison but he has also arrested the real murderer, his wife's dismissed French servant Hortense. With his world crumbling around him, Sir Leicester suffers a stroke but orders Bucket to find his wife, offering full forgiveness. Bucket and Esther track her all night, grasping only too late that Lady Dedlock has, once again, assumed a disguise to elude them. At dawn, they discover her dead body at the gate of the graveyard in which her lover is buried.

Having recovered from the shock, Esther and Jarndyce travel to London to visit Ada and Richard, who have secretly married. They find Richard wasting away and under the care of Allan Woodcourt, who finds an opportunity to declare his love to Esther. She informs him of Jarndyce's proposal and quickly sets a date for her wedding. Jarndyce, generous as ever, sets up a duplicate Bleak House for Woodcourt to occupy when he takes up a medical post in Yorkshire. Esther is called upon to provide the finishing touches and, once there, Jarndyce acknowledges that he is aware of their mutual feelings and is prepared to 'give' Esther to the younger man.

On the first day of the new Chancery term, Esther and Allan attend Court as another will has been found which may resolve the Jarndyce suit once and for all. When they arrive, however, they find that the entire estate has been eaten up in costs and the case has been dismissed. The shock proves too much for the already weakened Richard and he dies, conscious of his own mistakes and fully reconciled with Jarndyce who will, once again, look after Ada and her unborn child. The final chapters see all the loose ends neatly tidied up and leave Esther a happy wife and mother, restored to her former good looks and basking in the love of all around her.

Even such a brief outline of the novel's events should help to orient you when reading the following passages, but it may also be helpful to bear the following selection criteria in mind. In the first place, a number of passages relate directly to the critical material contained within this volume: these should help to elucidate the somewhat abstract notions of textuality, power and subjectivity that dominate so many recent readings of the novel. Others have been chosen to reflect Dickens's social criticism (especially the need for legal and sanitary reform) or, more generally, because they exemplify the central themes and concerns of the novel: responsibility, the family, paperwork, femininity, and so on. Still others allow the reader to engage with more overtly aesthetic issues such as Dickens's non-naturalistic style, his use of language and rhetoric and the double narrative. In any case, the individual headnotes will direct your attention to notable features within the passages and to their wider significance, whether theoretical, thematic or aesthetic. Taken together, these passages will give you a sense of the novel's richness and, above all, the intricate network of connections that render it one of the most tightly controlled novels of its time.

Key Passages

Chapter 1: In Chancery

The opening paragraphs of *Bleak House* are justifiably famous. Judged by anything other than the standards of realism, they constitute an extraordinary piece of writing. Not only do they establish the overall mood and style of the novel, they also introduce many of its central themes and set the stage for all that follows. The first sentence, comprising the single word 'LONDON', reminds us that Dickens was an urban novelist, recognised even by his peers as the pre-eminent chronicler of the capital and its inhabitants. With this one word, he conveys to the reader a multitude of images and impressions. Its very fecundity, however, renders its meaning ambiguous. It thus raises the issues of representability that faced all writers trying to capture the new urban reality. Indeed, one way to read *Bleak House* is as an attempt to uncover and display the hidden reality of this city.

The matter-of-fact tone of the first three sentences quickly gives way to a series of fantastic images and complex symbolism initiated by the reference to the Flood ('newly retired waters') and the introduction of a Megalosaurus. By these means, Dickens conveys the idea that, far from representing progress, urban life is best seen as a form of devolution, as a return to a more primitive and barbaric past. Everything and everyone – dogs, horses, people – is reduced to the same level in a primeval struggle against the mud, meanness and anonymity of the city's streets. Despite a closeness wherein they must jostle and literally compete for space on the pavement, the inhabitants of London share no sense of recognition or human empathy. Thus it seems that Dickens's critique of the city is closely linked to an implicit criticism of what Carlyle (see **p. 31**) called 'the cash-nexus', wherein the human bond between individuals is replaced by a purely economic relationship (hence the references to 'new deposits' and 'compound interest'). One should not assume, however, that Dickens's attitude towards the city was wholly negative; the sheer exuberance of his writing suggests otherwise. Whatever its faults, the city was always a source of creative and personal energy for Dickens: as he suggests elsewhere, London held for him the 'attraction of repulsion'.[1]

The opening paragraphs are dominated by repeated references to mud and fog. It is worth pointing out that the treatment of these two elements represents a perfect example of the process of defamiliarisation (making the familiar strange) that characterises the entire novel. As Schwarzbach suggests, this process forces readers to view a familiar, everyday world in an entirely new way (see **p. 75**). The most obvious point to make about the fog and mud in this passage is that they are omnipresent and inescapable. This is driven home by no fewer than thirteen references to fog in the second paragraph alone, references that gain added emphasis by their placement at the beginning of each sentence. Like so much else in this novel, the role played by fog is contradictory. On the one hand, it separates every individual from those around them, emphasising their fundamental isolation (as does 'the cash-nexus'). On the other, because it is all-pervasive, it conjoins all those it envelops, regardless of class or position. This connection between seemingly disparate characters and events is both a central theme and structuring principle of the novel, a fact to which Dickens draws attention by giving it such prominence within the opening. In this respect, one should also note the presence of the word 'infection', another important connecting principle of the novel (see Carlyle, **p. 32**). Hillis Miller argues (**p. 66**) that many of the connections within Bleak House are established through metaphor and metonymy (i.e. are based on principles of similarity and contingency), and a careful reading will reveal the prominent role they play within the opening paragraphs. Struggling through the mud and fog, individuals come to bear a striking similarity both to each other and the animals while the sense of being trapped emphasises their contingent relations.

In symbolic terms, the mud represents stagnation and delay while the fog conveys a sense of obfuscation and impenetrability. As we shall see, these are the very qualities that characterise Chancery Court (see Contextual Overview, **p. 18**) and one of the key functions of the opening is to establish a clear link between these conditions and the Court, where the qualities of the former are transferred to the latter (consider, for example, Key Passages, **p. 119**). Thus the Court is situated where 'the dense fog is densest, and the muddy streets are muddiest'. Locating it at the very epicentre of the fog and mud, Dickens is already intimating the centrality of the Court in the novel. '[T]ripping one another up' and 'groping knee-deep in technicalities', its members recall the fate of the foot passengers on the street. Similarly, the obfuscation associated with the fog finds its counterpart in the Chancery case where one looks 'in vain for Truth', meaning or resolution. Instead, one finds a proliferation of paperwork and writing: the means that Chancery Court employs to delay and obscure meaning (mud and fog again). As we shall see, written documents play an

---

1   C. Dickens, 'The City of the Absent', in *The Uncommercial Traveller* [1861], London: Collins' Clear-Type Press, no publication date, p. 275.

important role in the unfolding of the various plots and are depicted both as dangerous and as impediments to positive, practical action (for a discussion of the role of documents, see Hillis Miller and Schor, **pp. 67** and **97**). Finally, we should note that the opening paragraphs establish the influence of Chancery Court to be as all-pervasive as the fog itself. It is, quite simply, inescapable and, as D.A. Miller suggests, any attempt to contain its powers is co-opted back into it (**p. 82**). Butt and Tillotson (**p. 62**) argue that the critique of Chancery Court initiated in these opening pages mirrors in content, if not in form, the contemporary debate that was occurring within the pages of The Times. This acknowledgement, however, does not go far enough in recognising the importance of what can already be identified as Dickens's unique style of writing. The remainder of Chapter I is dedicated to introducing the case of Jarndyce and Jarndyce, the suit that affects so many of the novel's characters and events. Finally, the Lord Chancellor announces his intention to interview Ada and Richard, two orphans implicated in the Jarndyce suit.

LONDON. Michaelmas Term lately over, and the Lord Chancellor sitting in Lincoln's Inn Hall.[2] Implacable November weather. As much mud in the streets, as if the waters had but newly retired from the face of the earth, and it would not be wonderful to meet a Megalosaurus, forty feet long or so, waddling like an elephantine lizard up Holborn Hill. Smoke lowering down from chimney-pots, making a soft black drizzle, with flakes of soot in it as big as full-grown snow-flakes – gone into mourning, one might imagine, for the death of the sun. Dogs, undistinguishable in mire. Horses, scarcely better; splashed to their very blinkers. Foot passengers, jostling one another's umbrellas, in a general infection of ill-temper, and losing their foot-hold at street-corners, where tens of thousands of other foot passengers have been slipping and sliding since the day broke (if the day ever broke), adding new deposits to the crust upon crust of mud, sticking at those points tenaciously to the pavement, and accumulating at compound interest.

Fog everywhere. Fog up the river, where it flows among green aits[3] and meadows; fog down the river, where it rolls defiled among the tiers of shipping, and the waterside pollutions of a great (and dirty) city. Fog on the Essex marshes, fog on the Kentish heights. Fog creeping into the cabooses of collier-brigs; fog lying out on the yards, and hovering in the rigging of great ships; fog drooping on the gunwales of barges and small boats. Fog in the eyes and throats of ancient Greenwich pensioners, wheezing by the firesides of their wards; fog in the stem and bowl of the afternoon pipe of the wrathful skipper, down in his close cabin; fog cruelly pinching the toes and fingers of his shivering little 'prentice boy on deck. Chance people on the bridges peeping over the parapets into a nether sky of

---

2   Michaelmas Term lasted between 2–25 November and, outside of term, members of Chancery Court retired from Westminster Hall to Lincoln's Inn Hall.
3   Small islands in the Thames.

fog, with fog all round them, as if they were up in a balloon, and hanging in the misty clouds. [. . .]

The raw afternoon is rawest, and the dense fog is densest, and the muddy streets are muddiest, near that leaden-headed old obstruction, appropriate ornament for the threshold of a leaden-headed old corporation: Temple Bar.[4] And hard by Temple Bar, in Lincoln's Inn Hall, at the very heart of the fog, sits the Lord High Chancellor in his High Court of Chancery.

Never can there come fog too thick, never can there come mud and mire too deep, to assort with the groping and floundering condition which this High Court of Chancery, most pestilent of hoary sinners, holds, this day, in the sight of heaven and earth. [. . .]

[. . .] On such an afternoon, some score of members of the High Court of Chancery bar ought to be – as here they are – mistily engaged in one of the ten thousand stages of an endless cause, tripping one another up on slippery precedents, groping knee-deep in technicalities, running their goat-hair and horse-hair warded heads[5] against walls of words, and making a pretence of equity with serious faces, as players might. On such an afternoon, the various solicitors in the cause, some two or three of whom have inherited it from their fathers, who made a fortune by it, ought to be – as are they not? – ranged in a line, in a long matted well (but you might look in vain for Truth at the bottom of it), between the registrar's red table and the silk gowns, with bills, cross-bills, answers, rejoinders, injunctions, affidavits, issues, references to masters, masters' reports, mountains of costly nonsense, piled before them. [. . .] This is the Court of Chancery; which has its decaying houses and its blighted lands in every shire; which has its worn-out lunatic in every madhouse, and its dead in every churchyard; which has its ruined suitor, with his slipshod heels and threadbare dress, borrowing and begging through the round of every man's acquaintance; which gives to monied might the means abundantly of wearying out the right; which so exhausts finances, patience, courage, hope; so overthrows the brain and breaks the heart; that there is not an honourable man among its practitioners who would not give – who does not often give – the warning, 'Suffer any wrong that can be done you, rather than come here!' [. . .]

Chapter 2: In Fashion

> This passage forms the opening of the chapter and signals a move from Chancery Court in London to the country house of the Dedlocks in Lincolnshire. The narrator, however, immediately establishes a connection between the two. The 'world of fashion' associated with this aristocratic couple is, like Chancery,

4 Archway into the old walled city of London.
5 Refers to the wigs worn by Chancery lawyers.

an outmoded institution from the past. Both are based on 'precedent' and privilege. As Sucksmith suggests, Dickens engages in a thoroughgoing critique of the world represented by the Dedlocks (**p. 71**).

Lady Dedlock is introduced as a creature of movement – from Lincolnshire to London to Paris – driven on by restlessness and boredom. Her movements, however, lack purpose or direction and, in this respect, come to resemble the frenzied but ineffectual activity of the Court, as well as the fate of Jo, the crossing sweeper, being 'moved on' under Tulkinghorn's orders (Chapter 19). In much the same way as Jo is constantly under police scrutiny, so too is Lady Dedlock subject to the surveillance of the 'fashionable intelligence'. This provides us with yet another example of the novel's obsession with detection and interpretation, as well as its emphasis on the hidden connections between disparate elements (these issues are discussed by both Hillis Miller and D.A. Miller, **pp. 68** and **83**).

The description of Chesney Wold itself emphasises stagnation and decay. The repeated references to the rain and damp recall the fog and mud associated with Chancery Court, once again suggesting their similarities. As presented, it is the first in a whole series of unwelcoming or inadequate homes in the novel. The tone and language of the description also convey a dreary mood associated with the environment and Lady Dedlock herself. Of particular interest are the references to 'Indian ink', hinting at the role that written documents will play in her downfall (see Schor, **p. 95**), and the pointed statement that she 'is childless'. Its position, within parentheses, actually draws the reader's attention to it and thus subtly introduces one of the novel's two main plots, the uncovering of Esther's origins. Indeed, this plot is initiated by the final events of the chapter when Lady Dedlock's attention is arrested by the handwriting of a legal document brought by the family lawyer, Tulkinghorn, and, moments later, faints away.

The portrait of Sir Leicester Dedlock borders on caricature but as Sucksmith reminds us (**p. 72**), it is actually part and parcel of a topical debate about the changing nature of class positions and relations. Even at this very early stage, his love for his wife is introduced as his one redeeming feature and the emphasis given to it prepares the reader for his forgiving attitude towards her after he learns of her affair with Captain Hawdon.

It is but a glimpse of the world of fashion that we want on this same miry afternoon. It is not so unlike the Court of Chancery, but that we may pass from the one scene to the other, as the crow flies. Both the world of fashion and the Court of Chancery are things of precedent and usage; over-sleeping Rip Van Winkles, who have played at strange games through a deal of thundery weather; sleeping beauties, whom the Knight will wake one day, when all the stopped spits in the kitchen shall begin to turn prodigiously! [. . .]

My Lady Dedlock has returned to her house in town for a few days previous to her departure for Paris, where her ladyship intends to stay some weeks; after which her movements are uncertain. The fashionable intelligence says so, for the comfort of the Parisians, and it knows all fashionable things. To know things otherwise, were to be unfashionable. My Lady Dedlock has been down at what she calls, in familiar conversation, her 'place' in Lincolnshire. The waters are out in Lincolnshire. An arch of the bridge in the park has been sapped and sopped away. The adjacent low-lying ground, for half a mile in breadth, is a stagnant river, with melancholy trees for islands in it, and a surface punctured all over, all day long, with falling rain. My Lady Dedlock's 'place' has been extremely dreary. The weather, for many a day and night, has been so wet that the trees seem wet through, and the soft loppings and prunings of the woodman's axe can make no crash or crackle as they fall. The deer, looking soaked, leave quagmires, where they pass. The shot of a rifle loses its sharpness in the moist air, and its smoke moves in a tardy little cloud towards the green rise, coppice-topped, that makes a back-ground for the falling rain. The view from my Lady Dedlock's own win-dows is alternately a lead-coloured view, and a view in Indian ink. The vases on the stone terrace in the foreground catch the rain all day; and the heavy drops fall, drip, drip, drip, upon the broad flagged pavement, called, from old time, the Ghost's Walk, all night. On Sundays, the little church in the park is mouldy; the oaken pulpit breaks out into a cold sweat; and there is a general smell and taste as of the ancient Dedlocks in their graves. My Lady Dedlock (who is childless), looking out in the early twilight from her boudoir at a keeper's lodge, and seeing the light of a fire upon the latticed panes, and smoke rising from the chimney, and a child, chased by a woman, running out into the rain to meet the shining figure of a wrapped-up man coming through the gate, has been put quite out of temper. My Lady Dedlock says she has been 'bored to death.'

Therefore my Lady Dedlock has come away from the place in Lincolnshire, and has left it to the rain, and the crows, and the rabbits, and the deer, and the partridges and pheasants. The pictures of the Dedlocks past and gone have seemed to vanish into the damp walls in mere lowness of spirits, as the house-keeper has passed along the old rooms, shutting up the shutters. And when they will next come forth again, the fashionable intelligence – which, like the fiend, is omniscient of the past and present, but not the future – cannot yet undertake to say.

Sir Leicester Dedlock is only a baronet, but there is no mightier baronet than he.[1] His family is as old as the hills, and infinitely more respectable. He has a general opinion that the world might get on without hills, but would be done up without Dedlocks. He would on the whole admit Nature to be a good idea (a little low, perhaps, when not enclosed with a park-fence), but an idea dependent for its execution on your great county families. He is a gentleman of strict conscience, disdainful of all littleness and meanness, and ready, on the shortest notice, to die any death you may please to mention rather than give occasion for the least impeachment of his integrity. He is an honourable, obstinate, truthful, high-spirited, intensely prejudiced, perfectly unreasonable man.

1   The lowest of the inherited ranks.

Sir Leicester is twenty years, full measure, older than my Lady. He will never see sixty-five again, nor perhaps sixty-six, nor yet sixty-seven. He has a twist of the gout now and then, and walks a little stiffly. He is of a worthy presence, with his light grey hair and whiskers, his fine shirt-frill, his pure white waistcoat, and his blue coat with bright buttons always buttoned. He is ceremonious, stately, most polite on every occasion to my Lady, and holds her personal attractions in the highest estimation. His gallantry to my Lady, which has never changed since he courted her, is the one little touch of romantic fancy in him.

Indeed, he married her for love. A whisper still goes about, that she had not even family; howbeit, Sir Leicester had so much family that perhaps he had enough, and could dispense with any more. But she had beauty, pride, ambition, insolent resolve, and sense enough to portion out a legion of fine ladies. Wealth and station, added to these, soon floated her upward; and for years, now, my Lady Dedlock has been at the centre of the fashionable intelligence, and at the top of the fashionable tree. [. . .]

Chapter 3: A Progress

This passage is the first contribution from the novel's second narrator, Esther Summerson, and constitutes a retrospective account of her childhood. The change in tone and perspective is immediately apparent. Whereas the third-person narrator possessed a degree of knowledge that borders on the omniscient and speaks with a voice of assured, detached irony, Esther's voice is more obviously feminine (for a discussion of gender, see Contextual Overview, **p. 13**). The various hesitations and qualifications that characterise Esther's narrative represent an important clue to reading her character and passages such as this 'serve the important function of establishing Esther's sense of unworthiness and her continually recurring feeling that she has little or no right to existence or to the reader's attention'.[1] As Schor suggests (**pp. 95–6**), the denial of self implied by Esther's numerous negations may also be read as an exaggerated version of the self-constraint advocated by mid-century constructions of a 'proper' femininity, as well as a reflection of the legal status of women and illegitimate children. If 'Submission, self-denial [and] diligent work' are, according to Esther's aunt Barbary (a name that suggests both thorns and barbs), the only way to atone for an illegitimate birth, they are also the qualities attributed to any 'proper' middle-class woman.

While acknowledging that her narrative forms a 'portion' of a larger whole, it remains silent on how or why it might do so. Indeed, the relationship between the two narratives (and narrators) is very rarely acknowledged, thus allowing them to remain quite distinct throughout the course of the novel (for

---

1   Kennedy (see Schor, note 1), p. 335.

an alternative reading of this relationship, see Schor, **p. 96**). Speaking generally, Esther's portion of the story is confined to the domestic realm and deals with personal relationships. In contrast, the third-person narrator concerns 'himself' with public issues and events, such as those related to Chancery Court. Although Esther insists that she is neither clever nor in possession of a 'quick understanding', we should not take her at her own word. Her observations about her aunt's goodness – clearly Dickens doesn't equate Church attendance with true goodness – are a prime example of the way in which she often offers an indirect yet astute critique of all that goes on around her.

The conversation occasioned by Esther's birthday, a day that recalls her mother's sin, suggests how badly she wants and needs to understand her origins (this issue is discussed by Dever, **p. 88**). Esther's quest towards selfhood will occupy a significant place in the novel as a whole. Starting out from a position of isolation – 'You are set apart' – *Bleak House* documents her gradual integration into both a family and society at large. The placing of this story directly after Lady Dedlock's unexplained fainting spell encourages the reader to speculate whether the two events might not be related.

As I have suggested in the plot summary, this chapter continues the pre-history of Esther up to the point where she is brought to London to act as companion to Ada Clare who, incidentally, bears a certain resemblance to Esther's earlier confidant, a doll of 'beautiful complexion and rosy lips' (Chapter 3). For a psychoanalytic reading of Esther's relationship with her doll, see Dever, **p. 91**.

I have a great deal of difficulty in beginning to write my portion of these pages, for I know I am not clever. I always knew that. I can remember, when I was a very little girl indeed, I used to say to my doll, when we were alone together, 'Now, Dolly, I am not clever, you know very well, and you must be patient with me, like a dear!' And so she used to sit propped up in a great arm-chair, with her beautiful complexion and rosy lips, staring at me – or not so much at me, I think, as at nothing – while I busily stitched away, and told her every one of my secrets.[2]

My dear old doll! I was such a shy little thing that I seldom dared to open my lips, and never dared to open my heart, to anybody else. It almost makes me cry to think what a relief it used to be to me, when I came home from school of a day, to run upstairs to my room, and say, 'O you dear faithful Dolly, I knew you would be expecting me!' and then to sit down on the floor, leaning on the elbow of her great chair, and tell her all I had noticed since we parted. I had always rather a noticing way – not a quick way, O no! – a silent way of noticing what passed before me, and thinking I should like to understand it better. I have not by any means a quick understanding. When I love a person very tenderly indeed, it seems to brighten. But even that may be my vanity.

2   Note that the syntax of this sentence equates Esther to 'nothing', a particularly extreme example of the self-negation that characterises her narrative.

I was brought up, from my earliest remembrance – like some of the princesses in the fairy stories, only I was not charming – by my godmother. At least I only knew her as such. She was a good, good woman! She went to church three times every Sunday, and to morning prayers on Wednesdays and Fridays, and to lectures whenever there were lectures; and never missed. She was handsome; and if she had ever smiled, would have been (I used to think) like an angel – but she never smiled. [. . .]

It was my birthday. There were holidays at school on other birthdays – none on mine. There were rejoicings at home on other birthdays, as I knew from what I heard the girls relate to one another – there were none on mine. My birthday was the most melancholy day at home, in the whole year. [. . .]

Dinner was over, and my godmother and I were sitting at the table before the fire. The clock ticked, the fire clicked; not another sound had been heard in the room, or in the house, for I don't know how long. I happened to look timidly up from my stitching, across the table, at my godmother, and I saw in her face, looking gloomily at me, 'It would have been far better, little Esther, that you had had no birthday; that you had never been born!'

I broke out crying and sobbing, and I said, 'O, dear godmother, tell me, pray do tell me, did mama die on my birthday?'

'No,' she returned. 'Ask me no more, child!'

'O, do pray tell me something of her. Do now, at last, dear godmother, if you please! What did I do to her? How did I lose her? Why am I so different from other children, and why is it my fault, dear godmother? No, no, no, don't go away. O; speak to me!'

I was in a kind of fright beyond my grief; and I had caught hold of her dress, and was kneeling to her. She had been saying all the while, 'Let me go!' But now she stood still.

Her darkened face had such power over me, that it stopped me in the midst of my vehemence. I put up my trembling little hand to clasp hers, or to beg her pardon with what earnestness I might, but withdrew it as she looked at me, and laid it on my fluttering heart. She raised me, sat in her chair, and standing me before her, said, slowly, in a cold, low voice – I see her knitted brow, and pointed finger:

'Your mother, Esther, is your disgrace, and you were hers. The time will come – and soon enough – when you will understand this better, and will feel it too, as no one save a woman can. I have forgiven her;' but her face did not relent; 'the wrong she did to me, and I say no more of it, though it was greater than you will ever know – than any one will ever know, but I, the sufferer. For yourself, unfortunate girl, orphaned and degraded from the first of these evil anniversaries, pray daily that the sins of others be not visited upon your head, according to what is written.[3] Forget your mother, and leave all other people to forget her who will do her unhappy child that greatest kindness. Now, go!'

---

3 Esther's aunt is referring to Numbers 14.18: 'Visiting the sins of the fathers upon the children unto the third and fourth generations.'

She checked me, however, as I was about to depart from her – so frozen as I was! – and added this:

'Submission, self-denial, diligent work, are the preparations for a life begun with such a shadow on it. You are different from other children, Esther, because you were not born, like them, in common sinfulness and wrath. You are set apart.'

Chapter 4: Telescopic Philanthropy

Before travelling to the home of Jarndyce, Esther, Ada and Richard spend the night at the home of Mrs Jellyby, an eminent philanthropist dedicated to the natives of Borrioboola-Gha. They are conducted there by the law clerk, Guppy, who admires Esther. This passage is located near the beginning of Chapter 4 and describes their reception at the house. The 'child' referred to in the first sentence is Peepy, whom Esther has just freed from the railings. This act is significant because it establishes Esther as a model of caring femininity that contrasts strongly with the obvious lack of maternal concern exhibited in this passage by Mrs Jellyby. The middle-class wife was expected to be a good manager, supervising her home, children and servants (see Langland, **p. 86**). The fate of Peepy, combined with the inappropriate behaviour of the maid, alert the reader to Mrs Jellyby's inadequacies even before she appears on the scene. As 'Suckling Pigs' makes clear, Dickens did not approve of women with a mission (**p. 40**). This passage details the inevitable consequences of female involvement with the public sphere: the neglect of children, home and person. As Esther suggests, 'it is right to begin with the obligations of home [. . .] and [. . .] while those are overlooked and neglected, no other duties can possibly be substituted for them' (Chapter 6). The most obvious symbol of such neglect is the empty hearth, the traditional symbol of the comfortable middle-class home. It is worth noting that Mrs Jellyby's mission entails a preponderance of written documents – the room 'was strewn with papers and nearly filled by a great writing-table' – contributing to the theme of writing as a dangerous and evil activity. More specifically, it links her activities to those of Chancery Court and, in so doing, links parental irresponsibility to legal irresponsibility.

While Mrs Jellyby may represent both an irresponsible parent and a model of 'improper' femininity, Dickens's critique extends beyond this specific individual to her mission itself. While he played an active role in many charitable organisations and endeavours, he had no patience for overseas missionary projects such as that organised by Mrs Jellyby. Quite simply, he felt that it was absurd and irresponsible for so much effort to be expended abroad while there was still so much suffering and squalor at home. In this respect, one should also see the passage from Chapter 16 where 'the Society for the Propagation of the Gospel in Foreign Parts' exists in stoic indifference to the fate of Jo, sitting on its steps to eat his breakfast.

[. . .] Nobody had appeared belonging to the house, except a person in pattens,[1] who had been poking at the child from below with a broom; I don't know with what object, and I don't think she did. I therefore supposed that Mrs Jellyby was not at home; and was quite surprised when the person appeared in the passage without the pattens, and going up to the back room on the first floor, before Ada and me, announced us as, 'Them two young ladies, Missis Jellyby!' We passed several more children on the way up, whom it was difficult to avoid treading on in the dark; and as we came into Mrs Jellyby's presence, one of the poor little things fell down-stairs – down a whole flight (as it sounded to me), with a great noise. [. . .]

'I am very glad indeed,' said Mrs Jellyby, in an agreeable voice, 'to have the pleasure of receiving you. I have a great respect for Mr Jarndyce; and no one in whom he is interested can be an object of indifference to me.'

We expressed our acknowledgments, and sat down behind the door where there was a lame invalid of a sofa. Mrs Jellyby had very good hair, but was too much occupied with her African duties to brush it. The shawl in which she had been loosely muffled, dropped on to her chair when she advanced to us; and as she turned to resume her seat, we could not help noticing that her dress didn't nearly meet up the back, and that the open space was railed across with a lattice-work of stay-lace – like a summer-house.

The room, which was strewn with papers and nearly filled by a great writing-table covered with similar litter, was, I must say, not only very untidy, but very dirty. We were obliged to take notice of that with our sense of sight, even while, with our sense of hearing, we followed the poor child who had tumbled down-stairs: I think into the back kitchen, where somebody seemed to stifle him. [. . .]

'You find me, my dears,' said Mrs Jellyby, snuffing the two great office candles in tin candlesticks which made the room taste strongly of hot tallow (the fire had gone out, and there was nothing in the grate but ashes, a bundle of wood, and a poker), 'you find me, my dears, as usual, very busy; but that you will excuse. The African project at present employs my whole time. It involves me in correspondence with public bodies, and with private individuals anxious for the welfare of their species all over the country. I am happy to say it is advancing. We hope by this time next year to have from a hundred and fifty to two hundred healthy families cultivating coffee and educating the natives of Borrioboola-Gha, on the left bank of the Niger.' [. . .]

Chapter 5: A Morning Adventure

During an uncomfortable evening at the Jellybys, Esther entertains the children and makes a particular friend of Caddy, the eldest Jellyby child. In the morning,

1   Small wooden platforms strapped to one's shoes to protect them from the mud on the streets.

they all take a walk and find themselves back at Lincoln's Inn, where they come across the mad suitor Miss Flite, whom they met at Court on the previous day. Both Richard's comment – 'We are never to get out of Chancery!' – and their chance return to its environs are examples of dramatic irony borne out in his unhappy demise. Bringing the group to her lodgings, Miss Flite introduces them to her landlord Krook. Located in the first few pages of Chapter 5, this passage is the most explicit example of the ways in which *Bleak House* establishes connections between its various characters and events. As the description of Krook's shop suggests, the relation between this character and the Lord Chancellor is based on metaphoric similarity. As the collector of useless objects (including many written documents), Krook is very much like the Lord Chancellor who presides over a mass of useless paperwork. In addition, his refusal to sell any of his accumulated wares is reminiscent of how the Court generates enormous quantities of legal papers that serve no useful purpose (the relationship between Krook and the Lord Chancellor is discussed by Hillis Miller, **p. 66**). According to the critic for *Bentley's Monthly Review*, one of the flaws of *Bleak House* was that it identified the need for Chancery Reform but failed to offer any suggestions as to how this might be accomplished (**p. 61**). In linking the Lord Chancellor and Chancery Court to Krook and his warehouse, Dickens implicitly expresses a desire that they should suffer the same end – spontaneous combustion. While this hardly constitutes a realistic solution to the problem, it is wholly appropriate in symbolic terms. A system shown to blight and ruin so many lives must undergo complete and utter destruction. Finally, we should note that the advertisement placed by Nemo in Krook's window is actually written by Esther's father and represents the only contact she will ever have with him. The significance of this seemingly insignificant episode is lost upon a first reading. Only in subsequent re-readings does the care that Dickens lavished upon incorporating such details become apparent.

[. . .] 'So, cousin,' said the cheerful voice of Richard to Ada, behind me. 'We are never to get out of Chancery! We have come by another way to our place of meeting yesterday, and – by the Great Seal, here's the old lady again!'[1] [. . .]

She had stopped at a shop, over which was written, KROOK, RAG AND BOTTLE WAREHOUSE. Also, in long thin letters, KROOK, DEALER IN MARINE STORES. In one part of the window was a picture of a red paper mill, at which a cart was unloading a quantity of sacks of old rags. In another, was the inscription, BONES BOUGHT. In another, KITCHEN-STUFF BOUGHT. In another, OLD IRON BOUGHT. In another, WASTE PAPER BOUGHT. In another, LADIES' AND GENTLEMEN'S WARDROBES BOUGHT. Everything seemed to be bought, and nothing to be sold there. In all parts of the window, were quantities of dirty bottles: blacking bottles, medicines bottles, ginger-beer and soda-water bottles,

---

1   During their previous encounter, Miss Flite mentions the Great Seal from Revelations 6.12.

pickle bottles, wine bottles, ink bottles: I am reminded by mentioning the latter, that the shop had, in several little particulars, the air of being in a legal neighbourhood, and of being, as it were, a dirty hanger-on and disowned relation of the law. There were a great many ink bottles. There was a little tottering bench of shabby old volumes, outside the door, labelled 'Law Books, all at 9d.' Some of the inscriptions I have enumerated were written in law-hand, like the papers I had seen in Kenge and Carboy's office, and the letters I had so long received from the firm.[2] Among them was one, in the same writing, having nothing to do with the business of the shop, but announcing that a respectable man aged forty-five wanted engrossing or copying to execute with neatness and dispatch: Address to Nemo, care of Mr Krook within. [. . .]

'My landlord, Krook,' said the little old lady, condescending to him from her lofty station, as she presented him to us. 'He is called among the neighbours the Lord Chancellor. His shop is called the Court of Chancery. He is a very eccentric person. He is very odd. Oh, I assure you he is very odd!' [. . .]

'It's true enough,' he said, going before us with the lantern, 'that they call me the Lord Chancellor, and call my shop Chancery.' [. . .]

'You see I have so many things here,' he resumed, holding up the lantern, 'of so many kinds, and all, as the neighbours think (but *they* know nothing), wasting away and going to rack and ruin, that that's why they have given me and my place a christening. And I have so many old parchmentses and papers in my stock. And I have a liking for rust and must and cobwebs. And all's fish that comes to my net. And I can't abear to part with anything I once lay hold of (or so my neighbours think, but what do *they* know?) or to alter anything, or to have any sweeping, nor scouring, nor cleaning, nor repairing going on about me. That's the way I've got the ill name of Chancery. *I* don't mind. I go to see my noble and learned brother pretty well every day, when he sits in the Inn. He don't notice me, but I notice him. There's no great odds betwixt us. We both grub on in a muddle.' [. . .]

Chapter 7: The Ghost's Walk

Chapter 6 sees Esther and her companions happily established in their new residence, Bleak House. Located in the countryside near St Albans, Bleak House is distanced from both London and the Court of Chancery and is meant to represent a different world, characterised by more positive values. As soon as the group arrives, Jarndyce hands over the household keys to Esther, who will now assume responsibility for its housekeeping (the class implications of this role are discussed by Langland, **p. 84**). The following passage marks the narrative's return to the Dedlock's country seat, Chesney Wold, and forms part of an

2   Law-hand refers to a specific type of handwriting used in legal documents. The reader may see an example of it in the letter Esther receives from Kenge and Carboy's (Jarndyce's solicitors) in Chapter 3.

introduction to the workings of the house and its housekeeper, Mrs Rouncewell. In order to understand the significance of this description of her eldest son, we need to refer to the argument presented by Sucksmith (**p. 71**). As he suggests, the Ironmaster represented a new class and breed of man whose very existence was seen as a threat to the established power of the aristocracy (see the discussion of class and gender in the Contextual Overview, **pp. 12** and **13**). Except for the paranthetical description that reflects the authorial view of the Ironmaster, the perspective within this passage is clearly that of Sir Leicester. The erroneous 'general impression' that allows him to view the man solely in terms of 'some odd thousand conspirators' reveals Dedlock's ignorance of, and resistance to, the technological advancements of the day. Although Mrs Rouncewell is not a negligent parent, she does add to the growing list of unhappy families. The younger son briefly referred to is, as we shall see, Trooper George. The remainder of the chapter records the introduction of Rosa, Lady Dedlock's companion, and Watt, Mrs Rouncewell's grandson, as well as the arrival of Guppy, the law clerk, requesting a tour of the house. Seeing a portrait of Lady Dedlock, he is struck by the resemblance it bears to Esther. This event initiates his investigation into their relationship.

[. . .] Mrs Rouncewell has known trouble. She has had two sons, of whom the younger ran wild, and went for a soldier, and never came back. [. . .] Her second son would have been provided for at Chesney Wold, and would have been made steward[1] in due season; but he took, when he was a schoolboy, to constructing steam-engines out of saucepans, and setting birds to draw their own water, with the least possible amount of labour; so assisting them with artful contrivance of hydraulic pressure, that a thirsty canary had only, in a literal sense, to put his shoulder to the wheel, and the job was done. This propensity gave Mrs Rouncewell great uneasiness. She felt it, with a mother's anguish, to be a move in the Wat Tyler[2] direction: well knowing that Sir Leicester had that general impression of an aptitude for any art to which smoke and a tall chimney might be considered essential. But the doomed young rebel (otherwise a mild youth, and very persevering), showing no sign of grace as he got older; but, on the contrary, constructing a model of a power-loom, she was fain, with many tears, to mention his backslidings to the baronet. 'Mrs Rouncewell,' said Sir Leicester, 'I can never consent to argue, as you know, with any one on any subject. You had better get rid of your boy; you had better get him into some Works.[3] The iron country farther north is, I suppose, the congenial direction for a boy with these tendencies.' Farther north he went, and farther north he grew up; and if Sir Leicester Dedlock ever saw him, when he came to Chesney Wold to visit his mother, or ever thought of him afterwards, it is certain that he only regarded him as one of a body of some

---

1 Overall manager of the property.
2 Wat Tyler was the leader of the Peasants' Revolt of 1381 (see Sucksmith, **pp. 71–2**).
3 The general name for factories in the Industrial Midlands.

odd thousand conspirators, swarthy and grim, who were in the habit of turning out by torchlight, two or three nights in the week, for unlawful purposes. [. . .]

Chapter 8: Covering a Multitude of Sins

The conversation recorded in this passage occurs the day after Esther's arrival at Bleak House and may be found towards the beginning of the chapter. Although it does not advance the plot in any material way, it does develop a number of the novel's key themes, especially its critique of Chancery Court (see Contextual Overview, **p. 18**). Jarndyce's description of 'this Chancery business' foregrounds its two main faults: interminable delays and gross inefficiency. As Butt and Tillotson demonstrate, the nature and extent of these problems were already well known (**p. 62**). What is perhaps more interesting than the content of Dickens's critique is the manner in which it is presented. This particular passage has provoked a great deal of interest among post-structuralists such as Hillis Miller. As presented, Chancery Court may be seen as an analogy for the ways in which meaning is endlessly deferred by the language system itself (for a fuller discussion of this issue see Critical History, **p. 53**). If, as Hillis Miller suggests, the novel is a 'system of cross references among signs', where every element refers only to other elements within the same system, so too is Chancery (**p. 69**). The resulting 'infernal country-dance' sweeps up everything in its path. Thus Jarndyce's belief that he is able to keep himself separate from the case that bears his name – 'These are things I never talk about, or even think about' – is called into question.

Another interesting feature of this passage is its treatment of Esther and her accumulation of nicknames. Not only do these names age and de-sexualise Esther, they also impact negatively on her already vulnerable sense of identity (see Dever, **p. 88**). The final point to make is that in sweeping the cobwebs from the sky, Esther is associated with clarity and light (remember her name suggests the summer sun) as opposed to the obscurity and fog of Chancery Court.

[. . .] 'Of course, Esther,' he said, 'you don't understand this Chancery business?'
And of course I shook my head.

'I don't know who does,' he returned. 'The Lawyers have twisted it into such a state of bedevilment that the original merits of the case have long disappeared from the face of the earth. It's about a Will, and the trusts under a Will – or it was, once. It's about nothing but Costs, now. We are always appearing, and disappearing, and swearing, and interrogating, and filing, and cross-filing, and arguing, and sealing, and motioning, and referring, and reporting, and revolving about the Lord Chancellor and all his satellites, and equitably waltzing ourselves off to dusty death, about Costs.' [. . .]

[. . .] 'All through the deplorable cause, everything that everybody in it, except one man, knows already, is referred to that only one man who don't know it, to find out – all through the deplorable cause, everybody must have copies, over and over again, of everything that has accumulated about it in the way of cartloads of papers (or must pay for them without having them, which is the usual course, for nobody wants them); and must go down the middle and up again, through such an infernal country-dance of costs and fees and nonsense and corruption, as was never dreamed of in the wildest visions of a Witch's Sabbath.[1] Equity sends questions to Law,[2] Law sends questions back to Equity; Law finds it can't do this, Equity finds it can't do that; neither can so much as say it can't do anything, without this solicitor instructing and this counsel appearing for A, and that solicitor instructing and that counsel appearing for B; and so on through the whole alphabet, like the history of the Apple Pie. And thus, through years and years, and lives and lives, everything goes on, constantly beginning over and over again, and nothing ever ends. And we can't get out of the suit on any terms, for we are made parties to it, and *must* be parties to it, whether we like it or not. But it won't do to think of it!' [. . .]

[. . .] 'These are things I never talk about, or even think about, excepting in the Growlery,[3] here. If you consider it right to mention them to Rick and Ada,' looking seriously at me, 'you can. I leave it to your discretion, Esther.'

'I hope, sir' – said I.

'I think you had better call me Guardian, my dear.'

I felt that I was choking again – I taxed myself with it, 'Esther, now, you know you are!' – when he feigned to say this slightly, as if it were a whim, instead of a thoughtful tenderness. But I gave the housekeeping keys the least shake in the world as a reminder to myself, and folding my hands in a still more determined manner on the basket, looked at him quietly.

'I hope, Guardian,' said I, 'that you may not trust too much to my discretion. I hope you may not mistake me. I am afraid it will be a disappointment to you to know that I am not clever – but it really is the truth; and you would soon find it out if I had not the honesty to confess it.' [. . .]

'You are clever enough to be the good little woman of our lives here, my dear,' he returned, playfully; 'the little old woman of the Child's [. . .] Rhyme.'[4]

' "Little old woman, and whither so high?" –
"To sweep the cobwebs out of the sky." '

You will sweep them so neatly out of *our* sky, in the course of your housekeeping, Esther, that one of these days, we shall have to abandon the Growlery, and nail up the door.'

---

1 A midnight festival of witches and demons.
2 For a discussion of the difference between Equity and Law see Appendix 1 in the Penguin edition of *Bleak House*.
3 Jarndyce's name for his study. As he says in Chapter 8, 'When I am out of humour, I come and growl here'.
4 Jarndyce is referring to a character in the old nursery rhyme 'The Little Old Woman', who brushed the cobwebs off the sky.

This was the beginning of my being called Old Woman, and Little Old Woman, and Cobweb, and Mrs Shipton, and Mother Hubbard, and Dame Durden, and so many names of that sort, that my own name soon became quite lost among them. [. . .]

Located at the end of the chapter, this passage records Esther and Ada's visit to a slum dwelling, where they are conducted by Mrs Pardiggle, an associate of Mrs Jellyby. The description of the brickmaker's squalid dwelling and the moral bullying of Mrs Pardiggle add to the 'Multitude of Sins' indicated in the chapter's title. For an introduction to the issues of sanitary reform raised by this passage, you should see the relevant section of the Contextual Overview (**p. 15**), as well as Dickens's speech to the Metropolitan Sanitary Association (**p. 36**) and the extract by Gavin (**p. 32**). The only point I would make here is that the brickmaker's response to Mrs Pardiggle echoes Dickens's own belief that sanitary reform must precede all other types of reform, including moral reformation. As the man suggests, how can he be expected to abstain from gin given the state of the water he has to drink or, again, how can they be expected to keep clean and raise healthy children when their home is 'nat'rally dirty'?

Turning to Mrs Pardiggle herself, it is clear that Dickens had nothing but contempt and anger for her over-zealous and self-serving methods of dealing with the poor. Once again, Esther is set up as a model against which to judge the behaviour of this 'moral Policeman'. The quiet, sensitive and practical help she offers to the newly bereaved mother stands in direct opposition to the 'business-like and systematic' approach of Pardiggle (the reference to systems also reminds the reader of Chancery Court). Similarly, where the latter's tracts are shown to have no relevance to their lives, Esther's quote from the New Testament ('Suffer the little children to come unto me' (Mark 10.14)), offers genuine comfort and solace. The last point I would make is that Esther's comments about Mrs Pardiggle's behaviour constitute yet another example of the fact that she is, despite her protestations to the contrary, very perceptive.

[. . .] I was glad when we came to the brickmaker's house; though it was one of a cluster of wretched hovels in a brickfield, with pigsties close to the broken windows, and miserable little gardens before the doors, growing nothing but stagnant pools. Here and there, an old tub was put to catch the droppings of rain-water from a roof, or they were banked up with mud into a little pond like a large dirt-pie. At the doors and windows, some men and women lounged or prowled about, and took little notice of us, except to laugh to one another, or to say something as we passed, about gentlefolks minding their own business, and not troubling their heads and muddying their shoes with coming to look after other people's.

Mrs Pardiggle, leading the way with a great show of moral determination, and talking with much volubility about the untidy habits of the people (though I doubted if the best of us could have been tidy in such a place), conducted us into a cottage at the farthest corner, the ground-floor room of which we nearly filled.

Besides ourselves, there were in this damp offensive room – a woman with a black eye, nursing a poor little gasping baby by the fire; a man, all stained with clay and mud, and looking very dissipated, lying at full length on the ground, smoking a pipe; a powerful young man, fastening a collar on a dog; and a bold girl, doing some kind of washing in very dirty water. They all looked up at us as we came in, and the woman seemed to turn her face towards the fire, as if to hide her bruised eye; nobody gave us any welcome.

'Well, my friends,' said Mrs Pardiggle; but her voice had not a friendly sound, I thought; it was much too business-like and systematic. 'How do you do, all of you? I am here again. I told you, you couldn't tire me, you know. I am fond of hard work, and am true to my word.' [. . .]

[. . .] 'I wants a end of these liberties took with my place. I wants a end of being drawed like a badger. Now you're a going to poll-pry[5] and question according to custom – I know what you're a going to be up to. Well! You haven't got no occasion to be up to it. I'll save you the trouble. Is my daughter a washin? Yes, she *is* a washin. Look at the water. Smell it! That's wot we drinks. How do you like it, and what do you think of gin, instead! An't my place dirty? Yes, it is dirty – it's nat'rally dirty, and it's nat'rally onwholesome; and we've had five dirty and onwholesome children, as is all dead infants, and so much the better for them, and for us besides. Have I read the little book wot you left? No, I an't read the little book wot you left.[6] There an't nobody here as knows how to read it; and if there wos, it wouldn't be suitable to me. It's a book fit for a babby, and I'm not a babby. If you was to leave me a doll, I shouldn't nuss it. How have I been conducting of myself? Why, I've been drunk for three days; and I'd a been drunk four, if I'd a had the money. Don't I never mean for to go to church? No, I don't never mean for to go to church. I shouldn't be expected there, if I did; the beadle's too gen-teel for me. And how did my wife get that black eye? Why, I giv' it her; and if she says I didn't, she's a Lie!' [. . .]

Ada and I were very uncomfortable. We both felt intrusive and out of place; and we both thought that Mrs Pardiggle would have got on infinitely better, if she had not had such a mechanical way of taking possession of people. The children sulked and stared; the family took no notice of us whatever, except when the young man made the dog bark: which he usually did, when Mrs Pardiggle was most emphatic. We both felt painfully sensible that between us and these people there was an iron barrier, which could not be removed by our new friend. By whom, or how, it could be removed, we did not know; but we knew that. [. . .]

Mrs Pardiggle accordingly rose, and made a little vortex[7] in the confined room from which the pipe itself very narrowly escaped. [. . .]

She supposed that we were following her; but as soon as the space was left clear, we approached the woman sitting by the fire, to ask if the baby were ill. [. . .]

---

5 To pry (after the title character of the nineteenth-century comedy *Paul Pry* (1825) who intruded in the lives of others).
6 The Evangelicals distributed religious tracts in an attempt to convert the poor.
7 In other words, her exit leaves a space in the crowded room.

Ada, whose gentle heart was moved by its appearance, bent down to touch its little face. As she did so, I saw what happened and drew her back. The child died. [. . .]

Presently I took the light burden from her lap; did what I could to make the baby's rest the prettier and gentler; laid it on a shelf, and covered it with my own handkerchief. We tried to comfort the mother, and we whispered to her what Our Saviour said of children.[8] She answered nothing, but sat weeping – weeping very much. [. . .]

Chapter 10: The Law-Writer

The lawyer Tulkinghorn is the novel's most menacing representative of the law. As Lady Dedlock suggests, 'His calling is the acquisition of secrets, and the holding possession of such power as they give him' (Chapter 36). He is also one of the novel's most active detectives, determined to ferret out the secret that will ruin Lady Dedlock. Although he is murdered before he can inform Sir Leicester of her infamous past, he hounds her mercilessly until his death, making her a plausible suspect in Bucket's investigation. While the lawyer's desire to ruin her may, in part, be attributed to a desire for power, it is never wholly explained and is thus rendered all the more sinister (for a discussion of the relationship between power and the law, see D.A. Miller, p. 81 and Langland, p. 85). Located in the middle of Chapter 10, this description of Tulkinghorn's rooms is designed to reveal the essential aspects of his character. The 'old-fashioned' and 'obsolete' furniture remind the reader that Tulkinghorn is connected to the two outmoded institutions that dominate Bleak House: Chancery Court and the aristocratic Dedlocks. The likeness he bears to the former is reinforced by the dust and 'insufficient light' (suggesting obscurity) that characterise the room. The reference to maggots, in contrast, conjures up the presence of disease associated with slum districts such as Tom-all-Alone's (see Key Passages, p. 127). Indeed, by establishing the relationship between Lady Dedlock and Captain Hawdon, Tulkinghorn plays a key role in linking the novel's contrasting environments and characters. The statement that 'everything that can have a lock has got one', and the analogy between this character and an oyster, both contribute to the sense that Tulkinghorn is obsessed with secrets. His manipulation of the small objects – yet another example of the hermeneutic activity discussed by Hillis Miller (pp. 68–9) – represents an attempt to decipher Lady Dedlock's behaviour. As it was her reaction to a written document that initiated this investigation, the use of inkstand tops is particularly appropriate. His actions also suggest how he will go on to manipulate and toy with his victim once in possession of her secret. Finally, we should note that the phrase 'as the

---

8   See headnote to this extract.

crow came' echoes that used in Chapter 2 to introduce Chesney Wold. Its repetition in this context suggests that Tulkinghorn's actions will have some bearing on its inhabitants.

[. . .] Here, in a large house, formerly a house of state,[1] lives Mr Tulkinghorn. It is let off in sets of chambers now; and in those shrunken fragments of its greatness, lawyers lie like maggots in nuts. But its roomy staircases, passages, and antechambers, still remain; and even its painted ceilings, where Allegory, in Roman helmet and celestial linen, sprawls among balustrades and pillars, flowers, clouds, and big-legged boys, and makes the head ache – as would seem to be Allegory's object always, more or less.[2] Here, among his many boxes labelled with transcendant names, lives Mr Tulkinghorn, when not speechlessly at home in country-houses where the great ones of the earth are bored to death. Here he is today, quiet at his table. An Oyster of the old school, whom nobody can open.

Like as he is to look at, so is his apartment in the dusk of the present afternoon. Rusty, out of date, withdrawing from attention, able to afford it. Heavy broad-backed old-fashioned mahogany and horse-hair chairs, not easily lifted, obsolete tables with spindle-legs and dusty baize covers, presentation prints of the holders of great titles in the last generation, or the last but one, environ him. A thick and dingy Turkey-carpet muffles the floor where he sits, attended by two candles in old-fashioned silver candlesticks, that give a very insufficient light to his large room. The titles on the backs of his books have retired into the binding; everything that can have a lock has got one; no key is visible. Very few loose papers are about. He has some manuscript near him, but is not referring to it. With the round top of an inkstand and two broken bits of sealing wax, he is silently and slowly working out whatever train of indecision is in his mind. Now, the inkstand top is in the middle: now, the red bit of sealing-wax, now the black bit. That's not it. Mr Tulkinghorn must gather them all up, and begin again. [. . .]

The red bit, the black bit, the inkstand top, the other inkstand top, the little sand-box. So! You to the middle, you to the right, you to the left. This train of indecision must surely be worked out now or never. – Now! Mr Tulkinghorn gets up, adjusts his spectacles, puts on his hat, puts the manuscript in his pocket, goes out, tells the middle-aged man out at elbows, 'I shall be back presently.' Very rarely tells him anything more explicit.

Mr Tulkinghorn goes, as the crow came – not quite so straight, but nearly – to Cook's Court, Cursitor Street. To Snagsby's, Law Stationer's, Deeds engrossed and copied, Law-Writing executed in all its branches, &c., &c., &c. [. . .]

---

1   A property owned by the state and rented out to lawyers.
2   The painted figure of Allegory reappears in Chapter 48 to point down at Tulkinghorn's body and is linked with the pointing gesture made by Jo at the graveyard (Chapter 16).

Chapter 12: On the Watch

This passage, which occurs in the middle of the chapter, forms part of a lengthy description of the various guests present at a country-house party held at Chesney Wold. Focussing on the political contingent of the party, these paragraphs are an excellent example of Dickens's playful style and his ability to revel in the excesses of language. The endless permutations of 'Boodle' and 'Buffy' are an example of self-referential language where each signifier (i.e. each written word) refers only to the others within the list, rather than to an extra-textual reality. Such playfulness aside, the passage was also intended as a serious political satire. In the same way as Dickens's language bears no relation to reality, Boodle and Buffy's politics – concerned only with protecting their own vested interests – bear no relation to the pressing issues of the day, such as the urgent need for sanitary reform (a similar critique appears in Carlyle, **p. 31**). In fact, as described, the current state of government is shown to resemble the 'infernal country-dance' of Chancery Court. Dickens's use of the alphabet echoes that found in the first extract from Chapter 8, with 'this solicitor instructing and this counsel appearing for A, and that solicitor instructing and that counsel appearing for B; and so on through the whole alphabet, like the history of the Apple Pie' (**p. 119**). Dickens's lack of faith in the government's ability or willingness to effect positive change dated back to his days as a parliamentary reporter. Appearing in 1853, however, this attack was altogether topical. According to Butt and Tillotson, 'Throughout this period *The Times* was unsparing in its attacks upon Parliament and Government alike for failing to perform their duties.'[1]

[. . .] Then there is my Lord Boodle, of considerable reputation with his party, who has known what office is, and who tells Sir Leicester Dedlock with much gravity, after dinner, that he really does not see to what the present age is tending. A debate is not what a debate used to be; the House is not what the House used to be; even a Cabinet is not what it formerly was.[2] He perceives with astonishment, that supposing the present Government to be overthrown, the limited choice of the Crown, in the formation of a new Ministry, would lie between Lord Coodle and Sir Thomas Doodle – supposing it to be impossible for the Duke of Foodle to act with Goodle, which may be assumed to be the case in consequence of the breach arising out of that affair with Hoodle. Then, giving the Home Department and the Leadership of the House of Commons to Joodle, the Exchequer to Koodle, the Colonies to Loodle, and the Foreign Office to Moodle, what are you to do with Noodle? You can't offer him the Presidency of the Council; that is reserved for Poodle. You can't put him in the Woods and Forests; that is hardly

---

1   Butt and Tillotson (see Contextual Overview, note 20), p. 188.
2   The House of Commons and its Cabinet of ministers.

good enough for Quoodle. What follows? That the country is shipwrecked, lost, and gone to pieces (as is made manifest to the patriotism of Sir Leicester Dedlock), because you can't provide for Noodle!

On the other hand, the Right Honourable William Buffy, M.P., contends across the table with some one else, that the shipwreck of the country – about which there is no doubt; it is only the manner of it that is in question – is attributable to Cuffy. If you had done with Cuffy what you ought to have done when he first came into Parliament, and had prevented him from going over to Duffy, you would have got him into alliance with Fuffy, you would have had with you the weight attaching as a smart debater to Guffy, you would have brought to bear upon the elections the wealth of Huffy, you would have got in for three counties Juffy, Kuffy, and Luffy; and you would have strengthened your administration by the official knowledge and the business habits of Muffy. All this, instead of being, as you now are, dependent on the mere caprice of Puffy!

As to this point, and as to some minor topics, there are differences of opinion; but it is perfectly clear to the brilliant and distinguished circle, all round, that nobody is in question but Boodle and his retinue, and Buffy and *his* retinue. These are the great actors for whom the stage is reserved. A People there are, no doubt – a certain large number of supernumeraries, who are to be occasionally addressed, and relied upon for shouts and choruses, as on the theatrical stage; but Boodle and Buffy, their followers and families, their heirs, executors, administrators, and assigns, are the born first-actors, managers, and leaders and no others can appear upon the scene for ever and ever. [. . .]

Chapter 16: Tom-all-Alone's

Before proceeding to the next extract, it is worth taking a moment to remind ourselves of the key events that have occurred in relation to Tulkinghorn's investigation. The lawyer has learned from Mr Snagsby (a law stationer) that the document that caused Lady Dedlock to faint was copied by a man known only as Nemo (Latin for 'no one'). When Tulkinghorn goes to interview Nemo at his lodgings above Krook's shop, he finds the law-writer dead of an opium overdose. An inquest is held and Jo the crossing sweeper is called to give evidence. The Coroner, however, deems him too ignorant to participate and he is not allowed to testify. The next day, Nemo is buried in an overcrowded and diseased churchyard and Jo pays his respects by sweeping its steps. Armed with even this limited information, Tulkinghorn begins to torment Lady Dedlock and the pair watch each other ever more closely. In this extract, located near the beginning of Chapter 16, Lady Dedlock is, once again, engaged in frenetic but purposeless movement. At this point, however, her restlessness may be read, not simply as the product of boredom, but as a response to the threat posed by Tulkinghorn.

The importance of the second paragraph looms large in the novel. This series of rhetorical questions demands an answer on the part of the reader who is thereby forced to participate in the processes of detection and interpretation that dominate the lives of so many characters. As Hillis Miller suggests, it 'formulates the law of [. . .] interdependence' that dominates both the structure and content of *Bleak House*.[1] Despite Jo's insistence that he knows nothing, he is one of the most important means of 'connexion' within the novel. The portrait of Tom-all-Alone's, where Jo lives, is Dickens's most damning attack on the slum conditions in which many people were forced to live (for Browne's illustration of the slum, see Figure 3, p. 128). Comparing this representation to that of Gavin (p. 32), it becomes clear that Dickens was in no way exaggerating the filth and squalor that characterised certain districts of London. Tom-all-Alone's is, above all, a site of disease. Mirroring the language employed in 'On Duty with Inspector Field' (p. 38), the inhabitants are represented as scarcely human and are reduced to agents of contagion (for another contemporary discussion of contagion, see Carlyle, p. 31). Unsurprisingly, the 'dilapidated street' is linked back to the inefficiency and corruption of both the current government and Chancery Court. The final paragraphs concentrate on Jo's anomalous position within society. Not only is he ignored by the 'superior beings' who ought to help him; he is also alienated from the world of written signs by his illiteracy. This latter point does raise a puzzling question: in a novel in which written documents are the source of so much evil, one would suppose that the inability to read would represent a state of blissful ignorance. In the case of Jo, however, it all but strips him of his humanity.

[. . .] My Lady is at present represented, near Sir Leicester, by her portrait. She has flitted away to town, with no intention of remaining there, and will soon flit hither again, to the confusion of the fashionable intelligence. The house in town is not prepared for her reception. It is muffled and dreary. Only one Mercury in powder,[2] gapes disconsolate at the hall-window; and he mentioned last night to another Mercury of his acquaintance, also accustomed to good society, that if that sort of thing was to last – which it couldn't, for a man of his spirits couldn't bear it, and a man of his figure couldn't be expected to bear it – there would be no resource for him, upon his honour, but to cut his throat!

What connexion can there be, between the place in Lincolnshire, the house in town, the Mercury in powder, and the whereabout of Jo the outlaw with the broom, who had that distant ray of light upon him when he swept the churchyard-step? What connexion can there have been between many people in the innumerable histories of this world, who, from opposite sides of great gulfs, have, nevertheless, been very curiously brought together!

---

1   J. Hillis Miller, 'Interpretation in *Bleak House*' [1970], reprinted in *Victorian Subjects*, Durham, N.C.: Duke University Press, p. 180.
2   Refers to a footman in a powdered wig. In Roman mythology, Mercury is the messenger of the gods.

Jo sweeps his crossing all day long, unconscious of the link, if any link there be. He sums up his mental condition, when asked a question, by replying that he 'don't know nothink.' He knows that it's hard to keep the mud off the crossing in dirty weather, and harder still to live by doing it. Nobody taught him, even that much; he found it out.

Jo lives – that is to say, Jo has not yet died – in a ruinous place, known to the like of him by the name of Tom-all-Alone's. It is a black, dilapidated street, avoided by all decent people; where the crazy houses were seized upon, when their decay was far advanced, by some bold vagrants, who, after establishing their own possession, took to letting them out in lodgings. Now, these tumbling tenements contain, by night, a swarm of misery. As, on the ruined human wretch, vermin parasites appear, so, these ruined shelters have bred a crowd of foul existence that crawls in and out of gaps in walls and boards; and coils itself to sleep, in maggot numbers, where the rain drips in; and comes and goes, fetching and carrying fever, and sowing more evil in its every footprint than Lord Coodle, and Sir Thomas Doodle, and the Duke of Foodle, and all the fine gentlemen in office, down to Zoodle, shall set right in five hundred years – though born expressly to do it.

Twice, lately, there has been a crash and a cloud of dust, like the springing of a mine, in Tom-all-Alone's; and, each time, a house has fallen. These accidents have made a paragraph in the newspapers, and have filled a bed or two in the nearest hospital. The gaps remain, and there are not unpopular lodgings among the rubbish. As several more houses are nearly ready to go, the next crash in Tom-all-Alone's may be expected to be a good one.

This desirable property is in Chancery, of course. It would be an insult to the discernment of any man with half an eye, to tell him so. Whether 'Tom' is the popular representative of the original plaintiff or defendant in Jarndyce and Jarndyce;[3] or, whether Tom lived here when the suit had laid the street waste, all alone, until other settlers came to join him; or, whether the traditional title is a comprehensive name for a retreat cut off from honest company and put out of the pale of hope; perhaps nobody knows. Certainly, Jo don't know.

'For *I* don't,' says Jo, 'I don't know nothink.'

It must be a strange state to be like Jo! To shuffle through the streets, unfamiliar with the shapes, and in utter darkness as to the meaning, of those mysterious symbols, so abundant over the shops, and at the corners of streets, and on the doors, and in the windows! To see people read, and to see people write, and to see the postmen deliver letters, and not, to have the least idea of all that language – to be, to every scrap of it, stone blind and dumb! It must be very puzzling to see the good company going to the churches on Sundays, with their books in their hands, and to think (for perhaps Jo *does* think, at odd times) what does it all mean, and if it means anything to anybody, how comes it that it means nothing to me? To be hustled, and jostled, and moved on; and really to feel that it would appear to be perfectly true that I have no business, here, or there, or anywhere; and yet to be perplexed by the consideration that I *am* here somehow, too, and everybody

3   Tom Jarndyce, John's great uncle, was one of the original suitors.

Figure 3 'Tom-all-Alone's' (from Chapter 46).

overlooked me until I became the creature that I am! It must be a strange state, not merely to be told that I am scarcely human (as in the case of my offering myself for a witness), but to feel it of my own knowledge all my life! To see the horses, dogs, and cattle, go by me, and to know that in ignorance I belong to them, and not to the superior beings in my shape, whose delicacy I offend! Jo's ideas of a Criminal Trial, or a Judge, or a Bishop, or a Government, or that inestimable jewel to him (if he only knew it) the Constitution, should be strange! His whole material and immaterial life is wonderfully strange; his death, the strangest thing of all. [. . .]

Assuming the costume of a maid, a disguised Lady Dedlock instructs Jo to conduct her through the sordid urban environment of Captain Hawdon (Nemo). The tour culminates in a trip to the graveyard where he is buried. The importance of this passage, located at the end of Chapter 16, is twofold. In the first place, it is intended as part of the novel's attack on London's burial grounds, where the overcrowding that blighted so many lives continued after death. Jo's comment that 'They was obliged to stamp upon it [the coffin] to git it in' reflects the state of many urban cemeteries at mid-century. Such conditions inevitably produced a breeding ground for disease and hence constituted a serious health risk for the living. The rat noticed by Jo is just one of the ways in which such diseases were able to escape the iron bars that enclose the area. Indeed, the fever that Jo passes on to Esther may well find its origins in this graveyard. This episode also plays a decisive role in the future of many of the novel's characters. Most importantly, it will provide Tulkinghorn with a vital piece of evidence that he needs to establish Lady Dedlock's guilt and hence the stain she acquires is moral as well as physical (for another representation of the stain that taints Lady Dedlock's reputation, see Cohen, **p. 80** and Figure 2, **p. 92**). For Jo, this episode marks the beginning of his being 'moved on' by the police, a process that ends only with his death. Jo's gesture of pointing to Hawdon's grave with the handle of his broom receives attention from Hillis Miller, who views it as another example of the 'procedure of indication which is the basic structural principle of *Bleak House*' (**p. 67**).

[. . .] 'He was put there,' says Jo, holding to the bars and looking in.

'Where? O, what a scene of horror!'

'There!' says Jo, pointing. 'Over yinder. Among them piles of bones, and close to that there kitchin winder! They put him wery nigh the top. They was obliged to stamp upon it to git it in. I could unkiver it for you, with my broom, if the gate was open. That's why they locks it, I s'pose,' giving it a shake. 'It's always locked. Look at the rat!' cries Jo, excited. 'Hi! Look! There he goes! Ho! Into the ground!'

The servant shrinks into a corner – into a corner of that hideous archway, with its deadly stains contaminating her dress; and putting out her two hands, and passionately telling him to keep away from her, for he is loathsome to her, so remains for some moments. Jo stands staring, and is still staring when she recovers herself.

'Is this place of abomination, consecrated ground?'

'I don't know nothink of consequential ground,' says Jo, still staring.

'Is it blessed?'

'WHICH?' says Jo, in the last degree amazed.

'Is it blessed?'

'I'm blest if I know,' says Jo, staring more than ever; 'but I shouldn't think it warn't. Blest?' repeats Jo, something troubled in his mind. 'It an't done it much good if it is. Blest? I should think it was t'othered[4] myself. But *I* don't know nothink!'

The servant takes as little heed of what he says, as she seems to take of what she has said herself. She draws off her glove, to get some money from her purse. Jo silently notices how white and small her hand is, and what a jolly servant she must be to wear such sparkling rings.

She drops a piece of money in his hand, without touching it, and shuddering as their hands approach. 'Now,' she adds, 'show me the spot again!'

Jo thrusts the handle of his broom between the bars of the gate, and, with his utmost power of elaboration, points it out. At length, looking aside to see if he has made himself intelligible, he finds that he is alone. [. . .]

Chapter 22: Mr Bucket

The events of this passage require some contexualisation. In Chapter 19, Jo is harassed by a police officer for not 'moving on' and is found in possession of two half-crowns. Before being taken into custody, he claims to be known by Snagsby (whom he met at Nemo's inquest). This fact is confirmed by Guppy, who happens to be near. All proceed to the home of the stationer, who is, at the time, entertaining the preacher, Mr Chadband, and his wife. Jo's story about receiving the money from 'a lady in a wale as sed she was a servant' intrigues all present (Chapter 19). In the course of interrogating the child, Guppy reveals that he is employed at the law firm of Kenge and Carboy. Mrs Chadband (formerly Miss Rachael) reveals that she herself had connections with the firm while in charge of an orphan named Esther Summerson. This revelation is of great interest to Guppy, who continues to investigate Esther's past. Remembering Tulkinghorn's interest in Nemo, Snagsby takes it upon himself to inform him of these latest events. He is repeating the story for the second time when he is amazed to find himself in the presence of Inspector Bucket.

In this passage, near the start of Chapter 22, Bucket is introduced as an almost supernatural figure that is seemingly able to appear and disappear at will. It consistently emphasises the control and authority he is able to exert on both his environment and those around him, and reflects the virtually unbounded

---

4   In other words it is damned.

admiration of the Detective Branch evident in Dickens's 'On Duty with Inspector Field' (p. 38). The speed and efficiency with which this detective is able to formulate and execute a plan stand in direct contrast to the eternal delays and confusion associated with the law. And thus, as D.A. Miller suggests, his investigation is able to fulfil the reader's need for the clarity, understanding and resolution denied by Chancery (pp. 83–4). While the character of Bucket clearly has Dickens's approval, the reader's feelings towards him may be more ambivalent. However impressive his 'ghostly manner of appearing' may be, it is also vaguely threatening, as is his tendency 'to lurk and lounge'. Indeed, Bucket's impersonal, almost clinical, attitude towards the collection of information reminds us of Tulkinghorn. The image of Snagsby '[b]etween his two conductors' introduces an element of compulsion into the proceedings and, from this night forwards, the unfortunate stationer will feel himself to be inextricably trapped within mysteries beyond his understanding and control. In responding to Tom-all-Alone's with disbelief, Snagsby exemplifies Dickens's belief that many people were blind to the appalling conditions that existed at their very doorsteps (see Gavin, p. 32). This issue is discussed at some length by Schwarzbach (pp. 75–6).

[. . .] Mr Snagsby is dismayed to see, standing with an attentive face between himself and the lawyer, at a little distance from the table, a person with a hat and stick in his hand who was not there when he himself came in, and has not since entered by the door or by either of the windows. There is a press in the room, but its hinges have not creaked, nor has a step been audible upon the floor. Yet this third person stands there, with his attentive face, and his hat and stick in his hands, and his hands behind him, a composed and quiet listener. He is a stoutly-built, steady-looking, sharp-eyed man in black, of about the middle age. Except that he looks at Mr Snagsby as if he were going to take his portrait, there is nothing remarkable about him at first sight but his ghostly manner of appearing.

'Don't mind this gentleman,' says Mr Tulkinghorn, in his quiet way. 'This is only Mr Bucket.'

'O indeed, sir?' returns the stationer, expressing by a cough that he is quite in the dark as to who Mr Bucket may be.

'I wanted him to hear this story,' says the lawyer, 'because I have half a mind (for a reason) to know more of it, and he is very intelligent in such things. What do you say to this, Bucket?'

'It's very plain, sir. Since our people have moved this boy on, and he's not to be found on his old lay,[1] if Mr Snagsby don't object to go down with me to Tom-all-Alone's and point him out, we can have him here in less than a couple of hours' time. I can do it without Mr Snagsby, of course; but this is the shortest way.'

'Mr Bucket is a detective officer, Snagsby,' says the lawyer in explanation. [. . .]

---

1 His usual environment.

As they walk along, Mr Snagsby observes, as a novelty, that, however quick their pace may be, his companion still seems in some undefinable manner to lurk and lounge; also, that whenever he is going to turn to the right or left, he pretends to have a fixed purpose in his mind of going straight ahead, and wheels off, sharply, at the very last moment. Now and then, when they pass a police constable on his beat, Mr Snagsby notices that both the constable and his guide fall into a deep abstraction as they come towards each other, and appear entirely to overlook each other, and to gaze into space. In a few instances, Mr Bucket, coming behind some under-sized young man with a shining hat on, and his sleek hair twisted into one flat curl on each side of his head, almost without glancing at him touches him with his stick; upon which the young man, looking round, instantly evaporates. For the most part Mr Bucket notices things in general, with a face as unchanging as the great mourning ring on his little finger,[2] or the brooch, composed of not much diamond and a good deal of setting, which he wears in his shirt.

When they come at last to Tom-all-Alone's, Mr Bucket stops for a moment at the corner, and takes a lighted bull's-eye[3] from the constable on duty there, who then accompanies him with his own particular bull's-eye at his waist. Between his two conductors, Mr Snagsby passes along the middle of a villainous street, undrained, unventilated, deep in black mud and corrupt water – though the roads are dry elsewhere – and reeking with such smells and sights that he, who has lived in London all his life, can scarce believe his senses. Branching from this street and its heaps of ruins, are other streets and courts so infamous that Mr Snagsby sickens in body and mind, and feels as if he were going, every moment deeper down, into the infernal gulf. [. . .]

Chapter 32: The Appointed Time

In the course of Chapter 22, Guppy – who believes Krook to be in possession of some secret – establishes his friend Jobling as Krook's newest lodger. Assuming the name of Weevle, Jobling moves into Nemo's old rooms in order to spy on his landlord. Subsequently (Chapter 29), Guppy requests and is granted an interview with Lady Dedlock. As he informs her, he has been investigating Esther's past in an attempt to further her interests (and thereby his own, as he has amorous intentions towards her). Thus far, he tells her Ladyship, he has discovered from Mrs Chadband that Esther's true name is Hawdon and that she was brought up in secret by a Miss Barbary (Lady Dedlock's sister). In addition, he knows that a woman went to visit Hawdon's grave, and he suspects this woman to be Lady Dedlock herself. Finally, he informs her that certain letters

---

2   Memorial rings with the initials or mottoes of the deceased engraved on them.
3   A lantern with a single bulbous lens.

belonging to Hawdon are to come into his possession the following night. Throughout the interview, Lady Dedlock struggles to maintain her composure as she learns that Esther is her child whom she supposed died at birth.

The letters in question are currently held by Krook, who, unable to read, has agreed to hand them over to Jobling for interpretation (who will then pass them on to Guppy). This passage, the climactic ending of Chapter 32, describes how their plan is forestalled by the landlord's untimely death by spontaneous combustion. Krook's death received considerable attention from Dickens's contemporary critics (see, for example, Chorley, p. 57). The most significant of such attacks is that of G.H. Lewes (George Eliot's long-term partner and a staunch advocate of realism), who dismissed the episode as a scientific impossibility in a series of articles in *The Leader*. One of the advantages of serialisation was that it allowed Dickens to respond to the needs and concerns of his readers. Thus the next number continues the debate with Lewes by including a reference to 'men of science and philosophy' who insist 'that the deceased had no business to die in the alleged manner' (Chapter 33). Still smarting under Lewes's attack at the time of the novel's completion, Dickens used his Preface as a forum to defend his use of spontaneous combustion by citing a number of documented cases in which spontaneous combustion was alleged to have occurred.

It is much more profitable, however, to judge the episode on its own terms, that is, as a piece of non-naturalistic writing (see Schwarzbach, p. 73). This passage – in which Krook is reduced to a 'thick, yellow liquor' (Chapter 32) – has rightly been identified as 'the novel's most sensational instance of the grotesque'.[1] As such, it is entirely consistent with Krook's character, which is itself an embodiment of the grotesque. One should not forget, furthermore, that Krook is introduced to the reader with his 'breath issuing in visible smoke from his mouth, as if he were on fire within' (Chapter 5). The real significance of the passage, however, lies in its symbolic value. As Dickens suggests in the final paragraph, Krook has suffered the one form of death most appropriate to his status as the representative of the Lord Chancellor and Chancery Court.

[. . .] Mr Guppy takes the light. They go down, more dead than alive, and holding one another, push open the door of the back shop. The cat has retreated close to it, and stands snarling – not at them; at something on the ground, before the fire. There is very little fire left in the grate, but there is a smouldering suffocating vapour in the room, and a dark greasy coating on the walls and ceiling. The chairs and table, and the bottle so rarely absent from the table, all stand as usual. On one chair-back, hang the old man's hairy cap and coat. [. . .]

'What's the matter with the cat?' says Mr Guppy: 'Look at her!'

'Mad, I think. And no wonder, in this evil place.'

---

1   K. Hetherly Wright, 'The Grotesque and Urban Chaos in *Bleak House*', *Dickens Studies Annual*, 21, 1992, p. 103.

They advance slowly, looking at all these things. The cat remains where they found her, still snarling at the something on the ground, before the fire and between the two chairs. What is it? Hold up the light?

Here is a small burnt patch of flooring; here is the tinder from a little bundle of burnt paper, but not so light as usual, seeming to be steeped in something; and here is – is it the cinder of a small charred and broken log of wood sprinkled with white ashes, or is it coal? O Horror, he is here! and this, from which we run away, striking out the light and overturning one another into the street, is all that represents him.

Help, help, help! come into this house for Heaven's sake!

Plenty will come in, but none can help. The Lord Chancellor of that Court, true to his title in his last act, has died the death of all Lord Chancellors in all Courts, and of all authorities in all places under all names soever, where false pretences are made, and where injustice is done. Call the death by any name Your Highness will, attribute it to whom you will, or say it might have been prevented how you will, it is the same death eternally – inborn, inbred, engendered in the corrupted humours of the vicious body itself, and that only – Spontaneous Combustion, and none other of all the deaths that can be died.

Chapter 35: Esther's Narrative

At this point the reader might be forgiven for failing to remember the centrality of Esther Summerson. As she assumes a prominent place in the remaining extracts, it is worth taking a moment to indicate what has happened to her since her arrival at Bleak House. Much of her time (and narrative) has been spent witnessing the romantic attachments of those around her. She has watched Ada and Richard grow ever closer until they declare their love for one another. Esther has also been involved in trying to help Richard choose an appropriate career. At various points she expresses concern about his vacillating character, a flaw she attributes to his involvement in the Jarndyce suit. She has also been involved with Caddy's impending marriage to a dancing master (see Langland, pp. 86–7). Esther herself has received a proposal from Guppy, but has refused him and dedicates herself instead to the needs of Ada and Jarndyce, as well as managing Bleak House. Although she refuses to write openly about it in her narrative, a number of gaps and silences suggest that she has developed feelings for a young doctor, Allan Woodcourt. Although a promising physician, Allan is short of funds and has been forced to take a position as ship's doctor on a vessel bound for India. In Chapter 17, Jarndyce communicates to Esther what he knows of her history, namely, that he received a letter nine years previously asking him to provide for an illegitimate orphan in the case of her aunt's death. While this is hardly a revelation, it does prepare the reader for the events of the following chapter. There, Esther, Jarndyce and Ada visit the home of Boythorn, neighbour to the Dedlocks. One Sunday, Esther happens to see Lady Dedlock at church and wonders why 'her face should be, in a confused way, like a broken glass to [her], in which [she] saw scraps of old remembrances' (Chapter 18). Although she encounters her ladyship several times before they depart, the two never speak. Having returned to the house of her guardian, Esther learns that the brickmaker's wife is looking after a sick young boy. Together with her maid Charley, Esther goes to their dwelling to see if she is able to help and finds Jo, stricken with fever (probably smallpox). Jo reacts to the sight of Esther with terror. His comment, ' "She looks to me the t'other one" ' (Chapter 31), acknowledges the similarity between Esther and Lady Dedlock, whom he conducted to the burial ground. Attributing his reaction to fever, they take him back to Bleak House to be nursed only for him to disappear inexplicably during the night. Before he leaves, however, he passes the infection on to Charley, who, in turn, passes it on to Esther.

This passage, the opening of Chapter 35, records the worst crisis of Esther's illness. Its significance lies in the ways in which the fever affects her sense of selfhood and identity, both of which have already been rendered problematic by the mystery surrounding her origins. Until this mystery is solved, Esther is seemingly unable to progress and develop as an individual (for a discussion of Esther's relationship to her mother, see Dever and Schor, **pp. 88** and **93**). This situation finds its analogue in the description of her feverish state, where her life is presented as a series of overlapping but unconnected fragments. Also of note is her hallucinatory dream of being caught in 'a flaming necklace, or ring, or starry circle of some kind, of which *I* was one of the beads!' The image of the necklace, in which the position of each bead may be defined only in relation to the others, may be read as a metaphor for the language system itself. Thus Hillis Miller views it as a 'fit emblem for the violence exercised over the individual by language and other social institutions'.[1] Alternatively, it can be seen as a metaphor for the dependent and contingent status of the subject (see Critical History, **p. 55**).

I lay ill through several weeks, and the usual tenor of my life became like an old remembrance. But, this was not the effect of time, so much as of the change in all my habits, made by the helplessness and inaction of a sick room. Before I had been confined to it many days, everything else seemed to have retired into a remote distance, where there was little or no separation between the various stages of my life which had been really divided by years. In falling ill, I seemed to have crossed a dark lake, and to have left all my experiences, mingled together by the great distance, on the healthy shore. [. . .]

While I was very ill, the way in which these divisions of time became confused with one another, distressed my mind exceedingly. At once a child, an elder girl, and the little woman I had been so happy as, I was not only oppressed by cares

1 Hillis Miller (see the first passage from Chapter 16, note 1), p. 190.

and difficulties adapted to each station, but by the great perplexity of endlessly trying to reconcile them. I suppose that few who have not been in such a condition can quite understand what I mean, or what painful unrest arose from this source.

For the same reason I am almost afraid to hint at that time in my disorder – it seemed one long night, but I believe there were both nights and days in it – when I laboured up colossal staircases, ever striving to reach the top, and ever turned, as I have seen a worm in a garden path, by some obstruction, and labouring again. I knew perfectly at intervals, and I think vaguely at most times, that I was in my bed; and I talked with Charley, and felt her touch, and knew her very well; yet I would find myself complaining 'O more of these never-ending stairs, Charley, – more and more – piled up to the sky, I think!' and labouring on again.

Dare I hint at the worst time when, strung together somewhere in great black space, there was a flaming necklace, or ring, or starry circle of some kind, of which *I* was one of the beads! And when my only prayer was to be taken off from the rest, and when it was such inexplicable agony and misery to be a part of the dreadful thing? [. . .]

Chapter 36: Chesney Wold

Having recovered from the worst of her illness, Esther undergoes a lengthy period of convalescence. As all the mirrors have been removed from her rooms, she is unable to gauge the extent of the scarring left by the fever. She is heartened, however, that Jarndyce – who visits her at the first possible opportunity – seems to regard her as highly as ever. At this first meeting, her guardian informs Esther that Richard now views him as a rival suitor in the Chancery suit. He attributes the young man's distrust to his prolonged involvement with the case. Esther also receives a visit from Miss Flite, who, in addition to relating the history of her own involvement in Chancery, passes on two pieces of important information (such stories are, according to Schor, the means by which a female inheritance may be transmitted; see **pp. 97–8**). In the first place, Miss Flite has learned from Jenny, the brickmaker's wife, that 'there has been a lady with a veil inquiring at her cottage after my dear Fitz-Jarndyce's health [Flite's pet name for Esther], and taking a handkerchief away with her as a little keepsake' (Chapter 35). Believing the odd visitor to be Caddy, Esther thinks no more of the incident. The reference to the veil, however, leads the reader to suspect (quite rightly) that the woman is Lady Dedlock (see Key Passages, **pp. 129–30**). The second piece of information supplied by Miss Flite relates to Allan Woodcourt. As the old woman proudly informs her, the young man has survived a shipwreck and behaved admirably, saving many lives. At the close of Chapter 35, Esther admits for the first time that she is in love with Woodcourt and believes that he loved her. She is, however, relieved that such feelings were never acknowledged as her appearance is now so changed. Giving up all hope of romance, she resigns herself to pursuing her 'lowly way along the path of duty' (Chapter 35).

Chapter 36 sees Esther and Charley installed at the house of Boythorn, where she has gone to rest and recover. For the first time, she looks in the mirror to see her changed appearance. As she confides to the reader, 'I had never been a beauty, and had never thought myself one; but I had been very different from this. It was all gone now' (Chapter 36). Such changes in her appearance represent another example of the ways in which Esther's identity is problematised in the course of the novel.

The following extract, located towards the middle of the chapter, records a pivotal moment in Esther's history: Lady Dedlock's confession that she is her mother. It is only appropriate that the 'female shape' that haunts the Ghost's Walk should materialise into the figure of Esther's mother. According to family legend, the ghost of an ill-treated ancestor 'will walk here, until the pride of this house is humbled' (Chapter 7). Of course, this is exactly what will happen when the secret of Lady Dedlock's past is revealed. In offering her maternal love, Lady Dedlock fulfils a need that Esther has experienced since childhood (see Dever, **p. 91**). Thus, it is all the more surprising that Esther almost immediately expresses a 'burst of gratitude to the providence of God that I was so changed as that I never could disgrace her by any trace of likeness'. In so doing, she emphasises difference rather than similarity, separation rather than reunion. This reaction is never adequately explained and remains a mysterious reflection of Esther's complex psychological make-up. As a narrator, she has consistently withheld personal information from the reader. Thus it is hardly surprising that she remains silent about the contents of the letter she receives from her mother. Finally, we should note that Lady Dedlock's insistence that her past behaviour has placed her 'beyond all hope, and beyond all help' is altogether typical of the ways in which the fallen woman is represented in the Victorian novel.

When Esther eventually reveals the secret of her mother's identity to her guardian, Jarndyce takes the opportunity to write her a letter containing a proposal of marriage. While Esther acknowledges that his offer shows a generosity that rises 'above [her] disfigurement, and [her] inheritance of shame', she still feels 'as if something for which there was no name or distinct idea were indefinitely lost to [her]' (Chapter 44). She is clearly referring to the possibility of a marriage of love, rather than gratitude.

[. . .] I was resting at my favourite point, after a long ramble, and Charley was gathering violets at a little distance from me. I had been looking at the Ghost's Walk lying in a deep shade of masonry afar off, and picturing to myself the female shape that was said to haunt it, when I became aware of a figure approaching through the wood. The perspective was so long, and so darkened by leaves, and the shadows of the branches on the ground made it so much more intricate to the eye, that at first I could not discern what figure it was. By little and little, it revealed itself to be a woman's – a lady's – Lady Dedlock's. She was alone, and coming to where I sat with a much quicker step, I observed to my surprise, than was usual with her.

I was fluttered by her being unexpectedly so near (she was almost within speaking distance before I knew her), and would have risen to continue my walk. But I could not. I was rendered motionless. Not so much by her hurried gesture of entreaty, not so much by her quick advance and outstretched hands, not so much by the great change in her manner, and the absence of her haughty self-restraint, as by a something in her face that I had pined for and dreamed of when I was a little child; something I had never seen in any face; something I had never seen in hers before. [. . .]

I looked at her; but I could not see her, I could not hear her, I could not draw my breath. The beating of my heart was so violent and wild, that I felt as if my life were breaking from me. But when she caught me to her breast, kissed me, wept over me, compassionated me, and called me back to myself; when she fell down on her knees and cried to me, 'O my child, my child, I am your wicked and unhappy mother! O try to forgive me!' – when I saw her at my feet on the bare earth in her great agony of mind, I felt, through all my tumult of emotion, a burst of gratitude to the providence of God that I was so changed as that I never could disgrace her by any trace of likeness; as that nobody could ever now look at me, and look at her, and remotely think of any near tie between us.

I raised my mother up, praying and beseeching her not to stoop before me in such affliction and humiliation. I did so, in broken incoherent words; for, besides the trouble I was in, it frightened me to see her at *my* feet. I told her – or I tried to tell her – that if it were for me, her child, under any circumstances to take upon me to forgive her, I did it, and had done it, many, many years. I told her that my heart overflowed with love for her; that it was natural love, which nothing in the past had changed, or could change. That it was not for me, then resting for the first time on my mother's bosom, to take her to account for having given me life; but that my duty was to bless her and receive her, though the whole world turned from her, and that I only asked her leave to do it. I held my mother in my embrace, and she held me in hers; and among the still woods in the silence of the summer day, there seemed to be nothing but our two troubled minds that was not at peace. [. . .]

My unhappy mother told me that in my illness she had been nearly frantic. She had but then known that her child was living. She could not have suspected me to be that child before. She had followed me down here, to speak to me but once in all her life. We never could associate, never could communicate, never probably from that time forth could interchange another word, on earth. She put into my hands a letter she had written for my reading only; and said, when I had read it, and destroyed it – but not so much for her sake, since she asked nothing, as for her husband's and my own – I must evermore consider her as dead. If I could believe that she loved me, in this agony in which I saw her, with a mother's love, she asked me to do that; for then I might think of her with a greater pity, imagining what she suffered. She had put herself beyond all hope, and beyond all help. Whether she preserved her secret until death, or it came to be discovered and she brought dishonour and disgrace upon the name she had taken, it was her solitary struggle always; and no affection could come near her, and no human creature could render her any aid. [. . .]

Chapter 39: Attorney and Client

Encouraged by his solicitor, Vholes, Richard has become ever more entangled in the perverted machinery of Chancery. This involvement has affected his character (as it will his health) and 'his heart is heavy with corroding care, suspense, distrust, and doubt' (Chapter 39). As a representative of the law, Vholes suggests how Chancery Court resembles a vampire, or parasite, living off its suitors and destroying their lives in the process. As described in this passage, taken from the opening pages of Chapter 39, Vholes is clearly another example of the grotesque. Caught within the clutches of this man, who is likened to serpents, cats and other predators, Richard is constructed as the helpless victim of Vholes's 'professional appetite'. Throughout this novel, the word 'duty' is closely associated with Esther and her ability to help and guide those around her. When used to describe the actions of Vholes, Dickens clearly wishes the reader to make this comparison and judge him accordingly. The plate that accompanies this description (see Figure 4, p. 140) is discussed by Cohen (pp. 78–9). As she suggests, Browne used it as an opportunity to proliferate the images of entrapment that abound in Dickens's text.

[. . .] Mr Vholes, and his young client, and several blue bags hastily stuffed, out of all regularity of form,[1] as the larger sort of serpents are in their first gorged state, have returned to the official den. Mr Vholes, quiet and unmoved, as a man of so much respectability ought to be, takes off his close black gloves as if he were skinning his hands, lifts off his tight hat as if he were scalping himself, and sits down at his desk. The client throws his hat and gloves upon the ground – tosses them anywhere, without looking after them or caring where they go; flings himself into a chair, half sighing and half groaning; rests his aching head upon his hand, and looks the portrait of Young Despair.

'Again nothing done!' says Richard. 'Nothing, nothing done!' [. . .]

'Mr C,' returns Vholes, following him close with his eyes wherever he goes, 'your spirits are hasty, and I am sorry for it on your account. Excuse me if I recommend you not to chafe so much, not to be so impetuous, not to wear yourself out so. You should have more patience. You should sustain yourself better.'

'I ought to imitate you, in fact, Mr Vholes?' says Richard, sitting down again

---

1   The collection of legal documents pertaining to Richard's case.

Figure 4 'Attorney and Client, fortitude and impatience' (from Chapter 39).

with an impatient laugh, and beating the Devil's Tattoo[2] with his boot on the patternless carpet.

'Sir,' returns Vholes, always looking at the client, as if he were making a lingering meal of him with his eyes as well as with his professional appetite. 'Sir,' returns Vholes, with his inward manner of speech and his bloodless quietude; 'I should not have had the presumption to propose myself as a model, for your imitation or any man's. Let me but leave a good name to my three daughters, and that is enough for me; I am not a self-seeker. [. . .]

Mr Vholes, after glancing at the official cat who is patiently watching a mouse's hole, fixes his charmed gaze again on his young client, and proceeds in his buttoned up half-audible voice, as if there were an unclean spirit in him that will neither come out nor speak out:

'What are you to do, sir, you inquire, during the vacation. I should hope you gentlemen of the army may find many means of amusing yourselves, if you give your minds to it.[3] If you had asked me what *I* was to do, during the vacation, I

---

2   A rapid beating indicating impatience.
3   Having first attempted to train as a doctor, then a solicitor, Richard is currently in the army. His inability to decide on a career is meant to reflect the evil influence exercised by Chancery Court on his character.

could have answered you more readily. I am to attend to your interests. I am to be found here, day by day, attending to your interests. That is my duty, Mr C; and term time or vacation makes no difference to me. If you wish to consult me as to your interests, you will find me here at all times alike. Other professional men go out of town. I don't. Not that I blame them for going; I merely say, I don't go. This desk is your rock, sir!'

Mr Vholes gives it a rap, and it sounds as hollow as a coffin. [. . .]

Chapter 47: Jo's Will

In Chapter 45, Vholes travels to Bleak House to inform Jarndyce and Esther that Richard is in debt and in danger of losing his army commission. Ever helpful, Esther travels to Deal, where he is stationed, in order to offer her advice. While there, she unexpectedly sees Allan Woodcourt, who is just returning from his adventures abroad. Refusing to give in to her first impulse to run away and hide her scarred face, she forces herself to meet him and reveal her changed appearance. Allan is, as always, very kind and gentle and expresses his concern about Richard, whose health is deteriorating. He promises Esther that he will look after him when they both return to London. The following chapter sees Allan wandering around Tom-all-Alone's at daybreak, where he encounters Jenny, the brickmaker's wife (see Key Passages, p. 120). Having attended to an injury obviously inflicted by her husband, he is walking away when Jenny calls out to him to stop Jo, who is doing his best to run away from her. After a good deal of prompting, Jo tells Allan and Jenny that he was taken away from Bleak House by Bucket and has been 'moving on' ever since. Although horrified by the role Jo played in infecting Esther, Allan offers to find the homeless boy a place to rest as he is clearly close to death. Following the advice of Miss Flite, the doctor takes him to the shooting gallery owned by Trooper George, who is known to both Jarndyce and Esther (George was also a friend of Captain Hawdon and, having been wrongly arrested for Tulkinghorn's murder, will be revealed as Mrs Rouncewell's lost son). For the first time in his life, Jo experiences peace and comfort and, before dying, asks Snagsby to write an apology in 'Uncommon precious large' letters for infecting Esther (Chapter 47). This passage, the conclusion of Chapter 47, describes his death. Dickens was famous for his child death scenes (think of Paul Dombey in *Dombey and Son* or Little Nell in *The Old Curiosity Shop*), which were heavily invested with sentiment and tended to lapse into bathos. While certainly not free of these elements, the death of Jo registers an effective plea for the need for sanitary reform (for a non-fictional equivalent to this plea, see Dickens's speech to the Metropolitan Sanitary Association, p. 36).

In many ways, this scene parallels Esther's first encounter with the brickmaker's family, when she and Ada witness the death of Jenny's baby (see p. 122). Just as Esther's gentle reminder of the words of Christ contrasts with the harsh sermon of Mrs Pardiggle, so too does Allan's use of the Lord's Prayer contrast with the grandiose but irrelevant preaching of the hypocritical Reverand Chadband. Elsewhere in the novel, Jarndyce makes the distinction between those 'who did a little and made a great deal of noise' and those 'who did a great deal and made no noise' (Chapter 8). While Pardiggle and Chadband (as well as the government) belong to the former group, Esther and Allan belong to the latter and the similarities between them suggest how well suited they are to each other. It is significant that Jo dies before he is able to repeat 'HALLOWED BE THY NAME!' In a novel overrun with illegitimate children and orphans, he is one of many who cannot lay claim to a name and the sense of selfhood it instils. In the final paragraph, the narrator (who is closely aligned to Dickens here) is unable to restrain his rage any longer and indulges in an outburst that accuses everyone from the Queen down to the ordinary citizen of the wilful neglect of those 'dying thus around us, every day' (a similar tone is adopted by Carlyle, p. 31).

'Jo! Did you ever know a prayer?'

'Never know'd nothink, sir.'

'Not so much as one short prayer?'

'No, sir. Nothink at all. Mr Chadbands he wos a prayin wunst at Mr Sangsby's and I heerd him, but he sounded as if he wos a speakin' to his-self, and not to me. He prayed a lot, but *I* couldn't make out nothink on it. Different times, there wos other genlmen come down Tom-all-Alone's a prayin, but they all mostly sed as the t'other wuns prayed wrong, and all mostly sounded to be a talking to theirselves, or a passing blame on the t'others, and not a talkin to us. *We* never knowd nothink. *I* never knowd what it wos all about.' [. . .]

'Stay, Jo! What now?'

'It's time for me to go to that there berryin ground, sir,' he returns with a wild look.

'Lie down, and tell me. What burying ground, Jo?'

'Where they laid him as wos wery good to me, wery good to me indeed, he wos. It's time fur me to go down to that there berryin ground, sir, and ask to be put along with him. I wants to go there and be berried. He used fur to say to me, "I am as poor as you today, Jo," he ses. I wants to tell him that I am as poor as him now, and have come there to be laid along with him.'

'Bye and bye, Jo. Bye and bye.'

'Ah! P'raps they wouldn't do it if I wos to go myself. But will you promise to have me took there, sir, and laid along with him?'

'I will, indeed.'

'Thankee, sir. Thankee, sir! They'll have to get the key of the gate afore they can take me in, for it's allus locked. And there's a step there, as I used fur to clean with my broom. – It's turned wery dark, sir. Is there any light a comin?'

'It is coming fast, Jo.'

Fast. The cart is shaken all to pieces, and the rugged road is very near its end.

'Jo, my poor fellow!'

'I hear you, sir, in the dark, but I'm a gropin – a gropin – let me catch hold of your hand.'

'Jo, can you say what I say?'

'I'll say anythink as you say, sir, for I knows it's good.'

'OUR FATHER.'

'Our Father! – yes, that's wery good, sir.'

'WHICH ART IN HEAVEN.'

'Art in Heaven – is the light a comin, sir?'

'It is close at hand. HALLOWED BE THY NAME!'

'Hallowed be – thy –'

The light is come upon the dark benighted way. Dead!

Dead, your Majesty. Dead, my lords and gentlemen. Dead, Right Reverends and Wrong Reverends of every order. Dead, men and women, born with Heavenly compassion in your hearts. And dying thus around us, every day.

Chapter 59: Esther's Narrative

Lady Dedlock, fearing that her young companion Rosa may be harmed by continuing their association, sends her away with Rouncewell to receive a proper education before marrying his son. Tulkinghorn, who has previously instructed Lady Dedlock to maintain all outward signs of normalcy, warns her that he will soon be forced to act upon his knowledge of her past. Lady Dedlock goes for a walk and Tulkinghorn returns to his chambers where he is found murdered the next morning. Trooper George is arrested by Bucket for the crime. Returning to Esther's narrative in Chapter 50, we learn that she has gone to nurse Caddy, who is seriously ill after giving birth to a weak little baby. For several weeks she is in constant contact with Allan, Caddy's physician. On the occasion of Ada's twenty-first birthday, Esther finally tells her that she is to marry Jarndyce. Chapter 51 sees the narrative move back several weeks to offer an update on Richard's failing health. While visiting his chambers, Ada confesses that she secretly married him two months earlier and will not leave his side again. When Esther learns of Tulkinghorn's murder and the fact that a woman resembling Lady Dedlock was seen on his staircase, she fears for her mother.

In Chapter 54, Inspector Bucket is finally in a position to identify Hortense, Lady Dedlock's dismissed French maid, as the true murderer. He also informs Sir Leicester about his wife's unfortunate past. At this point, a number of minor characters arrive, in possession of Lady Dedlock's secret and wishing to blackmail Sir Leicester. Although Bucket himself is in possession of the incriminating letters they refer to (the same letters Guppy was to receive from Krook), he advises Dedlock to buy their silence. Chapter 55 takes the reader back in time to the previous day to record how Lady Dedlock – frightened by anonymous letters accusing her of Tulkinghorn's murder and believing her husband to be in possession of her secret – runs away. Before leaving, she writes her husband a farewell letter. When Sir Leicester eventually reads this letter, he suffers a stroke but manages to communicate to Bucket his desire for his wife to be found and offered 'Full forgiveness' (Chapter 56).

Searching Lady Dedlock's rooms, Bucket finds the handkerchief marked with Esther's name and, guessing their relationship, asks Esther to accompany him on his search in order to allay her mother's suspicions should he find her. They are able to track Lady Dedlock to Jenny's house in St Albans but cannot trace her movements after that point. Too late, Bucket realises that she has exchanged clothes with Jenny and returned to London. He does not, however, communicate this knowledge to Esther. Following Lady Dedlock back to London, they are directed to the house of Snagsby. On the way, they meet Woodcourt, who happens to be in the area. Once at Snagsby's, they retrieve a letter from Guster, Mrs Snagsby's servant who suffers from fits. Written by Lady Dedlock, it informs them of her intention to be lost and die (see Schor's discussion of tattered documents, disguises and narrative secrets, p. 97). Having been revived by the ministrations of Allan, Guster is able to tell them that she received the letter from a poor woman who was asking directions to the burial ground. This passage, the conclusion of Chapter 59, describes Esther's impressions of their journey there and what they find.

This is a more complex piece of writing than it initially appears. In exchanging places with Jenny, Lady Dedlock becomes what she believed herself to be for so long, 'the mother of the dead child'. By the same token, the exchange re-configures Esther as 'the dead child', the one who could not survive its inauspicious origins. One should also note that Esther's gesture of 'put[ting] the long dank hair aside' echoes that made earlier when she first studied her altered appearance: 'I put my hair aside, and looked at the reflection in the mirror' (Chapter 36). The repetition of this gesture, together with the moment of shocked recognition that follows in both episodes, establishes an unhappy parallel between Esther and her dead mother. Thus it is hardly surprising that Esther's recollection of the episode assumes a nightmarish and unreal quality. The final point to make is that Bucket's inability to save Lady Dedlock confirms Hillis Miller's argument that 'Bleak House is full of unsuccessful detectives' (p. 68).

[...] I have the most confused impressions of that walk. I recollect that it was neither night nor day; that morning was dawning, but the street-lamps were not yet put out; that the sleet was still falling, and that all the ways were deep with it. I recollect a few chilled people passing in the streets. I recollect the wet housetops, the clogged and bursting gutters and water-spouts, the mounds of blackened ice and snow over which we passed, the narrowness of the courts by which we went. At the same time I remember, that the poor girl seemed to be yet telling her story audibly and plainly in my hearing; that I could feel her resting on my arm;[1] that the stained house fronts put on human shapes and looked at me; that great water-gates seemed to be opening and closing in my head, or in the air; and that the unreal things were more substantial than the real.

At last we stood under a dark and miserable covered way, where one lamp was burning over an iron gate, and where the morning faintly struggled in. The gate was closed. Beyond it, was a burial-ground – a dreadful spot in which the night was very slowly stirring; but where I could dimly see heaps of dishonoured graves and stones, hemmed in by filthy houses, with a few dull lights in their windows, and on whose walls a thick humidity broke out like a disease. On the step at the gate, drenched in the fearful wet of such a place, which oozed and splashed down everywhere, I saw, with a cry of pity and horror, a woman lying – Jenny, the mother of the dead child.

I ran forward, but they stopped me, and Mr Woodcourt entreated me, with the greatest earnestness, even with tears, before I went up to the figure to listen for an instant to what Mr Bucket said. I did so, as I thought. I did so, as I am sure.

'Miss Summerson, you'll understand me, if you think a moment. They changed clothes at the cottage.'

They changed clothes at the cottage. I could repeat the words in my mind, and I knew what they meant of themselves; but I attached no meaning to them in any other connection.

'And one returned,' said Mr Bucket, 'and one went on. And the one that went on, only went on a certain way agreed upon to deceive, and then turned across country, and went home. Think a moment!'

I could repeat this in my mind too, but I had not the least idea what it meant. I saw before me, lying on the step, the mother of the dead child. She lay there, with one arm creeping round a bar of the iron gate, and seeming to embrace it. She lay there, who had so lately spoken to my mother. She lay there, a distressed, unsheltered, senseless creature. She who had brought my mother's letter, who could give me the only clue to where my mother was; she, who was to guide us to rescue and save her whom we had sought so far, who had come to this condition by some means connected with my mother that I could not follow, and might be passing beyond our reach and help at that moment; she lay there, and they stopped me! I saw, but did not comprehend, the solemn and compassionate look in Mr Woodcourt's face. I saw, but did not comprehend, his touching the other on the breast to keep him back. I saw him stand uncovered in the bitter air, with a reverence for something. But my understanding for all this was gone.

I even heard it said between them:

'Shall she go?'

'She had better go. Her hands should be the first to touch her. They have a higher right than ours.'

I passed on to the gate, and stooped down. I lifted the heavy head, put the long dank hair aside, and turned the face. And it was my mother, cold and dead.

---

1   Esther is referring to Guster.

Chapter 64: Esther's Narrative

Following the death of her mother, Esther undergoes a period of illness and remains in London where she can be close to Ada and Richard, whose health is fading quickly. Allan's mother comes to stay with them during Esther's recovery, ostensibly to be near her son who will shortly take up a post in Yorkshire, ministering to the poor. Ada confides to Esther that she is expecting a child. One evening, Allan takes the opportunity to declare his love to Esther, who informs him that she is to marry Jarndyce. The next morning, she and Jarndyce agree to be married in a month's time. Their conversation is interrupted by the appearance of Bucket, who has brought Smallweed (a distant relative of Krook, who has inherited his enormous collection of papers). Smallweed is in possession of a will relating to the Jarndyce suit. Having been forced to hand it over, Esther and Jarndyce take it to their solicitor, Kenge, and it is declared valid. In Chapter 64, Esther is busy preparing for her own modest wedding and is rather surprised when Jarndyce asks her to accompany him to Yorkshire to put the finishing touches on a house he has furnished for Allan. Towards the middle of the chapter, he takes her to a replicated Bleak House, where he makes the speech recorded in this next extract.

It is certainly true that Jarndyce's decision to sacrifice his own needs and feelings to further those of Esther is evidence of a generous nature. It is also true that his decision stops Esther from following in the footsteps of her mother, who married an older man while in love with a younger. At the same time, however, his gesture is quite troubling to readers today. For much of the novel, Esther has been caught in a series of circumstances that, while exercising a profound effect on her life, lay beyond her control. In 'giving' her to Woodcourt, however willingly, Jarndyce is simply perpetuating her forced passivity and helplessness. Allowing her to believe, furthermore, that she is preparing for a wedding with him, rather than Allan, is an extraordinary example of manipulation that is difficult to reconcile with Jarndyce's supposed benevolence.

[. . .] 'Hush, little woman! Don't cry; this is to be a day of joy. I have looked forward to it,' he said, exultingly, 'for months on months! A few words more, Dame Trot, and I have said my say. Determined not to throw away one atom of my Esther's worth, I took Mrs Woodcourt into a separate confidence. "Now madam," said I, "I clearly perceive – and indeed I know, to boot – that your son loves my ward. I am further very sure that my ward loves your son, but will sacrifice her love to a sense of duty and affection, and will sacrifice it so completely, so entirely, so religiously, that you should never suspect it, though you watched her night and day." Then I told her all our story – ours – yours and mine. "Now, madam," said I, "come you, knowing this, and live with us. Come you, and see my child from hour to hour; set what you see, against her pedigree, which is this, and this" – for I scorned to mince it – "and tell me what is the true legitimacy, when you shall have quite made up your mind on that subject." Why, honour to her old Welsh blood, my dear!' cried my guardian, with enthusiasm, 'I believe the heart it animates beats no less warmly, no less admiringly, no less lovingly, towards Dame Durden, than my own!'

He tenderly raised my head, and as I clung to him, kissed me in his old fatherly way again and again. What a light, now, on the protecting manner I had thought about!

'One more last word. When Allan Woodcourt spoke to you, my dear, he spoke with my knowledge and consent – but I gave him no encouragement, not I, for these surprises were my great reward, and I was too miserly to part with a scrap of it. He was to come, and tell me all that passed; and he did. I have no more to say. My dearest, Allan Woodcourt stood beside your father when he lay dead – stood beside your mother. This is Bleak House. This day I give this house its little mistress; and before God, it is the brightest day in all my life!'

He rose, and raised me with him. We were no longer alone. My husband – I have called him by that name full seven happy years now – stood at my side.

'Allan,' said my guardian, 'take from me, a willing gift, the best wife that ever a man had. What more can I say for you, than that I know you deserve her! Take with her the little home she brings you. You know what she will make it, Allan; you know what she has made its namesake. Let me share its felicity sometimes, and what do I sacrifice? Nothing, nothing.' [. . .]

Chapter 65: Beginning the World

Esther and Allan are to be married within a month. All three return to London, where Esther remains with Jarndyce, once again occupying the place of his ward rather than his fiancée. Guppy arrives at the house with his mother and Jobling to propose to Esther one last time. He is summarily dismissed by Jarndyce in yet another example of his tendency to act for Esther and maintain her passivity. Chapter 65 marks the beginning of the new Term of Chancery and, learning that the new will related to Jarndyce and Jarndyce is to be discussed, Allan and Esther proceed to Court. Located near the beginning of the chapter, this passage describes how, upon arriving, they discover that the interminable suit has finally been brought to an end by the entire estate being 'absorbed in costs'.

The demise of the suit is only slightly less absurd (and grotesque) than that of Krook. Although the case has ended, it has never been resolved. This termination without resolution emphasises the sheer wastefulness of the hundreds of thousands of documents, arguments and counter-arguments that it has generated. It also stands in marked and dramatic contrast to the extensive devastation it has wreaked upon so many lives. The reaction of the various solicitors, who find it all terribly amusing, reveals how utterly unfeeling the representatives of the Court really are. Furthermore, even now, when the case is at an end, lawyers such as Kenge and Vholes refuse to communicate the facts in a direct manner and continue to indulge in rhetoric designed to forestall and obscure meaning. Allan's premonition that this news will 'break Richard's heart' is literally, as well as metaphorically, true. He is found in the courtroom trying to address the judge but 'stopped by his mouth being full of blood' (Chapter 65). He dies several days later, but not before being reconciled with Jarndyce and passing on his blessings to Esther and Allan.

[. . .] when we came to Westminster Hall we found that the day's business was begun. Worse than that, we found such an unusual crowd in the Court of Chancery that it was full to the door, and we could neither see nor hear what was passing within. It appeared to be something droll, for occasionally there was a laugh, and a cry of 'Silence!' It appeared to be something interesting, for every one was pushing and striving to get nearer. It appeared to be something that made the professional gentlemen very merry, for there were several young counsellors in wigs and whiskers on the outside of the crowd, and when one of them told the others about it, they put their hands in their pockets, and quite doubled themselves up with laughter, and went stamping about the pavement of the hall.

We asked a gentleman by us, if he knew what cause was on? He told us Jarndyce and Jarndyce. We asked him if he knew what was doing in it? He said, really no he did not, nobody ever did; but as well as he could make out, it was over. Over for the day? we asked him. No, he said; over for good.

Over for good!

When we heard this unaccountable answer, we looked at one another quite lost in amazement. Could it be possible that the Will had set things right at last, and that Richard and Ada were going to be rich? It seemed too good to be true. Alas it was! [. . .]

At this juncture, we perceived Mr Kenge coming out of court with an affable dignity upon him, listening to Mr Vholes, who was deferential, and carried his own bag. Mr Vholes was the first to see us. 'Here is Miss Summerson, sir,' he said. 'And Mr Woodcourt.'

'O indeed! Yes. Truly!' said Mr Kenge, raising his hat to me with polished politeness. 'How do you do? Glad to see you. Mr Jarndyce is not here?'

No. He never came there, I reminded him.

'Really,' returned Mr Kenge, 'it is as well that he is *not* here to-day, for his – shall I say, in my good friend's absence, his indomitable singularity of opinion? – might have been strengthened, perhaps; not reasonably, but might have been strengthened.'

'Pray what has been done to-day?' asked Allan.

'I beg your pardon?' said Mr Kenge, with excessive urbanity.

'What has been done to-day?'

'What has been done,' repeated Mr Kenge. 'Quite so. Yes. Why, not much has been done; not much. We have been checked – brought up suddenly, I would say – upon the – shall I term it threshold?'

'Is this Will considered a genuine document, sir?' said Allan; 'will you tell us that?'

'Most certainly, if I could,' said Mr Kenge; 'but we have not gone into that, we have not gone into that.'

'We have not gone into that,' repeated Mr Vholes, as if his low inward voice were an echo.

'You are to reflect, Mr Woodcourt,' observed Mr Kenge, using his silver trowel, persuasively and smoothingly, 'that this has been a great cause, that this has been a protracted cause, that this has been a complex cause. Jarndyce and Jarndyce has been termed, not inaptly, a Monument of Chancery practice.'

'And Patience[1] has sat upon it a long time,' said Allan.

'Very well indeed, sir,' returned Mr Kenge, with a certain condescending laugh he had. 'Very well! You are further to reflect, Mr Woodcourt,' becoming dignified to severity, 'that on the numerous difficulties, contingencies, masterly fictions, and forms of procedure in this great cause, there has been expended study, ability, eloquence, knowledge, intellect, Mr Woodcourt, high intellect. For many years, the – a – I would say the flower of the Bar, and the – a – I would presume to add, the matured autumnal fruits of the Woolsack[2] – have been lavished upon Jarndyce and Jarndyce. If the public have the benefit, and if the country have the adornment, of this great Grasp, it must be paid for, in money or money's worth, sir.'

'Mr Kenge,' said Allan, appearing enlightened all in a moment. 'Excuse me, our time presses. Do I understand that the whole estate is found to have been absorbed in costs?'

'Hem! I believe so,' returned Mr Kenge. 'Mr Vholes, what do *you* say?'

'I believe so,' said Mr Vholes.

'And that thus the suit lapses and melts away?'

'Probably,' returned Mr Kenge. 'Mr Vholes?'

'Probably,' said Mr Vholes.

'My dearest life,' whispered Allan, 'this will break Richard's heart!' [. . .]

Chapter 67: The Close of Esther's Narrative

Chapter 65 sees all the characters, major and minor, accounted for before offering us the conventional happy ending of so many Victorian novels. The actual conclusion, represented in this final extract, is, however, slightly problematic. Esther's first contribution to the narrative is, appropriately enough, a chapter titled 'A Progress'. In the course of the novel, she has been transformed from an unloved and unwanted 'orphan' to a happy wife who is surrounded by

---

1   A reference to Shakespeare's *Twelfth Night*: 'She sat like Patience on a monument' (2, v, 115).
2   The official seat of the Lord Chancellor in the House of Lords. In this passage, Kenge is using the term as a metonym for the Lord Chancellor himself.

people who love her and is fully integrated into the community. Yet her sense of identity remains problematic (see Dever, **p. 88**). Jarndyce continues to call her by a host of names other than her own, while Esther still refers to herself in the most self-depreciatory manner. Those around her praise her 'as the doctor's wife' and like her 'for his sake' rather than for any of her own considerable merits. The most obvious marker of her continued inability to assert a strong sense of selfhood is, however, the final sentence of her narrative (and that of the novel), which trails off into one of the silences that characterised the story of her blighted youth.

On a more positive note, Allan's activities on behalf his patients (which find their counterpart in Esther's activities within the home) represent the one possibility of regeneration and hope that the novel offers. It is worth noting that these activities are undertaken by an individual and not by any official body or system, such as the government or the Church. Of course, when we consider the scale of the social problems documented by *Bleak House*, one is forced to question the efficacy of individual action. Furthermore, Allan and Esther undertake these activities not within the slums of Tom-all-Alone's, but in the rural retreat they create in Yorkshire. Such points aside, the lives of Allan and Esther embody Esther's belief that: 'I thought it best to be as useful as I could, and to render what kind services I could, to those immediately about me; and to try to let that circle of duty gradually and naturally expand itself' (Chapter 8). For Dickens, who had no faith in officialdom, individual social action was the best way forward.

[. . .] With the first money we saved at home, we added to our pretty house by throwing out a little Growlery expressly for my guardian; which we inaugurated with great splendour the next time he came down to see us. I try to write all this lightly, because my heart is full in drawing to an end; but when I write of him, my tears will have their way.

I never look at him, but I hear our poor dear Richard calling him a good man. To Ada and her pretty boy, he is the fondest father; to me, he is what he has ever been, and what name can I give to that! He is my husband's best and dearest friend, he is our children's darling, he is the object of our deepest love and veneration. Yet while I feel towards him as if he were a superior being, I am so familiar with him, and so easy with him, that I almost wonder at myself. I have never lost my old names, nor has he lost his; nor do I ever, when he is with us, sit in any other place than in my old chair at his side. Dame Trot, Dame Durden, Little Woman! – all just the same as ever; and I answer, Yes, dear guardian! – just the same.

I have never known the wind to be in the East for a single moment, since the day when he took me to the porch to read the name. I remarked to him, once, that the wind seemed never in the East now: and he said, No, truly; it had finally departed from that quarter on that very day.

I think my darling girl is more beautiful than ever. The sorrow that has been in her face – for it is not there now – seems to have purified even its innocent expression, and to have given it a diviner quality. Sometimes, when I raise my eyes and see her, in the black dress that she still wears, teaching my Richard, I feel – it is difficult to express – as if it were so good to know that she remembers her dear Esther in her prayers.

I call him my Richard! But he says that he has two mamas, and I am one.

We are not rich in the bank, but we have always prospered, and we have quite enough. I never walk out with my husband, but I hear the people bless him. I never go into a house of any degree, but I hear his praises, or see them in grateful eyes. I never lie down at night, but I know that in the course of that day he has alleviated pain, and soothed some fellow-creature in the time of need. I know that from the beds of those who were past recovery, thanks have often, often gone up, in the last hour, for his patient ministration. Is not this to be rich?

The people even praise Me as the doctor's wife. The people even like Me as I go about, and make so much of me that I am quite abashed. I owe it all to him, my love, my pride! They like me for his sake, as I do everything I do in life for his sake.

A night or two ago, after bustling about preparing for my darling and my guardian and little Richard, who are coming tomorrow, I was sitting out in the porch of all places, that dearly memorable porch, when Allan came home. So he said, 'My precious little woman, what are you doing here?' And I said, 'The moon is shining so brightly, Allan, and the night is so delicious, that I have been sitting here, thinking.'

'What have you been thinking about, my dear?' said Allan then.

'How curious you are!' said I. 'I am almost ashamed to tell you, but I will. I have been thinking about my old looks – such as they were.'

'And what have you been thinking about *them*, my busy bee?' said Allan.

'I have been thinking, that I thought it was impossible that you *could* have loved me any better, even if I had retained them.'

'—Such as they were?' said Allan, laughing.

'Such as they were, of course.'

'My dear Dame Durden,' said Allan, drawing my arm through his, 'do you ever look in the glass?'

'You know I do; you see me do it.'

'And don't you know that you are prettier than you ever were?'

I did not know that; I am not certain that I know it now. But I know that my dearest little pets are very pretty, and that my darling is very beautiful, and that my husband is very handsome, and that my guardian has the brightest and most benevolent face that ever was seen; and that they can very well do without much beauty in me – even supposing—.

4

Further Reading

Further Reading

There is a vast amount of critical material devoted to *Bleak House* and the follow-ing recommendations represent nothing more than a point of departure for your own further studies. Bearing the needs and relative experience of an undergradu-ate reader in mind, the texts that I am recommending are both accessible and informative.

Recommended Editions of *Bleak House*

Throughout this Sourcebook I have used the Penguin edition of *Bleak House* edited by Nicola Bradbury (2003). Like most recent editions, it is based on the first volume-edition of the novel (1853), which was established – by George Ford and Sylvere Monod in the Norton Critical Edition of 1977 – as the definitive text. Widely available, the Penguin edition has an insightful Preface by the Marxist critic Terry Eagleton, as well as all the original illustrations by Hablot Browne. It also includes useful appendices on Chancery Court and spontaneous combustion, as well as Dickens's complete number-plans for the novel.

Book-length Studies of Dickens

Butt, John and Tillotson, Kathleen, *Dickens at Work* (1957), 2nd edn, London and New York: Methuen, 1982. Providing a wealth of information, Butt and Tillotson's chapter on *Bleak House* is essential reading for those interested in Dickens as a social reformer. Relating the novel to such contemporary debates as legal and parliamentary reform, slums and sanitation, the Oxford Movement and the rise of the Metropolitan Police, their discussion will prove invaluable for those less familiar with the period. In addition, the introductory chapter offers a useful introduction to Dickens's habits as a writer (particularly his use of number-plans) and the effects of serialisation on his work.

Carey, John, *The Violent Effigy: A Study of Dickens' Imagination* [1973], 2nd edn, London: Faber and Faber, 1991. Primarily concerned with Dickens as an imaginative writer torn between a desire for neatness and order and an obsession with chaos and corpses, Carey's study does much to debunk the popular image of Dickens as a Father Christmas figure. The chapter devoted to *Bleak House* explores the novel in terms of its displacements and symbolism and contains helpful discussions of Esther, Lady Dedlock, Krook and Inspector Bucket. Dickens's ambivalent attitude towards order, children, humour, violence and sexuality (the last being particularly relevant to an understanding of Esther) are all discussed in the more general chapters.

Foor, Sheila M., *Dickens's Rhetoric*, New York: Peter Lang Publishing Ltd., 1993. Language is a central theme in *Bleak House* and, in this full-length study of the issue, Foor divides her attention between Dickens's own delight in wordplay and a more thematic discussion of the use and abuse of language in the novel. For obvious reasons, Chancery's obsession with documents receives considerable attention, but equally interesting are those sections in which Foor traces an intricate network of references to writing, paper, ink, the alphabet, and so on. The result is a much stronger appreciation of just how tightly constructed the novel is.

Hawthorn, Jeremy, Bleak House: *The Critics Debate*, Basingstoke: Macmillan, 1987. This short volume is accessible to even the most inexperienced reader and, like Morris (below), will help to prepare you for the more specialised titles included in this list. Although not overly detailed, Hawthorn's guide offers a succinct summary of the critical debates – both contemporaneous and current – surrounding the novel's social criticism, treatment of gender, symbolism, narration, and so on. It also contains informative shorter discussions of the opening chapter and the representation of systems, the family and humour.

Morris, Pam, Bleak House: *Open Guides to Literature*, Milton Keynes: Open University Press, 1991. Opening with a series of helpful exercises, this excellent little guide is an ideal point of departure for those who feel less confident about their ability to engage with the text. Without over-simplifying the issues at stake, Morris covers a good deal of material in an extremely lucid fashion. Topics under consideration include character, narrators and structures, topicality and Dickens as a social critic. The final chapter, devoted to recent theoretical approaches, provides a useful overview of the various positions and their relative strengths and weaknesses.

Newsom, Robert, *Dickens on the Romantic Side of Familiar Things*: Bleak House *and the Novel Tradition*, New York: Columbia University Press, 1977. As its title suggests, this book is an extended exploration of the phrase 'the romantic side of familiar things'. Newsom argues that *Bleak House* is characterised by an unresolved tension between reality and romance that remains ambiguous to the very end. Far reaching in its implications, Newsom's text remains accessible and will be of particular interest to those exploring Dickens's relationship to nineteenth-century conceptions of realism. Also of note is his extended discussion of the opening number and his useful gloss on the argument presented by J. Hillis Miller.

Page, Norman, Bleak House: *A Novel of Connections*, Boston, Mass.: Twayne Publishers, 1990. This small volume includes sensitive and accessible readings of the novel's topicality, narrative method, treatment of women and language. An introductory discussion of the historical context will help to orient readers who are less familiar with the period. The section devoted to the critical reception of the novel offers a comprehensive overview of the early critical response but, it has to be said, ignores more recent interpretations of it.

Collected Essays on *Bleak House*

Tambling, Jeremy (ed.), *Bleak House*, Basingstoke: Macmillan, 1998. This collection of essays reflects the most recent developments in critical theory and includes deconstructive, new historicist, psychoanalytic and feminist readings of the novel (including the complete texts of the Hillis Miller and D.A. Miller essays extracted in this Sourcebook). Tambling provides a general introduction to the various methodologies employed, as well as a gloss for each individual essay; however, without some previous experience of the theories in question, most readers will still find the material challenging. Although unquestionably the most demanding item included in this list, the extra effort it requires will be rewarded with a number of sophisticated and insightful analyses, especially of Esther, the issues of violence and power, and the question of interpretation itself.

Articles on *Bleak House*

Kennedy, Valerie, '*Bleak House*: More Trouble with Esther?', *Women's Studies in Literature* (1:4) 1979, pp. 330–47. In this article, Kennedy establishes a connection between Esther's self-denigration and the style of her narration. She suggests that Esther's feelings of inadequacy are the inevitable result of internalising the Calvinistic doctrine expounded by her aunt. Such feelings, moreover, find linguistic expression in her narrative through its hesitations, silences and negative or passive constructions. Kennedy's assertion that Esther's refusal to acknowledge certain feelings actually testifies to their significance provides a useful reminder that the reader must scrutinise closely the gaps and silences that characterise her narrative.

Wright, Kay Hetherly, 'The Grotesque and Urban Chaos in *Bleak House*', *Dickens Studies Annual* (21) 1992, pp. 97–112. Provoking both fear and laughter, the grotesque is fundamentally unstable and irrational; thus it becomes a productive concept through which Wright is able to discuss the illogical nature of Chancery Court in *Bleak House*. In this article, she traces Chancery's relation to the rest of the novel, relating it to Dickens's conception of modern urban life.

Wright offers illuminating discussions of the novel's opening, the character of Krook and his death by spontaneous combustion and, most importantly, the novel's preoccupation with questions of legitimacy and origins. In addition, she offers a thoughtful critique of the novel's conclusion, relating it to Dickens's ambivalent feelings towards the modern city.

Index